"The perfect blend of theory and practice is hard to achieve – especially at the intersection of sustainability, innovation, and transformation of business and society! Nevertheless, these authors have done it well – check out Sebhatu, Enquist, and Edvardsson *Business Transformation for a Sustainable Future* and start taking well-informed action today. Also, the book provides a solid roadmap to go from smarter to wiser service systems for the 'wicked problems' in business and society."

Jim Spohrer, IBM Director, Cognitive Open Technologies

"*Business Transformation for a Sustainable Future* is a key contribution to the PRME initiative and represents a powerful voice to draw attention to the sustainability challenges of our world. This book provides important lessons for businesses to transform from a strictly firm-centric and profit-driven approach toward a societal approach to achieve an inclusive and sustainable future. Onward!!!"

Robert Strand, Professor, Executive Director Center for Responsible Business, Haas School of Business, University of California, Berkeley

"This book thrives from the blended and well-integrated contributions of 16 thought leaders in sustainability, innovation and transformative thinking. The perspective is based on research related to the 'new social contract' that supports a more sustainable and people-centered world. At a time when so much is being rethought, this work is important to graduate and postgraduate students as well as practitioners seeking to strive for a better world."

O.C. Ferrell, Professor, James T. Pursell, Sr. Eminent Scholar in Ethics, Harbert College of Business, Auburn University and
Linda Ferrell, Roth Family Professor of Marketing & Business Ethics, Harbert College of Business, Auburn University

"The quest for transforming our world, making peace with nature and preserving our planet at the same time as ensuring equality and human well-being, demands transformations in science and education, and very much so in business research and at business schools. This book provides refined and novel intellectual tools – concepts and frameworks, as well as innovative practice-based and cocreated knowledge, immensely useful for reconsidering prevailing notions and formulating sustainable solutions for the business-society interface."

Marie Stenseke, Professor, Deputy Dean of the School of Business, Economics and Law, University of Gothenburg, Cochair of the Multidisciplinary Expert Panel of the Intergovernmental Platform on Biodiversity & Ecosystem Services (IPBES)

Business Transformation for a Sustainable Future

Interconnecting the concepts of sustainability, innovation, and transformation, this book explains how organizations have successfully transformed themselves and wider society to foster a more sustainable future, and identifies the difficulties and challenges along the way. Part of the Principle of Responsible Management Education (PRME) series, the book promotes a strong voice for meeting sustainability challenges for transformative change in a globalized world through business education and practice.

A transition to a more sustainable way of doing business can only be attained by combining technology with profound system innovations and lifestyle changes. The chapters in the book, each written by a strong and well-recognized team of researchers in the field, open up the discussion about a new partnership between sustainability, innovation and transformation that includes the global society (big world), the biosphere (small planet), and also requires a deep mind shift. The book presents cases from business (including Ikea and Eataly) and other service networks including the Base of the Pyramid (BoP) and illustrates how these organizations have transformed themselves for a sustainable future. The research perspectives are macro (policies and legislation), meso (institutional practices), and micro (business practices and individual behavior). This book is where research meets real-world business and societal practice. The chapters are grounded in business research, specifically the interdependencies between *sustainability*, *innovation*, and *transformation*, which makes for a robust basis for describing, explaining, and understanding the complex challenges faced by business and society in the 21st century.

The book is intended for graduate- and postgraduate-level students and executive education with implications for practitioners. Furthermore, it contributes to multidisciplinary research in the field of interaction between business and society with a view to extending the firm-centric view to encompass a broader, systemic, and dynamic understanding of business and societal transformation.

Samuel Petros Sebhatu, Ph.D., is Assistant Professor in Business Administration at Karlstad Business School and a researcher at the Service Research Center (CTF), Karlstad University, Sweden. His research focuses on management, corporate governance, corporate social responsibility, business models, and sustainability in different contexts of service research in both private and public sectors. Samuel has also studied sustainability in the city context from service ecosystem perspective. He conducted extensive studies of cities ecosystem. Currently, he is working on Transformation (Transformative Change) and Innovation in relation to multi-stakeholder dialogue and Agenda2030 – sustainable developmental goals (SDGs). Samuel is PRME manager at Karlstad Business School.

Bo Enquist is Professor of Business Administration and a research fellow at the Service Research Centre (CTF), Karlstad University, Sweden. Since 2006, he has been a member of the executive team and Deputy Director of the Vinn Excellent Center, Service and Market Oriented Transport research (SAMOT). Previously, he worked for more than 20 years in different businesses at management and executive levels. His research interests are focused on value-based service, business based on service logic, and social and environmental challenges in business transformation.

Bo Edvardsson, Ph.D., is Professor of Business Administration and former Vice-Rector at Karlstad University, Sweden. Bo is the founder of CTF-Service Research Centre at Karlstad University. He is also Professor II at Inland Norway University of Applied Sciences. His research includes new service development and innovation, complaints management and service recovery, service-dominant logic, and ecosystem transformation. Bo received several distinguished awards in service research and marketing and Honorary Doctorate. He is also an honorary Distinguished Professor of Service Management, EGADE Business School, Monterrey Tech, Mexico, and a distinguished Faculty Fellow of the Center for Excellence in Service, University of Maryland. Bo is a member of organizational committees for several research conferences. He is the former editor of the *Journal of Service Management.*

Principles for Responsible Management Education Series

Since the inception of the UN-supported Principles for Responsible Management Education (PRME) in 2007, there has been increased debate over how to adapt management education to best meet the demands of the 21st-century business environment. While consensus has been reached by the majority of globally focused management education institutions that sustainability must be incorporated into management education curricula, the relevant question is no longer why management education should change, but how.

Volumes within the Routledge/PRME book series aim to cultivate and inspire actively engaged participants by offering practical examples and case studies to support the implementation of the Six Principles of Responsible Management Education. Books in the series aim to enable participants to transition from a global learning community to an action community.

Books in the series:

Struggles and Successes in the Pursuit of Sustainable Development
Edited by Tay Keong Tan, Milenko Gúdic, and Patricia M. Flynn

The Sustainability Mindset Principles: A Guide to Develop a Mindset for a Better World
Isabel Rimanoczy

Business Transformation for a Sustainable Future
Edited by Samuel Petros Sebhatu, Bo Enquist, and Bo Edvardsson

Business Transformation for a Sustainable Future

Edited by
Samuel Petros Sebhatu, Bo Enquist, and Bo Edvardsson

Routledge
Taylor & Francis Group
LONDON AND NEW YORK

First published 2022
by Routledge
2 Park Square, Milton Park, Abingdon, Oxon OX14 4RN

and by Routledge
605 Third Avenue, New York, NY 10158

Routledge is an imprint of the Taylor & Francis Group, an informa business

British Library Cataloguing-in-Publication Data
A catalogue record for this book is available from the British Library

Library of Congress Cataloging-in-Publication Data
Names: Sebhatu, Samuel Petros, 1972– editor. | Enquist, Bo. editor. |
Edvardsson, Bo, 1952– editor.
Title: Business transformation for a sustainable future /
edited by Samuel Petros Sebhatu, Bo Enquist, Bo Edvardsson.
Description: First Edition. | New York : Routledge, 2021. |
Series: Business transformation for a sustainable future |
Includes bibliographical references and index. |
Identifiers: LCCN 2021011819 (print) | LCCN 2021011820 (ebook) |
ISBN 9781032037431 (hardback) | ISBN 9781032037455 (paperback) |
ISBN 9781003188773 (ebook)
Subjects: LCSH: Business–Technological innovations. |
Management–Study and teaching. | Social responsibility of
business–Study and teaching. | Business ethics–Study and teaching.
Classification: LCC HD45 .B875 2021 (print) |
LCC HD45 (ebook) | DDC 658.4/06–dc23
LC record available at https://lccn.loc.gov/2021011819
LC ebook record available at https://lccn.loc.gov/2021011820

ISBN: 978-1-032-03743-1 (hbk)
ISBN: 978-1-032-03745-5 (pbk)
ISBN: 978-1-003-18877-3 (ebk)

DOI: 10.4324/9781003188773

Typeset in Bembo
by Newgen Publishing UK

Contents

Illustrations

Figures

Tables

About the authors

Samuel Petros Sebhatu, Ph.D., is Assistant Professor in Business Administration at Karlstad Business School and a researcher at the Service Research Center (CTF), Karlstad University, Sweden. His research focuses on management, corporate governance, corporate social responsibility, business models, and sustainability in different contexts of service research in both private and public sectors. Samuel has also studied sustainability in the city context from service ecosystem perspective. He conducted extensive studies of cities ecosystem. Currently, he is working on Transformation (Transformative Change) and Innovation in relation to multi-stakeholder dialogue and Agenda2030 – sustainable developmental goals (SDGs). Samuel is PRME manager at Karlstad Business School.

Bo Enquist is Professor of Business Administration and a research fellow at the Service Research Centre (CTF), Karlstad University, Sweden. Since 2006, he has been a member of the executive team and Deputy Director of the Vinn Excellent Center, Service and Market Oriented Transport research (SAMOT). Previously, he worked for more than 20 years in different businesses at management and executive levels. His research interests are focused on value-based service, business based on service logic, and social and environmental challenges in business transformation.

Bo Edvardsson, Ph.D., is Professor of Business Administration and former Vice-Rector at Karlstad University, Sweden. Bo is the founder of CTF-Service Research Centre at Karlstad University. He is also Professor II at Inland Norway University of Applied Sciences. His research includes new service development and innovation, complaints management and service recovery, service-dominant logic, and ecosystem transformation. Bo received several distinguished awards in service research and marketing and Honorary Doctorate. He is also an honorary Distinguished Professor of Service Management, EGADE Business School, Monterrey Tech, Mexico, and a distinguished Faculty Fellow of the Center for Excellence in Service, University of Maryland. Bo is a member of organizational committees for several research conferences. He is the former editor of the *Journal of Service Management.*

Laura Di Pietro is Assistant Professor at University of Roma Tre, Department of Business Studies, Roma, Italy. She has a Ph.D. in Commodity Science and Quality Management and teaches "Corporate social responsibility and Business Ethics." She is interested in Service Innovation, Transformative Service, Sustainable Development, and Quality Management topics, applied in multiple contexts (e.g. healthcare, cultural heritage & tourism, public administration, transport).

Tina M. Facca-Miess, Ph.D., is Associate Professor of Marketing in the Boler College of Business at John Carroll University, Cleveland Ohio, USA. Her areas of research interest include applied statistics, marketing and entrepreneurship education, social innovation and entrepreneurship, and subsistence marketplaces. Her industry experience includes executive marketing positions with multinational franchised firms in varied industries including foodservice, hospitality, and executive recruiting. Dr. Facca-Miess founded Inspired Foresight, LLC, a nonprofit serving other nonprofits and faith-based institutions, with a focus on amplifying the voices of the poor and marginalized with innovative market research methods. Dr. Facca-Miess serves as a strategic advisor to the UNHCR/Worldbank Joint Data Center on Forced Migration. Dr. Facca-Miess earned a Ph.D. in Economics at Göttingen University, Germany. She holds an MS in Statistics from Case Western Reserve University as well as a Master of Applied Communication Theory and Methodology, and a B.A. in Communication from Cleveland State University.

Raymond P. Fisk is Professor of Marketing at Texas State University. He has taught in seven countries and given more than 100 international research presentations in 20 countries. His research focuses on services marketing, service design, and transformative service research. Ray has published numerous journal articles and six books including *Serving Customers: Global Services Marketing Perspectives*. In 1993, he founded the AMA Services Marketing Special Interest Group (SERVSIG). In 2005, Ray received the Career Contributions to the Services Discipline Award from SERVSIG. In 2012, he received the Grönroos Service Research Award from the Hanken School of Economics in Finland. In 2016, the American Marketing Association made him the Inaugural Recipient of the SIG Leadership Award. In 2018, Ray founded *ServCollab*, which seeks to serve humanity through collaborative service research. In 2020, he received the Steve Baron Award for Outstanding Contribution to the Service Community from the *Journal of Services Marketing*.

Maria Francesca Renzi is a full Professor and faculty member of the Department of Business Studies in Roma Tre University. Since 2010 she is Dean of the MSc in Economics and Management. From 2015 to 2017 she has been Deputy Rector of the Roma Tre University. She teaches "Quality management", "Corporate social responsibility and sustainability", and

"Quality Systems & Operations management." Her areas of interest involve service management in the public and private sectors, innovation management, quality management, and sustainability.

Margareta Friman is Professor and Pro-Vice Chancellor at Karlstad University. Margareta is researching travel behavioral change, accessibility, service quality, satisfaction, attitudes, and well-being. She publishes in academic journals in psychology, environmental studies, economics, and transportation. In 2014, she was rewarded the Håkan Frisinger Foundation for Transportation Research Award (given by the Volvo Research and Educational Foundations). She has edited "Handbook in Sustainable Travel" (2014), "Quality of Life and Daily Travel" (2018), and "Children´s Travel and Wellbeing (2019)."

Per Kristensson is Professor and the Director of the Service Research Center, Karlstad University, Sweden. He earned his Ph.D. from University of Gothenburg in 2003. Dr. Kristensson is also a visiting professor at Norwegian School of Economics (NHH) Initiative on Service Innovation (CSI) in Bergen, Norway. His research concerns mainly service management, service innovation, and various aspects of customer experience. Dr. Kristensson's research has been published in nearly all of the service journals. He has received Best Paper Award at Quality in Service, QUIS 12; International Product Development Management, IPDM 12; and was the runner-up for Best Article Award 2004 for *Journal of Service Research*. He won the Grand Prix speakers award at Karlstad University in 2013 and held a TedX-speech on the topic of service innovation and creativity at Karolinska Institute 2011.

Gene R. Laczniak, Professor of Marketing Emeritus, is the immediate-Past President of the *Macromarketing Society*. From 1998 to 2002, Laczniak was the Associate Vice-President/Associate Provost for Academic Affairs at the Marquette. He has been a visiting professor or visiting fellow at the University of Western Australia (Perth) on several occasions. Laczniak was a member of the editorial review board of the *Journal of Marketing* and continues to serve on two academic journal review boards. He is coauthor of six books on business ethics with his most recent being *Ethics in Marketing: International Cases and Perspectives, 2nd Ed.* (Routledge, 2017). He has been a member of the board of directors of four nonprofit organizations with 18 years of aggregate service. He has taught executive development classes in the US, Europe, and Asia winning several teaching awards. Laczniak has published over 150 journal articles and papers. In 2012, Gene received a lifetime achievement award from the American Marketing Association for his contributions to marketing ethics, corporate social responsibility, and public policy scholarship. In 2018, he received a career achievement award "for extraordinary and sustained contributions" to macromarketing thought from the Macromarketing Society.

Patrick E. Murphy, Professor of Marketing Emeritus, specializes in marketing and business ethics issues. His recent work has focused on normative perspectives for ethical and socially responsible marketing, distributive justice as it relates to marketing decision-making, emerging ethical concerns in advertising, and ethics and the ethical foundations of relationship marketing. His articles have won "best paper" awards from the *Journal of Advertising*, *Journal of Macromarketing*, and the *European Journal of Marketing*. Professor Murphy teaches courses in business ethics, marketing ethics, and corporate sustainability. He has taught previously at Marquette University and spent sabbaticals at the Federal Trade Commission and University College Cork in Ireland. His Ph.D. is from the University of Houston, M.B.A. from Bradley University, and B.B.A. from Notre Dame.

Lars E. Olsson is Head of Psychology and Professor at the Service Research Center, Karlstad University, Sweden. His research focuses on judgment and decision-making, idea management and innovation, sustainability, travel psychology, consumer behavior, and well-being. He has received awards for highly cited research, best reviewer, and for best practical implications of innovation management research. He has published more than 50 book-chapters and peer-reviewed articles in international journals in psychology, environmental studies, economics, innovation, and transportation, and has recently coedited two books on daily travel and quality of life together with professor Friman.

Lia Patrício is Associate Professor at the University of Porto, where she is the Director of the Master in Service Engineering and Management. Her research focuses on Service Design, Service Innovation and Customer Experience (particularly in Technology-Enabled Services), Value Networks, and Service Ecosystems. She coordinated the project with the Portuguese Ministry of Health for the design of the Portuguese Electronic Health Record and she was Principal Investigator of the Service Design for Innovation Marie Curie – Innovative Training Network. Lia Patrício is member of the editorial board of the *Journal of Service Research*, *Journal of Service Management*, and *Journal of Services Marketing*. She is Global Faculty Member of the Center for Services Leadership, Arizona State University and Academic Scholar at the Cornell Institute for Healthy Futures. Her research has been published in the *Journal of Service Research*, *Journal of Service Management*, *Design Studies*, *Journal of Business Research*, among others.

Javier Reynoso is Professor of Service Management at EGADE Business School, Monterrey Institute of Technology (ITESM) in Monterrey, Mexico. His main interest is to promote and develop research and academic activities on the service field in Mexico and Latin America. Javier is coauthor of the first textbook on Service Management written in Spanish, used in 20 countries. Listed in the Top 15 MBA Professors in Latin America, by Revista America Economia in 2012, he has received on three occasions, 1999, 2005 and 2013, the ITESM's Teaching and Research Faculty Award for his contributions to the service sector. In May 2013, Javier became the first Latin American researcher to join the Global Faculty Network, invited by the Center for Services Leadership (CSL), Arizona State University. He received the prestigious Christian Grönroos Service Research Award 2013 in recognition of his career achievements and significant originality in service research. In 2016, Javier Reynoso was awarded International Fellow of CTF, Service Research Center, Karlstad University, Sweden, for his significant career contributions in service research. In the same year, he became member of the Mexican Academy of Sciences, in recognition for the academic and scientific development of Service Management in Mexico.

Nicholas J.C. Santos, Ph.D., is Associate Professor of Marketing at the Heider College of Business, Creighton University, Nebraska, USA. His research interests include base of the pyramid markets, business ethics, business and society, catholic social teaching, corporate social responsibility, social innovation, and social entrepreneurship. Together with coauthors he has published in numerous journals such as *Business and Politics*, *Journal of Business Ethics*, *Journal of Catholic Social Thought*, *Journal of Macromarketing*, *Journal of Public Policy & Marketing*, among others and is an invited reviewer for a number of journals. He currently serves on the policy board of the Society of Macromarketing.

Ana Valdés-Loyola is a Ph.D. candidate in EGADE Business School. Her research is focused on increasing the understanding of service at the Base of the Pyramid context. Her scholarly work has been published in *The Service Industries Journal* and *Service Science*.

Preface

This book is about business transformation for a sustainable future. We are at a point now where we recognize that the old business models are not capable of responding to current global challenges. We need to move forward from the focus on growth and profit, in which sustainability is a public relations exercise – or "greenwashing/blue washing" as it is known. Sustainability needs to be embedded in a wider framework, both theoretically and in the context of what we refer to in this book as business-societal practice. Such a framework will be built on multiple dimensions – environmental, ethical, social, legal, and financial – to enable value creation in ecosystems that include business and society.

The book is being published a year after the world was first challenged by the COVID-19 pandemic and you will find reference to its impact in all the chapters here, alongside compelling arguments for transformation. The initiative behind this collection took shape at Karlstad Business School (KBS), Karlstad University, Sweden, as well as during discussions at CTF (Centrum för Tjänsteforskning; Service Research Center) at that same university. CTF is one of the world's leading research centers, focusing on "value creation through service." The book is also a contribution to the PRME ("Principles for Responsible Management Education") initiative for business schools, which is part of the UN Global Compact (KBS has been a PRME member since 2017). A project such as this would have been impossible for one individual or even a small number of researchers. We have, therefore, harnessed a collaborative team of well-known international scholars, the members of which draw on research contributions and publications from their own areas of specialization, with their findings brought together in this collection. The authors availed themselves of the opportunity to draw on the KBS network, the business ethics and CSR symposium network (Patrick Murphy's initiative), the service research global network, and PRME networks over the 2017–21 period.

The book's cocreation and realization have been an iterative process. The three editors held meetings – both formal and informal, physical and digital – with potential authors in the different networks during spring and summer 2019, in which the final authors were brought on board. First, the editors wrote a preliminary draft of Chapter 1 to set the stage and began the process of writing drafts of Chapters 2 and 3. In November 2019, they arranged a two-day workshop in Rome, hosted by the University of Roma Tre, where, together with Per Kristensson, CTF, and Maria Francesca Renzi and Laura Di Pietro, Roma Tre, they established the pillars of the book and finalized its structure. The original plan was to hold a second workshop in April/May 2020 at Arizona State University, USA, but COVID-19 made its appearance, forcing them to reorganize the process and make all meetings digital. Details about the background to the book are presented in Chapter 1.

From as early as KBS's first "Sustainability Day" back in 2016, Associate Professor Martin Lofgren, the director of KBS, was enthusiastic about being part of the PRME initiative and appreciated the need for a sustainability-related book to document the journey. Thank you Martin for your enthusiasm and for your support for this effort, without which the journey would have been much harder. We also want to thank Maria Francesca Renzi, not only for her chapter in the book, but also for hosting our first meeting at Roma Tre University. We would also like to thank all the authors – Laura, Lia, Ray, Margareta, Lars, Per, Ana, Javier, Nicholas, Tina, Patrick, and Gene – for their contributions and their eagerness to make this book happen.

Sustainability and transformation also mean thinking about future generations, the generation that includes Greta Thunberg; Samuel's children Miriam, Magda, Bruk-Mussie, and Mathilda-Sara; Bo Enquist's granddaughter Astrid; and Bo Edvardsson's granddaughters Flippa and Julia. They are transforming sustainability thinking and inspiring action and transformative practices for the generations to come.

The book is part of the Routledge Publishing/PRME series "Responsibility in Management Education."

Thank you!

Samuel Petros Sebhatu
Bo Enquist
Bo Edvardsson
Karlstad, June 2021

1 Business transformation for a sustainable future

Samuel Petros Sebhatu, Bo Enquist, and Bo Edvardsson

Setting the stage

This book is being published a year after the world was first impacted by the COVID-19 pandemic, which became a reality in spring 2020, creating a complex global challenge. Although the chapters were begun before it struck, they were finalized as it progressed. Before the pandemic, economic and social service systems were accelerating, in line with the upward trends of globalization and digital technology. However, the appearance of this highly contagious virus, spreading quickly across the world via global transportation systems and value networks, has had an unprecedented effect. The exact nature and extent of this effect on both business and society is still to be ascertained, but its influence on the contributors to this book is reflected in their chapters. These scholars all agree on the general point that the global economy will not go back to "business as usual." While it's clear that the crisis will contribute to a transformation of the world as we know it, dare we hope that it can transform to one that is more inclusive and sustainable?

This book focuses on business transformation meeting global challenges. The aim is to understand how sustainable societal practices can contribute to a broader view of business transformation, and vice versa, in a globalized world. A global transformation agenda that is already in place today is the UN's Agenda 2030, with its widely known Sustainable Developmental Goals (SDGs),[1] a plan of action for "people, planet, prosperity, peace, and partnership,"[2] in which nations, cities, companies, and civil society are encouraged to make the transformation to sustainability. Many businesses have already started to outline their own transformation agendas to meet the SDGs. Sustainability and the SDGs are complex and dynamic phenomena, however. Our focus is on transformation, based on proactive and innovative thinking, that results in both a societal and an environmental impact (Rockström & Klum, 2015). We look at transformation processes, presenting innovative and sustainable business practices and describing how to implement these practices in the real world. In a globalized world, businesses are going to need to transform from a strict firm-centric and economic perspective to embrace new societal practices (Laczniak & Murphy, 2012) in order to forge a sustainable future.

DOI: 10.4324/9781003188773-1

The book will also discuss the impact that PRME has made in the last decade with its ongoing fostering of the business transformation process. PRME – "Principles for Responsible Management Education" – is an initiative for business schools which, as part of the UN Global Compact, seeks to establish a process for continuous improvement among institutions of management education to develop a new generation of business leaders capable of managing the complex challenges facing business and society in the 21st century. PRME is helping business schools to focus on "a new era for responsible business."

This book is where research meets real-world business and societal practice. The chapters are grounded in business research, specifically the interdependencies between *sustainability*, *innovation*, and *transformation*, which makes for a robust basis for describing, explaining, and understanding the complex challenges faced by business and society in the 21st century. The book is intended for graduate- and postgraduate-level students and executive education with implications for practitioners. Furthermore, it contributes to multidisciplinary research in the field of interaction between business and society with a view to extend the firm-centric view to encompass a broader, systemic, and dynamic understanding of business and societal transformation.

The clear message from the Club of Rome's 50th Anniversary in 2018 was encapsulated by the remark "Don't tell me the current trends are sustainable" (von Weizsäcker & Wijkman, 2018). So, how to tackle this? There is a challenge for business and society to interpret and navigate the role of business and individuals in this new globalized landscape.

The foundation of the book rests on the following pillars:

- Real cases from business and other service networks;
- Illustrations of how these organizations have transformed themselves, and the society in which they operate, into a sustainable future;
- Identifying the difficulties and challenges that businesses are facing while undertaking their transformation;
- Academic research and theories from a broad range of areas;
- Research perspectives that are macro (policies, legislation), meso (institutional practices), and micro (business practices and individual behavior) and how these are intertwined;
- Its usefulness as a teaching resource (graduate and postgraduate level).

Sustainability is complex, and research needs to point to how the UN SDGs can be realized in different contexts. The 2030 Agenda outlines actions on sustainability for nations, cities, businesses, and civil society to transform the world. The plan includes 17 global goals, which include eliminating poverty, developing innovation and infrastructure, establishing sustainable cities and improving communities, responsible consumption, and climate action. These 17 SDGs demonstrate the scale and ambition of this new universal agenda. Paul Polman, former CEO of Unilever and now the cofounder and Chair of IMAGINE, Chair of the International Chamber of Commerce and board member of UN Global Compact, calls the SDGs "the world's greatest business plan – the growth story of the century" (Polman, 2020, p. 19). His message is that "we have a small window to act, but it's a window that's closing" (Polman, 2020, p. 19). This book focuses on transformation based on proactive and innovative thinking that has a societal and environmental impact (Rockström & Klum, 2015) and will have an effect during this window of opportunity, based on the understanding that business and ethics are intertwined and cannot be separated from each other (Freeman, 1994).

The UN Global Compact anticipates a new, inclusive, and sustainable era for responsible business (Global Compact, 2017). It claims, "Today's business landscape is characterized by an unprecedented, accelerating, and complex mix and opportunities. Every industry and every sector – in every country – is facing new challenges, which they must confront in a changing operating environment" (Global Compact, 2017).

These challenges should also be embraced by business schools. In the report *Business School Ranking for the 21st Century* (Pitt-Watson & Quigley, 2019), the authors pose an important question: "Are Business Schools prepared to meet this new era?" The report addresses how business schools, and the courses they offer, are evaluated and ranked. It concludes that the evidence suggests that ranking drives behavior, but perhaps not in the right direction: managers are not being trained to contribute to a sustainable and inclusive 21st-century economy (Pitt-Watson & Quigley, 2019, p. 23); the teaching of quality, sustainability, and business ethics is either minimal or absent. Business schools need to know how to train their students – with efficacy, inclusivity, humanity, and sustainability in mind (Pitt-Watson & Quigley, 2019, p. 5).

For the UN Global Compact's 20th anniversary a study on *Leadership for the Decade of Action* has been published (Global Compact, 2020). This Global Compact–Russell Reynolds Associates study on the characteristics of sustainable business leaders highlights that *sustainability is a leadership imperative.* The time to act is now to meet the 2030 deadline of the SDGs.

> With less than 4000 days remaining until the 2030 marker, we need to turn commitment into action. As we set out to recover from the COVID-19 pandemic, now it is the time for all companies to raise their ambition for people, planet and prosperity.
>
> Global Compact, 2020, foreword

Laczniak and Murphy (2012) argue for a broader and more inclusive stakeholder orientation in marketing, moving from a firm-centric to a societal perspective grounded in ethical, macro-oriented, and network views.

Global challenges

Business – and society as a whole – is facing many global challenges to be addressed in this business and societal landscape; they must be understood in a new manner by considering both the details and the landscape as a whole. In this book, we focus on the following global challenges:

- It is time to rethink the "Triple Bottom Line"
- A need for transformation
- Making and taking in the global economy
- Individual/group identity as a tool for inclusion
- Climate change
- The relationship between humanity and nature
- The age of acceleration

A common view of sustainability today is that it consists of three dimensions – social, environmental, and economic – a concept raised by John Elkington in 1993 which he referred to as the "Triple Bottom Line" (TBL) (see Elkington, 1998). Twenty-five years later he revisited the concept and insisted it was time to rethink the TBL (Elkington, 2019). He concludes that the Triple Bottom line has failed in its mission to bury the idea of the single bottom line. It was not intended as merely an accounting system but rather as working toward a triple helix of value creation, a genetic code for tomorrow's capitalism, spurring the regeneration of our economies, societies, and biosphere (Elkington, 2019).

Discussions about environmental sustainability first began with the publication of *Silent Spring* (Carson, 1962), which was a milestone and motivated a new "ecological" vision of society. Carson's book documented the adverse environmental effects caused by the indiscriminate use of pesticides. Carson accused the chemical industry of spreading disinformation and public officials of accepting the industry's marketing claims unquestioningly. In 1996, a follow-up appeared, *Beyond Silent Spring*, cowritten by H.F. van Emden and David Peakall (1996) and, in 2006, *Silent Spring* was named one of the 25 greatest science books of all time by the editors of *Discover* magazine. The environmental movement now has a long history, with concern continually increasing, especially after the establishment and growth of nongovernmental organizations (NGOs) such as the WWF, Greenpeace, Oxfam, and other consumer and environmental movements (Sebhatu, 2010).

In the late 1950s, before *Silent Spring* even, discussions were beginning about business social responsibility. Corporate social responsibility (CSR) was first used and defined as a concept by Bowen (1953), who defined it as "the obligations of businessmen to pursue those policies, to make those decisions, or to follow those lines of action which are desirable in terms of the objectives and values of our society" (Bowen, 1953, p. 6). At that time, CSR was considered an obligation and was linked to the power that business holds in society.

In his latest book, *Green Swans: The Coming Boom in Regenerative Capitalism* (Elkington, 2020), John Elkington has further developed this rethinking of his Triple Bottom Line and highlighted three "Rs": *responsibility*, *resilience*, and *regeneration* (Elkington, 2020, p. 248). The demands of sustainability challenges must be understood from multiple angles by listening to scientists, activists, and leaders.

On a macro level, Joseph E. Stiglitz described a "need for transformation" to cope with globalization's economic, social, and environmental challenges (Stiglitz, 2006). A later book by the same author asked the question: Why has inequality increased in the Western world – and what can we do about it? (Stiglitz, 2015). His opinion is that "We do not have to choose between capitalism and fairness. We must choose both" (Stiglitz, 2015, p. 131).

Economist Marina Mazzucato wants to reinvent value as a key concept and return to the question: What creates value? (Mazzucato, 2018). She is critical about the distribution of value and asks who are making and who are taking in the global economy. In her book *The Value of Everything* (Mazzucato, 2018), she argues for a more inclusive and collective creation of value: "If the goal is to produce growth that is more innovation-led (smart growth), more inclusive and more sustainable, we need a better understanding of value to steer us" (Mazzucato, 2018, p. xviii).

Francis Fukuyama tries to understand today's global challenges from a political science perspective. He focuses on the role that identity plays with regard to inclusion in larger groups and society as a whole. In his latest book, he analyzes the use of *identity as a tool* either for inclusion for democratic purposes or for the exclusion of different groups of people. The misuse of policies related to immigrants, refugees, and citizenship are at the heart of current identity debates (Fukuyama, 2019). With populism and nationalism burgeoning, and the internet enabling peer-to-peer interaction within "bubbles," issues around identity can divide a society into smaller, self-regarding groups; but the direction of travel can also go the other way to create identities that are broader and more integrative (Fukuyama, 2019, 166).

Al Gore (former US Vice President and activist) wrote an alarming book on climate change in 2006 entitled *An Inconvenient Truth: The Planetary Emergency of Global Warming and What We Can Do About It* (Gore, 2006); Greta Thunberg's activism took this to the next level by integrating the next generation into the debate. The message from Greta is simple and clear: *Listen to scientists and act according to what they tell us*. In a program broadcast on Swedish Radio in 2020, she made a comparison between COVID-19 and climate change action.

> The whole world is realizing that COVID-19 is a catastrophe and all actors are acting to treat it as a catastrophe waiting for a vaccine. The climate change challenge must be treated the same way, as a catastrophe, mobilizing action together for a real transformation realizing that there is no vaccine for climate change.[3]

This reminds us that sustainable development is the overriding issue of today, as we face a heated planet caused by climate change. This is related to Thomas L. Friedman's urgent message: the three largest forces on the planet – *technology*, *globalization*, and *climate change* – are all "accelerating" at once. As a result, so many aspects of our societies, workplaces, and geopolitics are being shaped and need to be reimagined (Friedman, 2016).

The voices are not just secular ones. Pope Francis's Encyclical letter *On Care of the Earth* calls for more balance between people and nature. He asserts that we now live in an ecological emergency in which technology and capitalism fail to imagine the mysterious "relationship between man and nature," where modern people look for the meaning of life and instead replace it with consumption (Papa Francis, 2015).

Key concepts of the book

In investigating this new landscape, this book is built around three key interrelated concepts: *sustainability*, *innovation*, and *transformation*. A brief explanation of the three concepts on how they are intertwined and relate to transformation from more an empirical phenomena to create a better understanding is presented as follows:

Sustainability

The term "sustainability" has become commonly used and widely accepted in both an ecological sense and a business sense. Sustainability is one of the world's biggest concerns and a global challenge. Sustainability – or sustainable development – in this book follows the now-standard definition of the World Commission on Environment and Development: "Sustainable development is development that meets the needs of the present without compromising the ability of future generations to meet their own needs" (WCED, 1987, p. 43). The publication in which that definition appeared, *Our Common Future*, was responsible for a significant early impetus to ecological awareness in society at large. This report contended that a balance between environmental issues and social development would be required in order to avoid jeopardizing the future of subsequent generations through unbalanced long-term economic development. The report outlined systemic key steps to be taken to achieve global sustainable development (within political, economic, social, production, technological, international, and administrative systems) (WCED, 1987, p. 65). These steps remain valid today, over 30 years later. The report stressed that these requirements are more like goals in nature, ones that should underlie national and international development action. Today, we have a set of goals for the 21st century: the SDGs.

Peter Kemp, writing about "the Utopia of Sustainability" (Kemp, 2011), identified five dimensions of sustainability: *ethical*, *social*, *scientific*, *economic*, and *legal*. For Kemp, the concept of sustainability begins in ethics and ends in law. The scientific dimension is distinct and more appropriately applied to the problem of climate change than the "softer" dimensions which might be applied to environmental sustainability, as is more common in today's business practice. The social dimension points to another current business concept: *corporate social responsibility* (CSR). This book emphasizes the link between sustainability and CSR, both being drivers of business and societal transformation. CSR is built on the interdependencies between individual, collective, and social responsibility. Taking the concept of CSR beyond a mere communication tool (in which so-called "greenwashing," "bluewashing," or "SDG-washing" substitute for real commitment) means that the business model for an organization working in a new era for responsible business is extended to include not only economic issues, but also ethical, social, and environmental ones.

Innovation

Innovation can be defined, drawing on Schumpeter (1934), as: *novel and useful combinations of new or existing resources, including goods, services, and technologies in the context of institutional arrangements.* Innovations are manifested in novel, smart, and institutionalized solutions in the market and society. They bring together novel ideas and collaborating actors, and integrate resources, including technology, in the context of institutional arrangements. Our focus here is on the creation and diffusion of smart solutions grounded in value-creating processes in both economic and social spheres (Christensen & Raynor, 2003; Ojasalo, 2015).

As the preceding paragraph demonstrates, innovation can be described in many different ways and with different emphases. There is an "innovation climate"; there are innovation processes or outcomes; and the diffusion or scaling-up of innovations in different markets is an important concern (for an overview, see Snyder, Witell, & Gustafsson, 2016). The Service-Dominant (S-D) logic approach focuses on how actors, resources, and institutional arrangements are integrated in ongoing service-for-service exchange processes to foster innovation (Edvardsson & Tronvoll, 2013; Lusch & Nambisan, 2015). Lusch and Nambisan (2015) have described service innovation as a collaborative process built on (1) service ecosystems, (2) service platforms, and (3) resource integration, emphasizing the underlying mechanisms that shape and direct actors' roles and resource integration, in which agency is crucial.

Innovations are grounded in the economic, social, environmental – as well as the ethical and legal – aspects of sustainability. This brings in a wide range of actors with different objectives and value propositions, resulting in both inhibiting and enabling as well as supporting or opposing activities (Skålén et al., 2015). Edvardsson and Tronvoll (2019) argue for the role of platforms in fostering innovations in cases where many different actors are collaborating. A platform is defined as a common structure and agreed method within which engaged actors can collaborate, and from which a stream of innovations can be created. Service platforms make it easier to orchestrate multiple collaborating actors to foster business and societal transformation.

This book defines innovation as novel, smart and scalable solutions to societal challenges that meet new requirements, unarticulated needs, or existing market and societal needs. Thus, innovation – and service innovation, in particular – contributes to business and societal transformation.

Transformation

Transformation represents a complete change, according to dictionary definitions. It refers to both process and outcome, and includes institutionalized change. Metamorphosis is a classic example of transformation. It is profound, fundamental change, altering the very nature of something; it is both radical and sustainable; something that has been transformed can never return to exactly what it was before. In this book we define transformation as *a map for a change of mindset in order to transcend old boundaries while addressing global challenges, guided by a vison- or values-based change process in a real-world context, to create something new and different.* An example of a successful transformation which revitalized a global enterprise can be seen in the case of Starbucks, when the company faced a crisis in 2008–2009 and "fought for its life without losing its soul" (Enquist et al., 2015).

In such a context, transformation is embedded in organizational values, and positions the organization, driven by new strategic thinking, at an entirely different level. This is an extension of the more common use of the term and relates to a change process (incremental progress) by which a change happens in form, nature, or appearance. In this book, transformative change is about societal transformation, innovation, and sustainability.

Transformation from a socioeconomic perspective can be seen in transition management for sustainable development, which focuses on the complexity of governance issues and societal challenges (Loorbach, 2010, 2014). Rockström and Klum (2015) are optimistic about harnessing innovation and transformation to meet global challenges, as long as this is implemented within planetary boundaries. They state that a transition to sustainability can only be attained by combining technology with profound system innovations and lifestyle changes (Rockström & Klum, 2015, p. 133). Such discourse reveals the potential for a new synergy between innovation and transformation (Loorbach, 2010), which includes global society (the big world), the biosphere (the small planet), and requires a deep mind shift (Rockström & Klum, 2015).

A summary of our definitions of these three key terms is presented in Table 1.1.

In this collection, each chapter has its own methodological approach. However, the last Chapter 13, in pursuit of a more holistic understanding and new meaning, applies its own approach. In that chapter, we will build on the contributions from previous chapters to present lessons learned and implications for a challenge-driven business and societal transformation. We are looking at the dialectic between the conceptual/theoretical frameworks and the real-world contexts. To understand complexity in today's world, a dialectic approach is required: acquiring new knowledge and searching for truth with the help of academic research and theories, but also understanding different practices and their history (Kristensson Uggla, 2019). Examples of such dialectic approach[4] are *explanation–understanding*; *explore–invent*; and *natural science–social science* (Kristensson Uggla, 2019).

Table 1.1 Definitions of the three key terms in this book

Term	*Definition*
Sustainability	Development that meets the needs of the present without compromising the ability of future generations to meet their own needs.
Innovation	A novel and useful combination of new or existing resources, including goods, services, and technologies in the context of institutional arrangements.
Transformation	A map for a change of mindset to transcend old boundaries while addressing global challenges guided by a vision- or values-based change process in a real-world context to create something new and different.

Contents and structure

Following this introductory chapter, Chapter 1 introduces business transformation for sustainable future based on the three concepts of sustainability, innovation, and transformation.This chapter also introduces the four parts of this book.

Part 1: *Transforming firm-centric business and societal practices*

The three chapters in this part tell stories of transformation change processes in real-world contexts. Chapter 2 focuses on the challenge-driven business ecosystem, addressing the fossil-free transformation of Sweden. Chapter 3 investigates circular economy thinking, centered on the values-based sustainability business practice of IKEA, embedded in its People & Planet Positive practice. Chapter 4 looks at sustainable business practices for transformative change based on the case of Eataly.

Part 2: *The role of the individual in business and social transformation*

The three chapters in this part follow the role of individuals in societal transformation. Chapters 5 and 6 focus on designing and steering such a transformation; Chapter 5 is about designing for transformative collaboration in complex service systems, while Chapter 6 looks at steering towards happiness in sustainable travel. Chapter 7 examines the role of individuals by discussing the transformation of people to a better life and better world – the real purpose of marketing.

Part 3: *Base of the Pyramid thinking for transforming business-societal practice*

This part focuses on the role of the Base of the Pyramid (BoP) in transforming business practices and integrating justice – both theoretically and empirically. Chapter 8 describes the advancement of service research at the BoP through a service ecosystems perspective based on a case study in Mexico. Chapter 9 presents the Integrative Justice Model (IJM) as a challenge-driven normative framework for sustainable and just business practice. Chapter 10 applies the IJM to predict the transformation in quality of life (TQL) for beneficiaries in varied settings by identifying the significant predictors of transformative outcomes, based on the voices of impoverished or marginalized beneficiaries.

Part 4: *Implications for a broader societal perspective for challenge-driven transformation practice*

The first of two chapters in this part, Chapter 11, discusses "Marketing ethics and corporate social responsibility for a broader societal perspective." Chapter 12 examines the role of PRME (Principles for Responsible Management Education) and its progress in meeting the goals of the UN 2030 Agenda while working toward transformative change in business schools.

The book's concluding and reflexive chapter looks at lessons learned and implications, asking "Why?", "What?", "Who?", and "How?".

Notes

1 https://www.un.org/sustainabledevelopment/development-agenda/
2 https://unfoundation.org/blog/post/the-sustainable-development-goals-in-2019-people-planet-prosperity-in-focus/
3 Greta Thunberg told her story and selected the music in the one-and-a-half-hour radio program *Summer*, on Swedish Radio on June 20, 2020. She was the youngest speaker ever to appear on this program – which is an institution in Sweden – on which one well-known Swedish-speaking guest appears every day during the eight weeks of summer. It has been broadcast every summer since 1959.
4 Dialectic means that the couples are interconnected. The opposite is the dualistic perspective where the couples are separated.

References

Bowen, H. (1953). *Social Responsibilities of the Businessman*. New York: Harper.

Carson, R. (1962). *Silent Spring* (10th edn). Boston, MA: Houghton Mifflin.

Christensen, C.M., and Raynor, M.E. (2003). *The Innovator's Solution: Creating and Sustaining Successful Growth*. Cambridge, MA: Harvard Business School Press.

Edvardsson, B., and Tronvoll, B. (2013). A new conceptualization of service innovation grounded in SD logic and service systems. *International Journal of Quality and Service Sciences*, 5(1), 19–31.

Edvardsson, B., and Tronvoll, B. (2019). How platforms foster service innovations. *Organization Dynamics*, 49(3), 1–8.

Elkington, J. (1998). *Cannibals with Forks: The Triple Bottom Line of 21st Century Business*. Gabriola Island, BC: New Society Publishers.

Elkington, J. (2019). 25 years ago I coined the phrase "Triple Bottom Line": here's why it's time to rethink it. Harvard Business Review, June 25, 2019.

Elkington, J. (2020). *Green Swans: The Coming Boom in Regenerative Capitalism*. New York: Fast Company Press.

Enquist, B., Sebhatu, S. P., and Johnson, M. (2015). Transcendence for business logics in value networks for sustainable service business. *Journal of Service Theory and Practice*, 25(2), 181–97.

Freeman, R.E. (1994). The politics of stakeholder theory: some future directions. *Business Ethics Quarterly*, 4(4), 409–21.

Friedman, T.L. (2016). *Thank You for Being Late: An Optimist's Guide to Thriving in the Age of Accelerations*. London: Allen Lane Penguin.

Fukuyama, F. (2019). *Identity: Contemporary Identity Politics and the Struggle for Recognition* (pbk edn). London: Profile Books.

Global Compact. (2017). *Making Global Goals Local Business: A New Era for Responsible Business*. New York: UN Global Compact. Retrieved from https://d306pr3pise04h.cloudfront.net/docs/about_the_gc%2FMakingGlobalGoalsLocalsBusiness2017.pdf

Global Compact. (2020). *Leadership for the Decade of Action: A United Nations Global Compact–Russell Reynolds Associates Study on the Characteristics of Sustainable Business Leaders*. New York: UN Global Compact. Retrieved from https://www.russellreynolds.com/insights/thought-leadership/Documents/Leadership%20for%20the%20Decade%20of%20Action.pdf

Gore, A. (2006). *An Inconvenient Truth: The Planetary Emergency of Global Warming and What We Can Do About It*. Emmaus, PA: Rodale.

Kemp, P. (2011). *Citizen of the World: The Cosmopolitan Ideal for the Twenty-first Century*. Amherst, NY: Humanity Books/Prometheus Books.

Kristensson Uggla, B. (2019). *Search for Truth: Scientific Theory and Practice*. Lund, Sweden: Studentlitteratur (Swedish language).

Laczniak, G.R., and Murphy, P.E. (2012). Stakeholder theory and marketing: moving from a firm-centric to societal perspective. *Journal of Public Policy and Marketing*, 31(2), 284–92.

Loorbach, D. (2010). Transition management for sustainable development: a prescriptive, complexity-based governance framework. *Governance: An International Journal of Policy, Administration, and Institutions*, 23(1), 161–83.

Loorbach, D. (2014). *To Transition! Governance Panarchy in the New Transformation*. Dutch Research Institute for Transitions, Erasmus University, Rotterdam.

Lusch, R.F., and Nambisan, S. (2015). Service innovation: a service-dominant (S-D) logic perspective. *MIS Quarterly*, 39(1), 155–75.

Mazzucato, M. (2018). *The Value of Everything: Making and Taking in the Global Economy*. London: Penguin.

Ojasalo, J. (2015). Open innovation platform in a smart city: empirical results. *Journal of American Business Review*, 4(1), 195–202.

Papa Francis. (2015). *On Care for Our Common Home*. Encyclical Letter "Laudato Si" of the Holy Father Francis. Retrieved from http://www.vatican.va/content/francesco/en/encyclicals/documents/papa-francesco_20150524_enciclica-laudato-si.html

Pitt-Watson, D., and Quigley, E. (2019). *Business School Ranking for the 21st Century*. Under the Aegis of United Nations Global Compact, Report. Retrieved from https://www.unglobalcompact.org/library/5654

Polman, P. (2020). Foreword. In J. Elkington, *Green Swans: The Coming Boom in Regenerative Capitalism*. New York: Fast Company.

Rockström, J., and Klum, M. (2015). *Big World Small Planet: Abundance within Planetary Boundaries*. Stockholm: Max Ström Publishing.

Schumpeter, J.A. (1934). *The Theory of Economic Development*. Cambridge, MA: Harvard University Press.

Sebhatu, S.P. (2010). *Corporate Social Responsibility for Sustainable Service Dominant Logic*. Doctoral dissertation, Karlstad University, Sweden.

Skålén, P., Gummerus, J., von Koskull, C., and Magnusson, P. (2015). Exploring value propositions and service innovation: a service-dominant logic study. *Journal of the Academy of Marketing Science*, 43(2), 137–58.

Snyder, H., Witell, L., Gustafsson, A., et al. (2016). Identifying categories of service innovation: a review and synthesis of the literature. *Journal of Business Research*, 69(7), 2401–8.

Stiglitz, J.E. (2006). *Making Globalization Work*. New York: W.W. Norton.

Stiglitz, J.E. (2015). *The Great Divide*. London: Penguin.

UN (United Nations) (2015). *Transforming our World: The 2030 Agenda for Sustainability Development*. Resolution adopted by the General Assembly United Nations on September 25, 2015.

van Emden, H.F., and Peakall, D.B. (Eds.), (1996). *Beyond Silent Spring: Integrated Pest Management and Chemical Safety*. Netherlands: Springer.

von Weizsäcker, E., and Wijkman, A. (2018). *Come On! Capitalism, Short-termism, Population and the Destruction of the Planet: A Report to the Club of Rome 50th Anniversary in 2018*. New York: Springer Science + Business Media.

WCED (World Commission on Environment and Development). (1987). *Our Common Future*. The Brundtland Report. New York: Oxford University Press.

Part 1

From firm-centric business to a broader sustainable business transformation

2 Business ecosystem for sustainability

Addressing fossil-free transformation

Bo Enquist and Samuel Petros Sebhatu

Takeaways

- Sustainability, innovation, and transformation will form the foundations of a business ecosystem model taking a societal perspective to achieve challenge-driven transformative change.
- The ecosystem has a multilevel nature (macro, meso, and micro), but the system also needs to be viewed from processual, systemic, and institutional perspectives, acknowledging its actor-to-nature relationships.
- The ecosystem, or the network of complexity, tackling global challenges under the guidance of the UN's 2030 Agenda, in addressing sustainability, innovation, and transformation issues can lead to fossil-free transformation in a real-world context.
- The transformative change process is vision- and goal-driven, addressing global challenges of complexity and wicked problems.

Introduction

Both business and society at large are facing a new reality. The COVID-19 pandemic, with its unpredictable effects, has brought this into sharp focus. The old business model – focusing only on economic value and viewing social and environmental issues as externalities – is now outdated. As we saw in Chapter 1, sustainability, innovation, and transformation are interrelated concepts. In this chapter, it is shown how these concepts form the foundation of a multidisciplinary framework in which transformative sustainability thinking brings ethical, social, and environmental dimensions into a business ecosystem where a balance between people and nature becomes prioritized. Challenge-driven transformative change is a vision- and goal-driven change process addressing complex global challenges and "wicked" problems.[1] A transformation agenda is used to break down old boundaries guiding the process in a real-world context to create something new and different, moving away from a firm-centric toward a societal perspective. Sustainable business practice will acquire a new meaning, relating not only to economic value but also to an open business model and a changed mindset.

DOI: 10.4324/9781003188773-2

The chapter will present a case study of a global transformation agenda in practice: the Sustainable Development Goals (SDGs) of the UN 2030 Agenda (see Chapter 1) as applied to address the global challenge of climate change via fossil-free transformation. "Fossil Free Sweden" is a case study of a national initiative to make Sweden one of the first fossil-free welfare countries in the world, not only as a responsibility to future generations but also because it makes economic sense.

Theoretical and conceptual framework

The interrelationship of sustainability, innovation, and transformation in an ecosystem

In Chapter 1 we learned about the three interrelated concepts of sustainability, innovation, and transformation. In this chapter, we will see how this interrelationship might look in a real-world context.

Today, sustainability is commonly viewed as consisting of three dimensions: social, environmental, and economic (Elkington, 1998). In the context of sustainable cities, many cities have made it clear that social sustainability is the goal, environmental sustainability sets the boundaries, and economic sustainability provides the resources (Enquist, 2016). Also in the context of cities, Enquist, from a research-driven perspective, took a processual approach to transformative change in a complex environment (see Enquist, 2016, pp. 380–90), in which sustainability is neither a standalone nor sequential process: it is interlinked with innovation and transformation. This broader view of the concept of sustainability also provides insights beyond the contexts of cities. The entire theoretical and conceptual framework in this chapter engages with the complexity of transformative change in the acknowledgment that such a change cannot be effected if understood as being a sequential and standalone process.

A dimension of sustainability advanced by Kemp (2011) is the social dimension as it is applied within business (i.e. corporate social responsibility (CSR)). The authors of the present chapter were among the first to introduce the CSR concept into service research (Enquist, Edvardsson, & Sebhatu, 2008; Edvardsson & Enquist, 2009; Sebhatu, 2010). An early article by Enquist, Edvardsson, and Sebhatu (2008) posed the following research question in its title: "Corporate social responsibility for charity or for service business?" The answer to that question is not simple and depends on the specific context. However, CSR practice is a reality for globally integrated enterprises (GIEs) (Palmisano, 2006) such as IKEA, IBM, Starbucks, and Unilever, because of CSR's important role in a sustainable business (Edvardsson, Enquist, & Sebhatu, 2014; Edvardsson & Enquist, 2009; Enquist, Sebhatu, & Johnson, 2015). Approaching CSR as a vehicle for charitable and philanthropic works is an outdated perspective on the concept (Vogel, 2005); a more proactive approach is to integrate CSR as part of the business model and not to view social and environmental issues as externalities. Seen like this, CSR can be approached as a strategy for innovative service business (Enquist, Edvardsson, & Sebhatu, 2008), but it is still not an easy task. Oliver Williams decoupled CSR from the history of business ethics, and, while admitting that corporations have a long way to go, argued for a paradigm shift in pursuit of a wider purpose for business in creating value for a community of stakeholders (Williams, 2014. p. 105). There is always the significant risk of CSR being used purely for "greenwashing," a practice that has now, in the age of the UN Global Compact Sustainable Development Goals (SDGs), been augmented by "bluewashing" and "SDG-washing."

In service research, innovation is related to customer needs and value cocreation, in which the purpose of the innovation part is to identify novel ways to cocreate value (Lusch & Vargo, 2014). Edvardsson and Enquist (2011) identified criteria for service innovation that differ from those for product innovation, one of which is that a service system is embedded in a social context and, therefore, is subject to social movements and norms that affect the value creation processes (Edvardsson & Enquist, 2011). Ostrom et al. (2015) argued for an expansion of service innovation research; this is categorized as one of the strategic priorities in helping shape how service processes and systems are conceptualized.

The social component is important for challenge-driven innovation for transformative change. Social innovation is the concept that addresses this. *The Evolution of Social Innovation: Building Resilience through Transitions* (Westley, McGowan, & Tjörnbo, 2017) uses historic cases to explore the role of social innovation as an engine of transformation. In the book's concluding chapter, entitled "Recognizing transformative potential," one of the editors, Professor Frances Westley of Canada, finds some patterns in the preceding chapters. Where social innovation is used as a proactive tool for transformation, the patterns emerging include: the importance of meaning; it takes time to unfold; each situation is unique; adaptation and pairing with adjacent opportunities shape the innovation itself; paradox and tensions characterize social innovation; conflict and opposition stimulate novel combinations; positive policy changes create stable zones for development and new experimentation; and negative policy changes stimulate shadow networks and lay the foundations for opportunistic behavior (Westley, McGowan, & Tjörnbo, 2017, pp. 240–48).

Common features of service research are value cocreation and innovation, embedded in an ecosystem in which actor-to-actor interaction is prominent (Lusch & Vargo, 2014; Di Pietro et al., 2017). The ecosystem perspective is important as a platform for stakeholder interaction (Lusch & Webster, 2011). The ecosystems are also multilevel in nature and can be viewed on different levels – i.e. the *macro*, *meso*, and *micro* levels – by zooming out (rather than zooming in) to see the bigger picture (see Lusch & Vargo, 2014). In her dissertation, Kaisa Koskela-Huotari (2018) extended the ecosystem perspective in service research, highlighting the *processual*, *systemic*, and *institutional* views. The present chapter takes a broader view of an ecosystem in the context of business addressing global challenges. It is not only about value cocreation in an actor-to-actor configuration, it is also about transformative change addressing global challenges in the context of a business network viewing a value network as a business ecosystem for sustainability. This is a transformative change process in which business practice is dynamic and reflects the interactions of sustainability, innovation, and transformation.

The transformation agenda: the 2030 Agenda for Sustainable Development

The societal perspectives can be found in the challenges presented in the SDGs of the UN's 2030 Agenda for Sustainable Development. Many companies and cities have begun to outline their transformation agendas to meet the challenges of SDGs, as related in Chapter 1. In this chapter, we tell the story of the *Fossil Free Sweden* initiative, a proactive initiative by the Swedish government to support the creation of transformation agendas in different Swedish industries. The devil, we discover, is in the detail – or, to be precise, the implementation (von Weizsäcker & Wijkman, 2018, p. 38). The socio-economic goals (SDGs 1–12) cannot be tackled using conventional growth policies if the environmental goals (13–15) are to be achieved. To facilitate a full dialogue that effectively illustrates the interdependence of the 17 SDGs, Johan Rockström and Pavan Sukhdev from the Stockholm Resilience Center developed a systemic hierarchy of the SDGs (Stockholm Resilience Center, 2016) based on the three bottom lines – *biosphere*, *society*, and *economy* – as presented in Figure 2.1.

Sustainability – as pursued by applying the SDGs – is the key guiding principle for business in meeting the challenges of a complex and dynamic world (Waddock et al., 2015; van Tulder, 2018). As a framework for business globally, the Global Compact initiative represents an example of a transformative change perspective to launch a new business and societal practice for the future (Global Compact, 2017).

Management research has a strong influence on real-world business practice. For example, the Rotterdam School of Management (RSM) at Erasmus University launched a new mission statement in May 2017, in which it claimed "RSM is a force for positive change in the world," and undertook to use the SDGs as a reference framework. The RSM publishes its Series on Positive Change, in which it aims to inform managers and business students about critical trends for a sustainable future, and about opportunities for businesses to contribute to positive change. Rob van Tulder, Professor of International Business at RSM, has conducted a critical assessment of the SDGs in *Business and Sustainable Developments Goals: A Framework for Effective Corporate Involvement* (van Tulder, 2018), in which he presents a framework for making corporate strategies effective for sustainable development. It is divided into three parts:

- *Part I: Why?* The creation of the SDGs – a new paradigm for progress?
- *Part II: What and Who?* The SDGs as "wicked problems." Who should address what?
- *Part III: How?* A framework for corporate strategies in support of the SDGs.

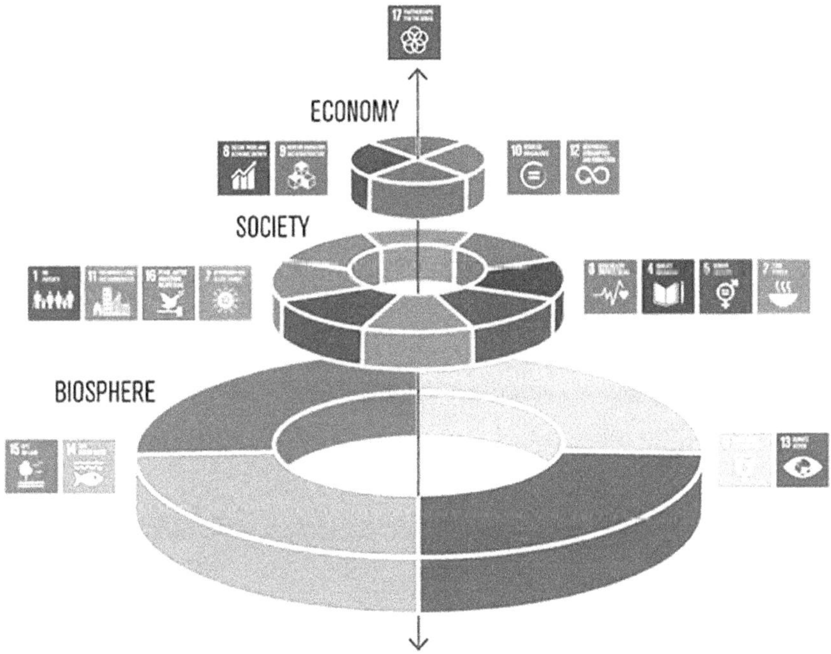

Figure 2.1 A systemic hierarchy of the SDGs, as illustrated by Rockström and Sukhdev (Stockholm Resilience Center, 2016).

A strong message of this framework is that transformative change should be part of a new paradigm for positive change in a complex environment (van Tulder, 2018). An important reference here is Waddock et al. (2015), who, in their article "The complexity of wicked problems in large scale change," explain that successful organizational change needs to incorporate the concept of large system change (LSC) in the direction of greater sustainability and social justice (Waddock et al., 2015, p. 994). Their article also addresses complex adaptive systems (CAS) and "wicked problems." Complexity theory, which is required to understand wicked problems, is outlined as follows (Waddock et al., 2015, p. 999, Table II):

- **Problem definition and boundaries.** Wicked problems are characterized by uniqueness, complexity, and the interactive dynamism of issues, making each one unique and definitive problem definition impossible, in part because each stakeholder brings different perspectives to the problem at hand.
- **Holistic.** Both wicked problems and CAS need to be viewed holistically rather than in piecemeal or fragmented ways because their various components are interconnected, interdependent, and interrelated.

- **Dynamics.** Wicked problems and CAS are both characterized by nonlinear, coevolving, and emergent dynamics that are inherently unpredictable.

In Part III of van Tulder (2018), the author uses this insight about the complexity of wicked problems to help explain how companies can contribute to the SDGs. He identifies four levels of corporate engagement with the SDGs, each with its own logic:

- **Level 1.** The classic business case revolves around cost savings; in this situation, CSR stands for "corporate self-responsibility."
- **Level 2.** The defensive business case; CSR here stands for "corporate social responsiveness."
- **Level 3.** The strategic or active business case; CSR here stands for the more proactive principle of "corporate social responsibility" (it requires companies to go beyond "liability-oriented" reasoning to embrace responsibility and "positive duty-oriented" reasoning).
- **Level 4.** The systemic or social business case (also known as the "new economy business case"); CSR here stands for "corporate societal (or sustainable) responsibility" (wicked challenges, in particular, play out at the level of whole systems).

In this chapter, we focus on levels 3 and 4, which is where companies are looking at stakeholder engagement and working with the SDGs: levels where transformative change addresses global challenges of complexity and wicked problems.

Transformative change to address global challenges: climate change

Climate change is a major global challenge that is embedded in the fabric of the SDGs. According to Rockström and Klum (2015), this challenge requires a transition to sustainability which can be attained only by combining technology with deep system innovations and lifestyle changes (Rockström & Klum, 2015, p. 133). They identify five areas in which such a transition is ongoing and being achieved through new technologies, novel system integration, and new behavioral strategies; they are: a renewable and sustainable energy system; sustainable and healthy food systems; circular economic models for business, societies, and communities; sustainable urban futures in a world where 70% of all people live in cities; and sustainable transportation systems (Rockström & Klum, 2015). Theirs is an optimistic view in which technology and innovation form at least part of the solution, as long as it is implemented within planetary boundaries. The solution also lies partly in the ability of natural sciences and social sciences to learn from and inspire one another (Rockström & Klum, 2015).

Following a similar line of thinking is the "Doughnut" model developed by Kate Raworth, which includes two boundaries: the *planetary boundary* (built on nine planetary limits proposed by an international group of earth-system scientists, led by Johan Rockström and Will Steffen) and the *social boundary* (built on the social-economic SDGs) (see Raworth, 2018). Between the two sets of boundaries lies the ecologically safe and socially just space in which humanity can thrive (Raworth, 2018, p. 295).

Framework summary: a framework of complexity and an ecosystem model for challenge-driven transformative change

In this summary section, we sketch a preliminary framework and a model of a business ecosystem for sustainable transformative change. This framework will be further developed later in the chapter. So far, from our preliminary framework, we have learned the following:

- **Business ecosystem.** A platform for stakeholder interaction between people and nature. An ecosystem can be viewed from a processual, systemic, and institutionalized point of view and at different levels (micro, meso, macro).
- **Service innovation and social innovation.** Service innovation differs from product innovation and is embedded in a social context; social innovation is an important engine for transformation.
- **Sustainability.** For business practices, a balance between economic, social, and environmental thinking, in a holistic way. It starts with ethics and ends with law, with the scientific dimension setting the boundary.
- **Corporate social responsibility.** Doing well by doing good. CSR practice can be used as a proactive tool for transformational change as part of the business model.
- **2030 Agenda SDGs.** The devil is in the implementation. The strong interdependence between humanity and nature cannot be neglected in any transformative change processes. SDG implementation for transformative change is related to the complexity of wicked problems.
- **Transformative change addressing global challenges: the climate change issue.** Climate change is a huge issue but the problems are solvable. Natural sciences and social sciences can learn from one another. There is room for prosperity and growth within social and planetary boundaries.

With this in mind, we suggest the model shown in Figure 2.2.

We will develop this framework and model further below in the "Discussion/analysis" section.

Research methodology

Collaborative research methods are required to address the "Why?", "What?", "Who?", and "How?" questions of transformative change. We would like to share here the experience we have gained from our stakeholder- and learning-based

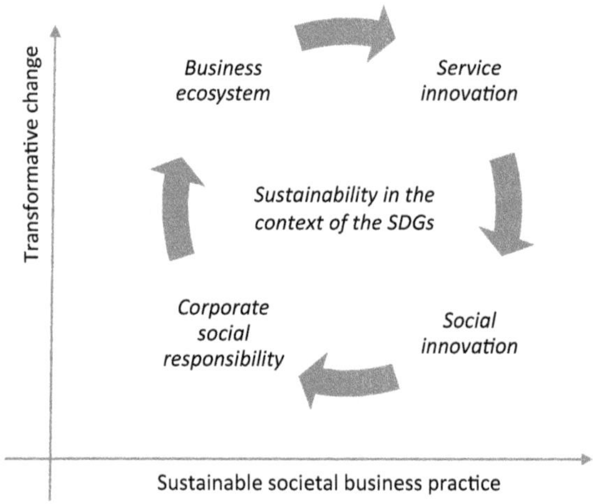

Figure 2.2 A model of complexity in which service innovation, social innovation, CSR, and the business ecosystem address global challenges for transformative change in the context of the Sustainable Development Goals (SDGs).

lab research, which is still at an early stage and requires further development and institutionalization.

Our *Service Innovation Lab* is situated at the Innovation Park, close to the Karlstad University campus. A T-Lab (Transformation-Lab) session is a means of providing a distributed method independent of place, allowing the collaboration of multiple actors. It is a reflexive, explorative methodological approach (Alvesson & Sköldberg, 2010) which maintains a focus on real-world implementation. The lab is used as a platform for orchestrating innovation and transformation to develop ideas, create interaction and dialogue, and integrate and allocate resources. The learning process is a consequence of the engagement of different stakeholders learning collectively in an interaction between academia and reflective practitioners. We will return to this concept in the discussion and the conclusion.

Our methodological approach generates new meaning in the dialectic between the theoretical framework and the real-world context. The interpretative research element involves tacking back and forth among previous theory, the data, and theory development.

The case of fossil-free transformation

The following case on fossil-free transformation comes from our own research and has been compiled to assist in learning from stakeholder engagement in transformative change processes that address global challenges of complexity and wicked problems.

Fossil Free Sweden

There is still hope for solutions to climate change. The 2015 Paris Agreement represented progress for global stewardship. At the Paris Climate Conference (COP21) in December 2015, 195 countries adopted the first-ever universal, legally binding global climate deal. The agreement sets out a global action plan to put the world on track to avert the worst of the climate change forecasts by limiting global warming to below 2°C and pursuing further efforts to limit it to 1.5°C. So what kind of transformative change can a developed Western country like Sweden make to contribute to its commitments?

Fosilfritt Sverige ("Fossil Free Sweden") was started by the Swedish government ahead of the Paris climate summit, with Svante Axelsson as national coordinator; today over 400 players are involved.

The conditions in Sweden are well aligned with the government´s ambition to become one of the world's first fossil-free welfare country to tackle the climate crises. The first step in realizing such a vision was taken when seven parliamentary parties adopted a common target for Sweden to be climate-neutral by 2045. With the new Climate Act and the establishment of the Climate Policy Council, clear rules have been created for government and parliament to follow up on the climate goals. A second step was the development, by 21 industrial sectors, within the framework of the Fossil Free Sweden initiative, of roadmaps[2] for fossil-free competitiveness during 2019 and 2020. This roadmap jigsaw demonstrates that Swedish industries are taking the climate targets seriously, and at the same time shows that competitiveness can also be boosted by pursuing fossil-free/climate-neutrality strategies. But it is also clear that industry cannot handle the transformation alone.

Political lessons must now be drawn from these roadmaps, which represents a third step in the process. In October 2019, Fossil Free Sweden put forward to parliament 27 policy proposals based on the roadmaps (Fosilfritt Sverige, 2019). These will be a necessary prerequisite for the roadmaps being put into practice and their intent is to influence the government's 2019 climate action plan.

Fossil Free Sweden has been given an extension of its mandate – by four years until December 2024 – which allows step four to be taken. The initiative can now focus on creating the conditions for implementation of the roadmaps. In developing concrete strategies to achieve the challenges presented in the roadmaps, we will see a holistic approach being brought to climate change adaptation within Swedish industry.

A narrative from a roundtable discussion

As part of the learning process, the Fossil Free Sweden national coordinator Svante Axelsson arranged roundtable discussions for conflict resolution among different stakeholders, to find constructive ways forward, and to find common ground for policy proposals to accelerate the transition to a fossil-free society. The two authors of this chapter attended one of these, a regional meeting on 18

January 2018 under the title of "Fossil-free Värmland" (Värmland is a province in west-central Sweden, with Karlstad its main city), with approximately 200 other participants, and with Svante Axelsson.

The authors also attended a workshop in Stockholm on 6 February that year. That day's mission was to attend a workshop entitled "How can we stretch the goals?" which was arranged by Fossil Free Sweden with Svante Axelsson as moderator for the day. It was to be a "Talanoa Dialogue"[3] designed to find more ambitious solutions to avoiding the worst of the effects of climate change by limiting global warming to 1.5°C. The speakers were: Johan Rockström, professor of water systems and, at that time, director of the Stockholm Resilience Center; Johanna Lissinger Peitz, EU climate negotiator for Sweden; and Nina Ekelund, executive director of the Haga Initiative, a business network that strives to reduce the business sector's climate impact. The authors participated in a constructive dialogue in a workshop session. (Lunch was vegetarian and vegan with a low carbon footprint.) In the workshop Johan Rockström presented a roadmap for rapid decarbonization (Rockström et al., 2017) – "carbon law" – which he and his colleagues have published worldwide, Rockström was skeptical about the Paris Agreement: although its goals are aligned with science and can, in principle, be technically and economically achieved, alarming inconsistencies remain between science-based targets and national commitments. The research group's solution is a global decadal roadmap based on their so-called "carbon law" which applies to all sectors and countries and involves halving gross anthropogenic carbon dioxide (CO_2) emissions every decade. The final remarks from the research group concerned the need for global governance/stewardship to implement the roadmap.

The "carbon law" is a call to action, and it is already happening in many firms and public sector organizations in Sweden. It can be a catalyst for transformation change. One example is an ongoing innovation project to eliminate coal from stainless steel production, replacing it with hydrogen and thereby making this process fossil-free. Another example is the huge transformation taking place within the forestry industry driven by the "bio-economy" innovation.

Roadmaps from Swedish industry

Against the background of the Swedish parliament's 2045 climate-neutrality targets, the Fossil Free Sweden initiative has encouraged business sectors to draw up their own roadmaps for how to become fossil-free while also increasing competitiveness. The industries must describe when and how they will be fossil-free, what technological solutions need to be developed, what investments need to be made, and what obstacles need to be removed. The roadmaps also include proposals for stakeholder commitments and political solutions. Thirteen roadmaps were delivered to the Swedish government in 2019 and a further eight in spring 2020.

One roadmap was from the forestry sector. Its vision was encapsulated by the slogan "The forest sector drives growth in the global bioeconomy." It is a vision that goes beyond its own sector by including the transformation of society into a bio-based economy. In a growing bioeconomy, the forestry sector can contribute to climate change mitigation in three ways: substitution, whereby bio-based products replace those produced from raw fossil materials or those with major carbon emissions during production; carbon capture by forests; and reduction in use of fossil energy sources.

The following conditions are critical for implementation of the roadmap: a clear political ambition to create a bio-based society; competitive conditions for the forestry sector; assured access to biomass from sustainable forestry; increased focus on goods transportation; improved efficiency of transportation; electrification; and continued investment in research and innovation.

Paper Province is a world-leading business cluster within the Swedish forestry bio-economy, owned and operated by its over 100 member companies. Based in Karlstad, it operates in Värmland and the surrounding area and collaborates closely with Karlstad University. Its mission is to make a decisive contribution to society by working toward sustainable development and the achievement of the SDGs. The SDGs help Paper Province and its members to accelerate the development of renewable materials as substitutes for fossil-based materials. Four of the SDG goals are relevant:

- **Goal 8**: *Decent work and economic growth*. This is crucial for the transition to a forestry bio-economy – lasting, inclusive, and sustainable.
- **Goal 9**: *A sustainable industry, innovation, and infrastructure*. This is about the competitiveness of the forestry industry in the region, spreading sustainable innovative technologies and gaining market share.
- **Goal 12**: *Responsible consumption and production*. For Paper Province, the main focus is the creation of new products in which the forest bio-economy substitutes for raw fossil materials. It aims to contribute to the building of a circular economy in pursuit of waste reduction.
- **Goal 5**: *Gender equality*. The forestry industry is a male-dominated industry and this needs to change – not least because it has both a direct and indirect impact on the industry's long-term competitiveness and capacity for innovation. (Goal 5 serves as a horizontal goal in all its operations.) In making this shift, Paper Province argues that the forest can be a goldmine: a great asset with great opportunities. And this is where the cluster can make a difference.

Discussion/analysis

In this part, we will present a discussion of what we have learned from our fossil-free transformation framework case in order to provide a more theoretical reflection on innovative and sustainable transformation. Van Tulder's (2018) message is that transformative change should be part of a new paradigm of positive change in a complex environment. Our discussion will borrow Van Tulder's set of questions – *Why?*, *What?*, *Who*, and *How?* – but place them within a broader framework, one that covers the main purpose of this chapter, which is to understand how a multidisciplinary approach can be used as a foundation to develop a more dynamic business ecosystem for challenge-driven transformative change by using an actual global transformation agenda in practice (i.e. the UN 2030 Agenda for Sustainable Development). This section proceeds as follows:

- **Part I: Why?** Innovation, sustainability, CSR practices, and beyond – meeting the global challenges of the SDGs to engage with transformation, cocreation, and sustainability issues. A new paradigm for progress is required?
- **Part II: What? and Who?** The transformative change process as being vision- and goal-driven to address global challenges of complexity and wicked problems. Who should address what?
- **Part III: How?** A framework for business ecosystem with a business and societal perspective for challenge-driven transformative change.

Part I: Why?

The insight that sustainability starts with ethics and ends in law is not yet well established. The Brundtland Report of 1987 (WCED, 1987) is widely known, but its effect has been minimal, perhaps because it is too general for implementation purposes. *Corporate social responsibility* as a communication tool for business, NGOs, and public institutions can be used for good, but can also be misused. Seeing CSR as a challenge but also as a promise requires a broader view and the understanding that business and ethics cannot be separated.

But what about the purpose of *transformation*? The concepts of service innovation, sustainability, and CSR practices can meet cocreation and sustainability issues within a management perspective, as we have seen above. Business practice also must engage with transformative change by addressing "people and nature" challenges with a perspective that transcends management view. Why do we need some form of paradigm shift? Because the societal perspective of business practice has also to come into focus.

Part II: What? and who?

To tackle global challenges, we need to be aware of the complexity of wicked problems inherent in large-scale change. They have to be addressed in a holistic way because their various components are interdependent and interrelated. Wicked problems are also dynamic and unpredictable. There is a need for a more multidisciplinary methodological approach to face the complexity of wicked problems and to organize a vision- and goal-driven transformative change process to meet global challenges. The micro, meso, and macro levels and the processual, systemic, and institutional issues have to be handled in a holistic way in which both management and societal practice incorporate the concept of large-scale system change. We suggest using the lab method as a platform for orchestrating innovation and transformation to *further develop ideas*, to *create interaction and dialogue*, and to *integrate and allocate resources* between researchers and practitioners *to create a new meaning*. *Service innovation* can be used for transformational change answering the question "Good for whom?" in a broader stakeholder view that includes more than just customers. The management perspective must be expanded to allow for more inclusive societal thinking. Yet this is still too limited. The *SDGs* can be a proactive tool for identifying global challenges and developing a transformation agenda in multiple institutions and organizations in the direction of greater sustainability and social justice, as we learned from the above framework. *Who should address what* requires time for reflection in an open-source, stakeholder-oriented environment. The lab setting – a platform where researchers and practitioners meet in an organized way for explorative learning – can be of great help in enabling a deeper understanding and interpretation of transformative change and innovative processes in real contexts in which the intention is to make a difference.

Part III: How?

As we have seen in Parts I and II above, it is not easy to tackle the complexity of wicked problems on the macro, meso, and micro levels simultaneously. This book represents a search for a new innovative and sustainable business-societal practice, and later chapters will present business cases and service networks. In these cases we will learn that business-societal practice in real contexts is about a combination of what van Tulder called "level 3," where the cases are strategic or active business cases, and "level 4," where the cases are systemic or social business cases of corporate societal responsibility. However, the context is not only about business, but also includes the public sector, business society, and/or civil society, or a mixed context such as actor-to-actor interaction in networks embedded in a social context. Our preliminary model from our theoretical and conceptual framework (Figure 2.2) must therefore be further developed and restructured in order to understand the *How?* (see Figure 2.3).

We will do this in two steps. First, we need to develop a new model of an ecosystem: *a dynamic ecosystem in a business-societal perspective*. We start with a multilevel service ecosystem model inspired by Lusch and Vargo (2014), whose model included an actor-to-actor perspective of processes in different levels of exchange. Our theoretical and conceptual framework brings out an actor-to-actor-to-nature interaction. The ecosystem can also be seen from systemic, institutional, and processual points of view (Koskela-Huotari, 2018).

- **Macro level**. Focusing on the planet/global society to identify planetary boundary/global challenges. The level is more *systemic* in character.
- **Meso level**. The level that focuses on societal and business institutional networks searching for societal practice. This level is more *institutional* in character.

- **Micro level.** The level that focuses on a stakeholder-centric point of view searching for a new business-societal practice. This level is more *processual* in character.

The fossil-free transformation case in this chapter illustrates the ongoing processes of *how* transformative change addresses global challenges. These are ongoing transformative processes and demonstrate the need for a mind shift, a roadmap, or a transformation agenda for action. The implementation phase of a Fossil Free Sweden starts at the macro level by identifying the planetary boundaries and the global challenges around climate change. The case described here, illustrated by the forestry sector, has concentrated primarily on the meso level in terms of how a country like Sweden wants to be one of the world's first fossil-free welfare countries and how the business sector organizes different roadmaps at the meso level and starts implementation processes at the micro level. It also shows that the roadmaps also need radical governmental reforms to support the fossil-free transformation.

The dynamic ecosystem model in Figure 2.3 shows the different levels, but the *mission* of transformative change is still missing. We need to develop our model still further. Our solution is a combination of Figures 2.2 and 2.3 to build a new, final model: *a dynamic ecosystem in a business-societal perspective for challenge-driven transformative change*. We will do this in the concluding part of our chapter in which we will also reflect on business-societal implications.

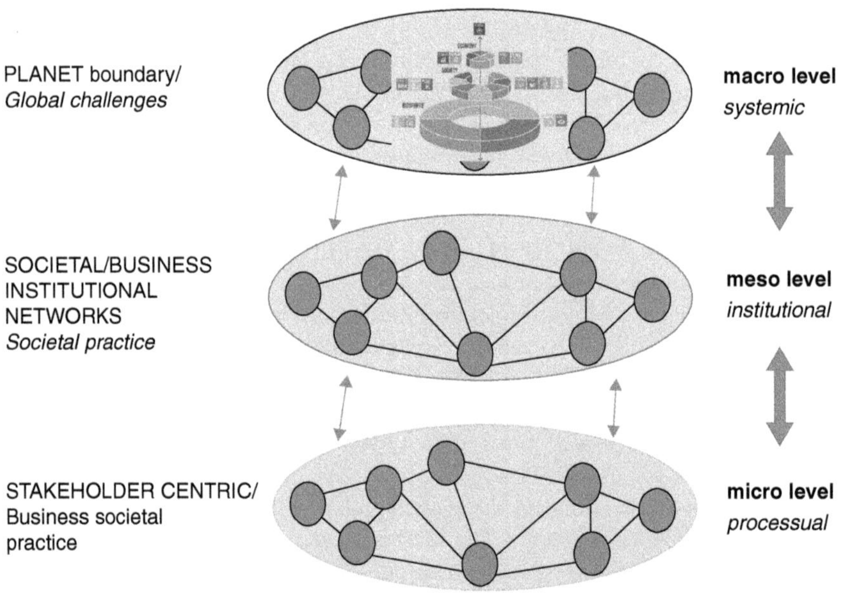

Figure 2.3 A business ecosystem in a business-societal perspective.

Conclusion and implications

The final model is a combination of a framework in which sustainable business-societal practice in real-world contexts addresses transformative change processes of complexity and wicked problems within a dynamic ecosystem in a business-societal perspective (see Figure 2.4).

The main purpose of this chapter has been to discuss how a multidisciplinary approach based on sustainability, innovation, and transformation can be used as a foundation on which to develop a more dynamic business ecosystem for challenge-driven transformative change. In the discussion/analysis section, our theoretical framework was combined with the other two components – the research methodology and the fossil-free transformation case – to find a new meaning. Figure 2.3 outlined a dynamic and systemic ecosystem with a business-societal perspective. The model was extended (Figure 2.4) to configure the transformative change process as being vision- and goal-driven to address the global challenges of complexity and wicked problems. The extension shows the transformative change loop where the SDGs are used as a proactive tool for identifying global challenges and also for developing a transformation agenda for change in multiple institutions and organizations in the direction of greater sustainability and social justice. The network of complexity – where service innovation, social innovation, and corporate social responsibility address global challenges, under the guidance of Agenda 2030, in order to tackle transformation, innovation, and sustainability issues, needs to move from a firm-centric to a societal perspective by combining what van Tulder (2018) called "level 3" (strategic or active business cases) and "level 4" (systemic or social business cases of corporate societal responsibility).

The following challenges and implications can be identified:

- Ecosystems are multilevel in nature and can be viewed on micro, meso, and macro levels as well as from processual, institutional, and systemic perspectives.
- A business ecosystem can be seen as platform for stakeholder interaction consisting of people and nature.
- An understanding of how sustainable societal practices can contribute to business transformation and vice versa can only be acquired via a stakeholder view that asks "Good for whom?"
- Sustainability, including CSR practice, has to be seen in a wider perspective and in a context of transformative change.
- The societal perspective of business practice has to be brought into focus in order to move beyond the management perspective.
- To tackle global challenges, we need to be aware of the complexity of wicked problems on a large scale.
- A multidisciplinary methodological approach is needed to confront the complexity of wicked problems and to organize vision- and goal-driven transformative change that meets global challenges.

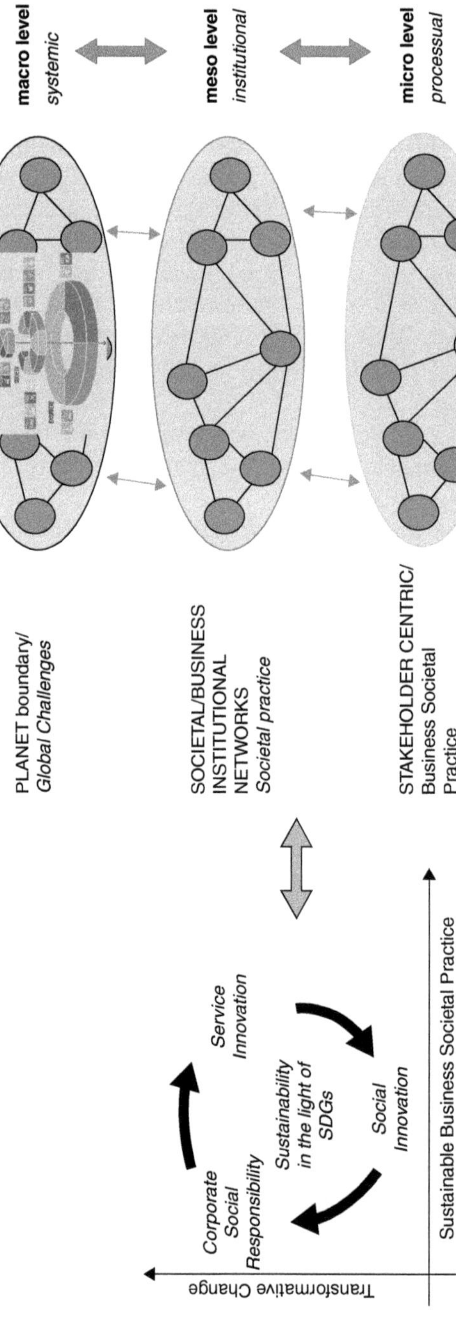

Figure 2.4 A business-societal ecosystem for sustainability-driven transformative change.

- The SDGs can be a proactive tool for identifying global challenges and for developing a transformation agenda for change in multiple institutions and organizations at all levels in directions of greater sustainability and social justice.
- The actors in change processes at the micro level need to be aware of the possibility that the institutional setting at the meso level will protect the status quo and not permit changes in the broader institutional structures (values, laws, routines, policies).
- The network of complexity, where service innovation, social innovation, and corporate social responsibility address global challenges, under the guidance of Agenda 2030, to tackle transformation, innovation, and sustainability issues, needs to move from a firm-centric to a societal perspective.

Notes

1 A wicked problem is a complex social or cultural problem that is large scale, difficult or impossible to solve.
2 Roadmaps are planning instruments that link short term targets to longer-term goals.
3 https://cop23.com.fj/talanoa-dialogue/

References

Alvesson, M., and Sköldberg, K. (2010). *Reflexive Methodology: New Vistas for Qualitative Research* (2nd ed.). London: Sage Publications.

Di Pietro, L., Edvardsson, B., Reynoso, J., Renzi, M.F., Toni, M., and Guglielmetti Mugion, R. (2017). A scaling up framework for innovative service ecosystems: lessons from Eataly and KidZania. *Journal of Service Management*, 29(1), 146–75.

Edvardsson, B., and Enquist, B. (2009). *Values-Based Service for Sustainable Business: Lessons from IKEA*. London: Routledge.

Edvardsson, B., and Enquist, B. (2011). The service excellence and innovation model: lessons from IKEA and other service frontiers. *Total Quality Management and Business Excellence,* 22(5) (May), 535–51.

Edvardsson, B., Enquist, B., and Sebhatu, S. P. (2014). The important role of shared values in a sustainable service business. In Raymond P. Fisk, Rebekah Russell-Bennett, and Lloyd C. Harris (Eds.), *Serving Customers: Global Services Marketing Perspectives* (pp. 229–48). Melbourne: Tilde University Press.

Elkington, J. (1998), *Cannibals with Forks: The Triple Bottom Line of 21st Century Business*. Gabriola Island, BC: New Society Publishers.

Enquist, B. (2016). *Kollektivtrafik som transformativ kraft för levande och hållbara städer* ("Public transit as transformative power for living and sustainable cities"). Karlstad University Studies, Vol. 19. Karlstad: Karlstad University.

Enquist B., Edvardsson, B., and Sebhatu, S. P. (2008). Corporate social responsibility for charity or for service business? *Asian Journal of Quality*, 9(1), 55–67.

Enquist, B., Sebhatu, S., P. and Johnson, M. (2015). Transcendence for business logics in value networks for sustainable service business. *Journal of Service Theory and Practice*, 25(2), 181–97.

Fosilfritt Sverige (Fossil Free Sweden). (2019). Politics for fossil-free competitiveness: compilation and development of policy proposals based on the roadmaps for fossil-free competitiveness. Agenda from Fosilfritt Sverige, October 28, 2019 (in Swedish).

Global Compact (2017). *Making Global Goals Local Business: A New Era for Responsible Business*. New York: UN Global Compact. Retrieved from https://d306pr3pise04h.cloudfront.net/docs/about_the_gc%2FMakingGlobalGoalsLocalsBusiness2017.pdf

Kemp, P. (2011). *Citizen of the World: The Cosmopolitan Ideal for the Twenty-first Century*. Amherst, NY: Humanity Books/Prometheus Books.

Koskela-Huotari, K. (2018). *The Evolution of Markets: A Service Ecosystems Perspective*. Doctoral Thesis. Karlstad Universities Studies 2018:6.

Lusch, R., and Vargo, S. (2014). *Service Dominant Logic: Premises, Perspectives, Possibilities*. Cambridge: Cambridge University Press.

Lusch, R.F. and Webster, F.E. (2011). A stakeholder-unifying, co-creation philosophy for marketing. *Journal of Macromarketing*, 31 (June), 129–34.

Ostrom, A.L., Parasuraman, A., Bowen, D.E., Patrício, L., and Voss, C.A. (2015). Service research priorities in a rapidly changing context. *Journal of Service Research*, 18(2), 127–59.

Palmisano, S.J. (2006). The globally integrated enterprise. *Foreign Affairs*, 85(3), 127–36.

Raworth, K. (2018). *Doughnut Economics: Seven Ways to Think Like a 21st-century Economist* (pbk ed.). London: Penguin/Random House Business Books.

Rockström, J., and Klum, M. (2015). *Big World Small Planet: Abundance within Planetary Boundaries*. Stockholm: Max Ström Publishing.

Rockström, J., Gaffney, O., Rogelj, J., Meinshausen, M., Nakicenovic, N., and Schnellhuber, H.J. (2017). A roadmap for rapid decarbonization: emissions inevitably approach zero with a "carbon law." *Science*, 355(6331), 1269–71.

Sebhatu, S. (2010). *Corporate Social Responsibility for Sustainable Service Dominant Logic*. Karlstad University Studies, no. 10. Karlstad: Karlstad University.

Stockholm Resilience Center. (2016). A systemic hierarchy of the SDGs, as illustrated by Rockström and Sukhdev. Available from https://www.stockholmresilience.org/research/research-news/2017-02-28-contributions-to-agenda-2030.html (2020).

United Nations (UN) (2015). *Transforming our World: The 2030 Agenda for Sustainable Development*. Resolution adopted by the General Assembly United Nations on September 25, 2015. Retrieved from https://sustainabledevelopment.un.org/post2015/transformingourworld/

van Tulder, R. (2018). *Business and Sustainable Developments Goals: A Framework for Effective Corporate Involvement*. Rotterdam School of Management, Erasmus University, Rotterdam.

Vogel, D. (2005). *The Market for Virtue: The Potential and Limits of Corporate Social Responsibility*. Washington, DC: Brooking Institution Press.

von Weizsäcker, E., and Wijkman, A. (2018). *Come On! Capitalism, Short-termism, Population and the Destruction of the Planet: A Report to the Club of Rome 50th Anniversary in 2018*. New York: Springer Science + Business Media.

Waddock, S., Meszoely, G.M., Waddell, S., and Dentoni, D. (2015). The complexity of wicked problems in large scale change. *Journal of Organizational Change Management*, 28(6), 993–1012.

Westley, F., McGowan, K., and Tjörnbo, O. (Eds.). (2017). *The Evolution of Social Innovation: Building Resilience through Transitions*. Cheltenham, UK: Edward Elgar Publishing.

Williams, O. (2014). *Corporate Social Responsibility: The Role of Business in Sustainable Development*. New York: Routledge.

World Commission on Environment and Development (WCED). (1987). *Our Common Future*. The "Brundtland Report." New York: Oxford University Press.

3 The circular economy and values-based sustainability business practice

People & Planet Positive at IKEA

Bo Enquist and Samuel Petros Sebhatu

Takeaways

- A values-based sustainable business practice outlines a shift from efficiency and control to a values-based perspective that includes social and ethical responsibility, circular and regenerative thinking, and a stakeholder orientation.
- IKEA represents a values-based enterprise which thinks long term in pursuit of a positive sustainability footprint. It aims for innovative change within a circular economy model under a continuous transformative change process which addresses complexity. Led by a strong culture, stakeholder engagement, and its "IKEA values," its mission is to "create a better life for the many people."
- IKEA represents a good example of a company guided and inspired by the UN Sustainable Development Goals (SDGs) to meet global challenges by adopting sustainability thinking; at the same time, it plays an important role in contributing to the SDG outcomes.

Introduction

This chapter will relate a story of a modern sustainable business practice and demonstrate what we can learn about sustainability challenges acting as a driving force to forge a new business landscape for the future. The business context is that of IKEA, being a values-based global enterprise, with a dynamic and developing track record embedded in its Scandinavian heritage and management; in particular, we examine its "People & Planet Positive 2030" strategy. In 2015 IKEA introduced a "circular economy" model; this operates across business, societies, and communities. This model has now been implemented at full scale across the different steps of the IKEA value chain: from sourcing of raw materials, through to production and transportation of IKEA products. The company aims to be resource- and energy-independent by only using raw materials within ecological limits and by transforming all waste into inputs – for

DOI: 10.4324/9781003188773-3

example, wood, water, cotton, and plant-based food ingredients – with full supply chain control over all critical material. IKEA addresses sustainability in a holistic way, considering how the IKEA business impacts both environmental and social dimensions (see IKEA SR, 2019 pp. 37–77).

IKEA case study (Part I)

IKEA was founded in 1943 by the entrepreneur Ingvar Kamprad in the county of Småland, a poor part of Sweden, and its journey to become the world-leading global home furnishings enterprise and brand that we know today was a long one. It currently employs 211,000 staff or "coworkers," with retail sales of €41.3 billion in 2019 up from €4.5 billion in 1996 – and a mere €160 million in 1970 (IKEA, 2019). In FY19 it had 433 stores in over 50 markets; there were over 1 billion visits to its stores; there were around 2.8 billion visits to IKEA websites; it had nearly 1,000 home furnishing suppliers in over 50 countries; and there were over 9,550 products in the IKEA range (IKEA SR, 2019).

IKEA can be described as a values-based company (Edvardsson & Enquist, 2009), grounded in a strong culture and a set of core values. The values form the compass that guides IKEA coworkers in their day-to-day work, and the IKEA culture is what is formed when these values are put into practice. The eight IKEA "Key Values" are: "Togetherness"; "Caring for people and planet"; "Cost-consciousness"; "Simplicity"; "Renew and improve"; "Different with a meaning";"Give and take responsibility"; and "Lead by example." Most of these values date to when IKEA first became a values-based company in the mid of 1970s, but the "Caring for people and planet" value has become more salient in the last decade. Sustainable business is a continuous transformative change process embedded in IKEA's history and heritage and underpins the IKEA culture (Edvardsson & Enquist, 2009). The Inter IKEA *Sustainability Report* highlights a number of sustainability challenges which represent the focus of the IKEA transformation change process: addressing unsustainable consumption; remaining affordable; limiting climate change to 1.5°C; sourcing recycled materials; improving working conditions; and inclusion of vulnerable groups in society (IKEA SR, 2019, p. 5).

Many authors, in media and academia, as well as practitioners, have written about IKEA in an attempt to grasp its "soul." The best-known book is Bertil Torekull's *Leading by Design: The IKEA Story* (Torekull, 1999), which tells the inside story of founder Ingvar Kamprad and his visionary concepts and strategies which turned a small, Swedish mail-order company into a global enterprise. It is an important document in revealing how the IKEA values have their roots in the company's founder, how his vision and values were realized through trial and error to build a dynamic business model outside the mainstream, and how his view of ownership is centered on cost-consciousness and financial independence. Further insight into Kamprad's vision is his first-person disclosure in "A Furniture Dealer's Testament" (Kamprad, 1976).

Anders Dahlvig, IKEA Group CEO from 1999–2009, revealed the inside story in *The IKEA Edge: Building Global Growth and Social Good at the World's Most Iconic Home Store* (Dahlvig, 2012), published after his resignation. In his conclusion about the basis of IKEA's success in "doing good business while being a good business," he distills it into four key points:

- A vision with a social ambition and a strong value base;
- Differentiation through control of the value chain;
- Market leadership and a balanced market portfolio;
- Company control by a committed owner with a long-term perspective (Dahlvig, 2012, p. 185).

Scholars have contributed several studies. Two doctoral dissertations worthy of mention are, firstly, Miriam Salzer's *Identity across Borders A Study in the "IKEA-World"* from 1994. This is a culture study about organizational identity: how people in a global, complex company construct collective and shared views of the "organizational self" across borders not as an idea of a global integrating supra-identity but rather an idea of multiple identities. She introduced the term "IKEA Saga" as an interpretative tool for a deeper understanding of the IKEA culture and IKEA's organizational identity (Salzer, 1994). This idea was further developed by Edvardsson and Enquist (2002; 2009). A second is Anna Jonsson's *Knowledge Sharing across Borders: A Study in the IKEA World* from 2008. This is a study about internationalization focusing on knowledge sharing, and, in the IKEA context, how firms learn from their experiences of entering new international markets. The study was undertaken from an organizational not a management perspective (Jonsson, 2008).

The present authors' prior contributions have had a more values-based and sustainable business perspective (Edvardsson and Enquist, 2009; Edvardsson, Enquist, & Sebhatu, 2014; Enquist, Sebhatu, & Johnson, 2015). (We will elaborate on this in the theoretical and contextual part of this chapter.) Our studies have been undertaken more with a service logic perspective with a stakeholder view rather than with a service management perspective.

Sara Kristoffersson, guest professor of Design History and Theory at Konstfack University College of Arts, Crafts and Design in Stockholm, published *Design by IKEA: A Cultural History*, in which she argued that the company's commercial success has been based on a neat alignment of the brand with a particular image of Swedish national identity, and its material expression in a pared-down, functional design aesthetic (Kristoffersson, 2014).

The above works focus on different aspects of the IKEA story and help us piece together a picture of the keys to IKEA's success: its strong values and culture, leading by design, sharing knowledge across borders, the founder's vision built on a trial-and-error conceptualization, and the IKEA ownership model and financial independence. The IKEA story is dynamic in character not least because of its phenomenal scaling-up in both size and complexity. The founder was prescient in making sure that he bequeathed a structure and ownership model for IKEA that would prepare it for the long term and minimize its dependence on the stock market. An independent company group was created around 1980, consisting of foundations and two IKEA groups: the Inter IKEA Group, which owns the brand and the IKEA system; and the IKEA Group, now known as Ingka Group, which is the biggest franchisee of the IKEA concept and runs most of the IKEA stores. Under this arrangement, Kamprad aspired to provide, as a legacy, a model in which the money remained within the IKEA sphere so it could continue to develop and flourish after he had gone (Torekull, 1999). So, when Kamprad died in 2018, IKEA was well prepared. In August 2016, the two IKEA groups had undergone an important reorganization to address the new business reality of digitalization, lifestyle changes owing to urbanization, and the challenge of climate change. The Inter IKEA Group became owner not only of the IKEA Systems, but also of IKEA Range & Supply and IKEA Industry. More on this transformation can be found in IKEA's 2018 *Sustainability Report* (IKEA SR, 2018).

The People & Planet Positive strategy, which was launched in 2012 and relaunched in 2018 (IKEA, 2018), will be a major cornerstone of the IKEA story as it moves forward. It was launched initially by the franchisee Ingka Group, well before the 2016 acquisition of Range & Supply and production activities from Ingka Group. It included ambitious goals, looking forward to 2030, to transform the IKEA business, the industries in the IKEA value chain, as well as life in the home for people around the world (IKEA SR, 2018).

Crucial in understanding IKEA today is, first, its vision – "to create a better everyday life for the many people":

> The IKEA vision has been with us from the very beginning and that continues to influence everything we do. It guides the products we develop, the ideas we share, the raw materials we use and the way we act in the world. Yes, every little thing. You could say it's the compass that keeps us on track. It helps us keep our feet on the ground and to become more accessible and inclusive.[1]

Second is its business idea:

> While the IKEA vision expresses why we exist, the IKEA business idea says how we realize the vision. We want "to offer a wide range of well-designed, functional home furnishing products at prices so low that as many people as possible will be able to afford them." We love these words because they capture the very essence of the IKEA brand.[2]

The business idea is also linked to the concept of "Democratic Design," which we will come to later, but here we will focus on its sustainability commitment. Torbjörn Lööf and Lena Pripp-Kovac, CEO and Chief Sustainability Officer, respectively, of Inter IKEA Group, wrote in their introductory letter in the 2019

IKEA Sustainability Report about the journey to transform the IKEA business to become People & Planet Positive. This is a transformational change and it means rethinking every aspect of how IKEA do business. "As a global home furnishing and food business, our focus is to make IKEA products more affordable and accessible for many more of the many people, and at the same time, to create a positive impact for people, society and the planet. … By relying on our own culture of entrepreneurship, always moving forward and not waiting for perfection, we can, and must, all work together to achieve breakthrough improvements" (IKEA SR, 2019, pp. 9–10).

In this chapter, we will undertake an empirical study of IKEA's transformative change by relating today's IKEA story, which we will construct with reference to: the People & Planet Positive 2030 strategy, IKEA's response to the 2030 Agenda SDGs; the relaunch of the "Democratic Design" concept; and IKEA's commitment to the goal of circularity in all aspects of the business. But first we will present the chapter's theoretical framework and research design.

Theoretical framework

A values-based stakeholder view and sustainable business

Pruzan (1998) argues for a shift from a focus on efficiency and control to a values-based perspective that includes social and ethical responsibility and a stakeholder orientation. His 1998 article presents a series of arguments for why it is good business, both in a traditional economic sense as well as in an ethical sense, for business leaders to actively introduce the notion of organizational and stakeholder values into the managerial culture – and to develop a values-based perspective on management (Pruzan, 1998, p. 1381). Quinn and Thakor (2019) argue the importance for business organizations to discover a higher purpose, but also assert that this insight alone is insufficient: the organization has to connect its purpose to people and their emotions (Quinn and Thakor, 2019, p. 168). Edvardsson and Enquist (2009) introduced the notion of values-based service for sustainable business, supported by the real-world context of IKEA. IKEA is unified by shared values (strong company values in resonance with foundational values of society and customer values) and shared meanings: the answers are not found in IKEA handbooks but rather from narratives in the field which IKEA coworkers share with one another in a continuous learning and transformative process. In the introductory chapter to the 2009 title, the authors made a distinction between two different categories of values: company core values and foundational values (Edvardsson and Enquist, 2009, pp. 1–2). Since that title was published, the concepts of sustainability and CSR have been further developed, and examples of contemporary foundational values can be found in the 17 SDGs. A decade after that publication, there is more to be learned from IKEA and its People & Planet Positive strategy, including signposts toward a more circular economy.

Values-based thinking was further developed in these authors' chapter in *Serving Customers: Global Services Marketing Perspectives* (Edvardsson, Enquist, & and Sebhatu, 2014), whereby economic, social, and environmental perspectives are handled interdependently from a holistic point of view as part of a more integrative business model. In Enquist et al. (2015), the values-based position is presented as a *transcendence* phenomenon found in sustainable business practices in real contexts, with four values-based organizations – Patagonia, IKEA, Starbucks, and Mayo Clinic – offered as examples. The premise of the article is to show that the business model needs to be broadened from the narrow neo-classical economic business model that focuses only on economic and financial issues. Values derived from the whole business network, along a process of cocreation, form the basis for the dialectic around the different transcendence phenomena whereby a broader spectrum of logics become part of the business model: exchange logic; steering logic; value creation logic; business interaction logic; responsibility logic; and communication logic.

In this chapter, we argue that the transformation to a new business practice related to our theoretical and conceptual framework is based on values, adopting a stronger stakeholder orientation and aiming for real societal and sustainability impact. In short, business practice needs to learn more about its interaction with people and planet. Gaia Vince is a science writer and broadcaster with an interest in the interplay between humans and the natural environment. In her book about the transcendence of our human culture (Vince, 2019), she analyzes this interplay and describes how Homo sapiens became a super-organism via the human evolutionary triad of genes, environment, and culture. Her interpretation of human evolution is underpinned by four transcendence phenomena: fire, language, beauty, and time.

- **Fire.** Making and controlling fire gave humans the amazing ability to transform the natural stuff of our planet into the materials of our human-made world. Fire mastery marks a turning point in the story of us, but also in the story of the earth, because it was the first step toward a new planetary force (Vince, 2019, p. 62).
- **Language.** Our group identity is woven into the words we speak, but this also makes language a vital tool for bridging cultural divides. Our success as a species depends both on competition between our tribal groups and the necessity of cross-cultural exchange (Vince, 2019, p. 124).
- **Beauty.** We are made human by the contemplation of beauty. We seek meaning in our lives and beauty gives us purpose, even immortality, through our modes of expression. Our greatest collaborations have been driven by beauty; it has enabled us to become global players. Beauty builds our human world (Vince, 2019, p. 125).
- **Time.** We have our stories, and they tell us about the past and help us imagine the future. We observe, predict, measure, and reason out our mysteries to decipher the future, and in doing so we have recreated the world and ourselves within it (Vince, 2019, p. 199).

Vince demonstrates how we as humans are continually remaking ourselves through the genes, environment, and culture triad. Humanity is seen as a super-organism which she calls *Homo omnis*, or *Homni* for short (Vince, 2019, p. 234). Although Vince does not discuss business practice per se, the four transcendence phenomena of fire, language, beauty, and time can be useful in providing new meaning to the collective mind in a business context.

An early work on the need for a transformation of business practice is *Reframing Business: When the Map Changes the Landscape* (Normann, 2001), which doesn't address environmental issues per se but rather focuses on transformative change and the need for a broader business logic that uses resources in a more innovative way. The book offers two potent concepts: *reconfiguration* and *reframing*. On the one hand, it examines the changing logic of today's business context and presents the *logic of value creation*, expressed in opportunities for dramatic *reconfiguration* of business systems. On the other hand, it investigates *the mental, symbolizing processes of the collective mind* which allow institutions to change themselves and function in this new context. This counterpoint to the reconfiguration process of the mental realm, but taking place in the business realm, is called *reframing* (Normann, 2001, p. 4). Transformative change is about a duality of ideas: those of *materialization* (using physical resources) and *dematerialization* (using mental and symbolizing processes and the collective mind in a proactive way), driven by a strong vision. The point behind the book's subtitle – *When the Map Changes the Landscape* – is that a strong vision for reframing the business can serve as the new *business mission*. It is also about mobilizing, managing, and using resources in a more proactive way and a way that is not limited to the boundary of the company itself. "The ability to reconfigure, to use resources inside and particularly outside the boundaries of the traditional corporation more effectively, becomes a mandatory skill for management" (Normann, 2001, p. 10).

In the area of service research, Lusch and Vargo (2014) offer a state-of-the-art reflection about research into S-D logic. Normann was an influence on their thoughts on the split between materialization and dematerialization of resources and how those resources are intertwined. They investigate these interrelationships in three chapters. In "The nature, scope and integration of resources," they identify resources as being either *operand* (must act on some other resource to create an effect) or *operant*, which is in the realm of knowledge and skills for use in action (i.e. resources that are capable of acting on other resources – operand or operant – to create an effect). In "Collaboration," they discuss actor-to-actor collaboration (collaborate in a network, coproduce, and cocreate for mutual gain). In "Service ecosystems," they explain how a service ecosystem is a relatively self-contained, self-adjusting system of resource-integrating actors that are connected by shared institutional and mutual value creation through service (Lusch & Vargo, 2014, p. 161). (See also Chapter 2 in this book, in which there is a broader discussion of an ecosystem characterized by "actor-to-actor-to-nature.")

The circular economy and regenerative transformation

The above framework makes it explicit that business practice cannot decouple people and planet from each other. Sustainable business needs to go beyond greenwashing, bluewashing, or SDG-washing. There are methodological implications in giving sustainability a more regenerative and societal meaning in the light of Agenda 2030. This idea is illuminated by the Club of Rome's 50th anniversary book (von Weizsäcker & Wijkman, 2018). With the help of system theory, the book introduces two metaphors – *empty world* and *full world* – which offer a deeper understanding of the conflict between economics and ecology, as well as perhaps a "way out" to solve this conflict.

- In an *empty world* (von Weizsäcker & Wijkman, 2018, pp. 50–1), the human economy is an open subsystem of the larger ecosphere, which is finite (the first law of thermodynamics). More human economy (more people, more commodities, more waste dumps) means less natural ecosphere. Both neoclassical and Keynesian economic theories were developed on the basis of the empty-world vision and still embody many assumptions from a past era (von Weizsäcker & Wijkman, 2018, p. 52).
- In a *full world*, total welfare (the sum of economic and ecological services) is maximized when the marginal benefit of added economic services is equal to the marginal cost of sacrificed ecosystem services (the second law of thermodynamics). In a full world, there is no vast natural sink to absorb wastes. Carbon dioxide accumulation in our atmosphere today is a salient example. In the full world, "externalities" are not external, but affect people and planet alike (von Weizsäcker & Wijkman, 2018, p. 52).

Sustainability acquires a more regenerative and societal meaning with transformative change and innovation based on the "full world" logic. Circular-economy thinking is related to this regenerative thinking because it shifts the linear system to a circular one. At its core, the circular economy focuses on three activities: *reuse at the product level* (repair or refurbishment), *reuse at the component level* (remanufacturing), and *reuse at the material level* (recycling) (Zink & Geyer, 2017). The foundation of economic growth in a circular economy is the reuse of materials from end-of-life products instead of extraction of resources (Ellen MacArthur Foundation, 2013). Products in a circular economy are designed for reuse, refurbishment, or recycling. Circular systems employ reuse, sharing, repair, refurbishment, remanufacturing, and recycling to create a closed-loop system, minimizing the use of resource inputs, the creation of waste, pollution, and carbon emissions (Geissdoerfer et al., 2017). A circular economy, according to the Ellen MacArthur Foundation (2013), is "an economic system aimed at eliminating waste and the continual use of resources." A circular economy aims to keep products, equipment, and infrastructure in use for longer, thus improving these resources' productivity. All "waste" should become "food" for another process: either a by-product or recovered resource for another industrial process, or as regenerative resources for nature (e.g. compost). Compared to the linear economy which follows a "take–make–dispose" approach, circular economic models allow business to have a positive societal impact at the end of the value chain on societies and communities.

Rockström and Klum (2015) assert that a transition to sustainability can be attained only by combining technology with deep system innovations and lifestyle changes (Rockström & Klum, 2015, p. 133). They identify five key global transformations to achieve sustainability in which technology and innovation can play an important role. One of these is the circular economy – "circular economics models for business, societies, and communities" (Rockström & Klum, 2015, p. 133). Each of the five global transformations has a societal impact where technology and innovation must be accompanied by lifestyle changes in which people and nature provide a new meaning. A circular economy is restorative by intention and design.

Transcendence for the circular economy and values-based sustainability business practice

The interdependences between *sustainability*, *transformation*, and *innovation* are central to this book as a whole, and to this chapter in particular. We will use the idea of transcendence to shape and narrate these interlinkages. Transcendence is simply defined as the quality or state of being transcendent, which can be understood as a "state of excelling or surpassing or going beyond usual limits." Going further, transcendence can be seen as a cultural movement in which physical (materialistic) influences that have dominated culture are ebbing while metaphysical (experiential) influences become stronger (see Enquist, Sebhatu, & Johnson, 2015).

What can we learn in a business context from Gaia Vince (2019) and her four transcendence phenomena? *Fire* means material and resources, important for a human-made world; *language* means group identity, corporate culture, and cross-cultural exchange, important in building an integrated global enterprise; *beauty* means using the links between design and brand-building for interactive marketing communication; and *time* means using time to predict, measure, and reason the transforming change by coming to terms with the past, understanding the reality of today, and imagining the future.

Based on the above conceptual/theoretical framework for transcendence, the circular economy, and values-based sustainable business practice, we propose a matrix (Table 3.1) which will be used in Part II of the IKEA case study in order to analyze and interpret the transformative change in IKEA.

Research design

Our case is designed to follow IKEA's transformation process, which involves scaling up in both size and complexity, to see if there has been a shift of thinking toward sustainable practice – from "empty world" to "full world" thinking.

Table 3.1 Transcendence, the circular economy, and values-based sustainable business practice for transformative change: matrix

Time/transformative change	*Time frame*
Values/culture	
Material resources	
Immaterial resources/vision, strategy, knowledge, and skill	
Sustainability/responsibility, as well as circular and regenerative thinking	
Communication/interactive	
Steering/governance structure and stewardship	

The data collection process for the case study has been ongoing for the last three years. However, as researchers, we have been following and reporting on IKEA in different studies over two decades. This study is based on the grounded theory method of inquiry for multiple types of information-gathering based on interviews with key persons, documents, workshops (lab sessions), on-site observations at IKEA, as well as ongoing research on business transformation by practitioners and researchers from a multidisciplinary point of view. Case theory (Gummesson, 2017) has broadened our multidisciplinary perspective with the insight of pragmatic wisdom and the importance of case theory for understanding business and sustainable management practices.

The most recent primary data were collected through interviews with company leaders and management, and through observation and a T-Lab (Transformation-Lab) session in an innovation park. More specifically:

- We have been following IKEA for several years. We have met with key individuals at executive and management levels (including the sustainability director), examined open and internal documents from the organization, and we are in possession of scientific articles and memos from our research into the company.
- We visited the IKEA's Design Center in Älmhult in spring 2016, meeting with the previous Head of Design, Marcus Engman, and Sustainability Manager Lena Pripp Kovac, who is currently Head of Sustainability, Inter IKEA Group.
- We arranged and conducted a joint Transformation-Lab (T-Lab) session in fall 2016 in a neutral location: an innovation park in a service innovation lab. Collaborating with us in this were: a designer and a project manager from IKEA's global design and supply chain company; IKEA of Sweden; two professors in business ethics and CSR from distinguished American universities; and three leaders of the innovation park including the chairman and sustainability director of another business. In this session, we sought to

identify the transformation agenda for meeting the sustainability challenges of a values-driven enterprise like IKEA in order to provoke a more general discussion about stewardship, hyper-norms, and sustainable service innovation.

- We acquired insights about IKEA from two keynote speakers at Sustainability Day 2016 at Karlstad University Business School who were speaking about Democratic Design. At the same event in 2019, we met with three people from IKEA to discuss IKEA's ambitions around a circular economy.
- We held a follow-up meeting in March 2020 with Emma Gullstrand Edbring, Circular Business Designer and team leader at Ingka Group, to further enquire into circular business the IKEA way. The meeting was at IKEA Hubhult Malmö, which is a meeting space as well as being home to Scandinavia's most experienced homemakers. The building has the honor of being the most environmentally friendly office building in Scandinavia.

The collected materials were analyzed using a case analysis (Eisenhardt, 1989). The case was analyzed based on the description, understanding, and interpretation of the research material.

IKEA case study (Part II)

In Part I of the case study, we identified IKEA as a values-based global enterprise driven by shared values and shared meanings. In Part II we will show how IKEA employs sustainability thinking for innovation and transformation guided by its culture and values, and we will see how sustainability has acquired a new more regenerative and societal meaning with a view to making a real transformation and meeting global challenges in a way that makes a real difference. "Democratic Design" and the "People & Planet Positive" strategy are two tools already discussed for transformative change. But there are other concepts also of great importance for the ongoing transformative change process; these include *experience* (for example, seeing the IKEA showrooms as experience rooms) for the cocreation of value, *brand and marketing communication* for values resonance (as opposed to dissonance), and *leadership* by living the values (Edvardsson & Enquist, 2009). There is also a major transformation that has been ongoing since 2015 which involves efforts to come closer to customers. Ingka Group, the retail group that accounts for 90% of IKEA sales, claims that it is in the midst of its biggest transformation change process yet, with strong movements in digital development, store transformations, city expansion, services, and sustainability initiatives, "bringing IKEA to more people in new ways," always in pursuit of becoming more affordable, accessible, and sustainable (Ingka Group, 2019). The big flagship stores, the "blue boxes," outside city centers are being augmented with new concepts in the bigger cities. The different channels are seen as a joint experience, bringing IKEA into people's lives, something supported by a new app – "Ikea Place" – which makes the experience "phygital" (where the physical and digital shopping worlds merge); it is an augmented-reality app which allows consumers to visualize how furniture will look in their homes (it is being introduced in some European markets in 2020). There is also an ongoing transformation of the business model: simultaneous physical and digital; a lower cost structure so products can reach new markets outside Europe; and the drive to make the IKEA network more sustainable – all happening concurrently.

The IKEA sustainable business: a continuous transformative change process

Ever since it was founded, IKEA has been a company that makes efforts to avoid wasting resources: which goes for everything, from natural resources to other resources such as time and money. Over time, the "IWAY" – IKEA's supplier code – has been introduced for different areas such as wood, child labor protection, food, etc. In *Values-Based Service for Sustainable Business* (Edvardsson & Enquist, 2009), we showed that IKEA's sustainability was embedded in its history and heritage. The environmental issues IKEA has faced over the years have been transformed in numerous small steps from being a reputational (and potentially existential) threat to an opportunity to address social and environmental issues in a proactive manner by virtue of the company's vision in which daily business can contribute to genuine long-term sustainability.

The Democratic Design concept for transformative change

Fifty years after it first launched as a home furnishing company, IKEA devised its first version of Democratic Design. The concept was outlined in a 1995 booklet entitled *Democratic Design: A Book about Form, Function and Price – The 3 Dimensions at IKEA* (IKEA, 1995). Michel Hay, at the time head of Global Communication at IKEA, who collaborated with two of the authors of this chapter on an article entitled "Values-based service brands: narratives from IKEA" (Edvardsson, Enquist, & Hay, 2006), recounted the narrative about Democratic Design, a notion that was first announced outside IKEA at the Milan Design Fair of 1995. The concept was part of IKEA sustainability thinking and the way it was embedded in IKEA products. In the booklet (IKEA, 1995) was a reflection by Victor Papanek, an Austrian-American Professor of Architecture and Design (who died in 1998), who was a strong advocate of socially and ecologically responsible design of products, tools, and community infrastructures. Papanek's personal view of how IKEA could use sustainability as a driving force in the future turned out to prophetic:

> When thinking about the future of IKEA I also think about the future design, manufacture and distribution. It is a future that will be closely linked to ecology and the environment. ... The future isn´t what it used to be. Everyone talks about it, yet no one has been there. One thing is certain: IKEA will continue in the forefront – ecologically, socially and culturally – of making things that work, possess beauty and are affordable.
>
> (IKEA, 1995, pp. 255–61)

Democratic Design has developed since 1995: the original three-dimensional concept has been reconceptualized and is now five-dimensional, the two new dimensions being *sustainability* and *quality* to add to *function*, *form*, and *low price*. Democratic Design has a key role to play in realizing the IKEA business idea. What do the dimensions mean?

> The form is for beauty, it's what attracts the eye, and the object has to be functional, otherwise it won't be used. When objects and materials last over time, that's quality. Being mindful of resources is something that has been with us since the start. We don't like complicated solutions and wastefulness, it's bad for everyone. Part of sustainability is about using exactly the right materials for the function, and using them sparingly, but sustainability also means taking responsibility all the way through a product's life. It starts with how we source materials, to the people who produce the product, all the way through to our clients.[3]

People & Planet Positive strategy 2030

The IKEA sustainability strategy, "People & Planet Positive," was published in June 2018 (IKEA, 2018) as an updated version of the first People & Planet Positive strategy of 2012. The new strategy has ambitious goals to transform the IKEA business, the industries in the IKEA value chain, and life at home for people all across the world. The commitments are set for 2030 in line with the UN SDGs. The following statement accompanies the strategy outlining what sustainability means to IKEA: "We want to have a positive impact on people and the planet. For us it's about balancing economic growth and positive social impact with environmental protection and regeneration" (IKEA, 2018, p. 3).

The idea is one of being positive in a rapidly changing world. Three major challenges have been identified that are relevant for the IKEA business: *climate change*, *unsustainable consumption*, and *inequality*. The UN SDGs act as a guide for IKEA business and are used as a compass to mobilize change. The IKEA People & Planet Positive strategy will remain transparent and will be followed up in the company's Sustainability Reports, benchmarked against the SDG Index to demonstrate IKEA's contribution to achieving the goals (IKEA SR, 2018).

The Ingka story: becoming people- and planet-positive

The Ingka Group – which, as revealed, is the biggest franchisee of the IKEA concept, running most of the IKEA stores – is implementing the P&P strategy in its daily operations as a means toward transformation to become people- and planet-positive. The Ingka Group message is: "We want to play our part in creating a movement in society – one that encourages everyone to live within the limits of our planet, and one which is truly inclusive" (Ingka Group, 2019, p. 58). According to Pia Heidenmark Coock, Chief Sustainability Officer at Ingka Group, 2019 was a turning-point year when the world finally woke up to the urgency of climate change and biodiversity loss. "We need everyone – from shop floor to senior leadership – to take responsibility for creating a more sustainable business." She points out three areas where sustainability is the key for this transformation (Ingka Group, 2019).

- **Leading a sustainable transformation.** As we transform our business to come closer to customers and their needs and dreams, we know the greatest opportunities will come when we're more sustainable, more affordable, and more accessible – all at the same time.
- **Meeting customer needs for affordable sustainable living.** We have also made good progress at integrating sustainability into our customer offer and the way we communicate the sustainable stories behind the products in a clear and compelling way.
- **Taking a stand on the issues that matter.** In what can feel like an increasingly polarized world, we believe we have a responsibility to demonstrate our vision, values, and commitment to inclusive growth. How we treat and care for each other is more important today than ever before, and we know that customers and coworkers increasingly look to companies like ours to drive progressive change in society.

An example of more effective use of resources inside and, particularly, outside the boundaries of the traditional corporation, spurred on by sustainability thinking, can be found in Inkga Group's proactive tackling of travel and delivery emissions. Around 15% of Ingka Group's emissions are attributable to customers traveling to and from stores, coworker travel, and last-mile delivery of products to customer homes (Ingka Group, 2019, p. 78).

In a magazine produced by Trivector, a leading Swedish consultancy firm in mobility management, Angela Hultberg, Ingka Group's Head of Sustainable Mobility, describes the intended transformation to being fossil-free by 2025 (Lindskog, 2020), which includes all deliveries of IKEA goods worldwide. Since Ingka does not operate its own transport, the transition involves cooperation with carriers, car manufacturers, government, customers, energy producers, and many others. Hultberg is confident of success with home delivery transport (the "last mile"):

> When we set the goal in September 2018, it was slow at first. We knew where we wanted to go, but not how to reach the goal. The first year we only managed to electrify a few percent of our transport, but now I see an exponential development. There will be more electric vehicles, cheaper batteries, and more cities that limit transport with fossil fuels. I also know what's going on in the future, so I'm pretty confident we will reach our goal.
> (Lindskog, 2020, p. 8)

It is not just electric cars. "We have started testing bicycle transport. This is good because the bikes can take other, often faster, roads than cars" (Lindskog,

2020, p. 9). Five focus cities have been selected as frontrunners to learn from, each with different challenges: Shanghai, Amsterdam, Paris, New York, and Los Angeles. Shanghai has already reached the goal of being fossil-free, and Amsterdam, Paris, and New York are almost fossil-free for last-mile transport. Los Angles is a bigger challenge, but is proving instructional (Lindskog, 2020, p. 10).

This is also about influencing how the 160,000 coworkers of the Ingka Group get to work and how customers travel to stores. Here, too, there are some workplaces that have acted as test beds to learn more about what does not work. Tools that have been tested are bikes, shuttle buses from public centers, and buses running on routes where there are many commuters. The Ingka Group's preference is for customers to travel on the same buses as the coworkers in order to maximize capacity (Lindskog, 2020). The e-commerce model and other store concepts in city centers are of use to customers without cars or can encourage customers not to use their cars. Hultberg closes the article with the words: "If we are not a sustainable company, we cannot remain in business."

Long-term transformative change at IKEA

The matrix shown in Table 3.2, constructed from the conceptual and theoretical framework, presents a summary of transformative change in IKEA.

A reflection on innovative and sustainable transformation

In this section, we reflect on IKEA's transformative change process over the last decade. For this purpose, we will draw on a model developed by Johan Asplund, a sociology professor, who was influenced by Marx, particularly his concepts of *base* (related to production and property) and *superstructure* (related to culture, art, immaterial resources, etc.). In developing these concepts for modern society, Asplund spoke of *praxis* rather than material base and *discourse* rather than superstructure. He also expanded this duality with a connective aspect he referred to as *thought figure* (Asplund, 1991). This model will help us to visualize IKEA's transformative change process. As per Asplund, praxis represents material resources, and system structures and discourse are related to immaterial resources. Instead of "thought figure," however, we use *transcendence* as the link between discourse and praxis.

The transcendence of IKEA

It is clear that the transcendence of IKEA during this transformative change period can be described as a cultural movement in which physical (materialistic) influences that dominated the culture are ebbing while metaphysical (experiential) influences become stronger. Major changes are taking place in IKEA values, which are becoming more innovative, circular/regenerative, and caring/responsible. Papanek's prophetic view from 1995, whereby sustainability

Table 3.2 The transcendence circular economy and values-based sustainability business practice for transformative change in IKEA

Time/ transformative change	*IKEA prior to 2010*	*IKEA since 2010*
Values/culture	• IKEA culture embedded in history and heritage. • Nine values: togetherness and enthusiasm; constant desire for renewal; cost-consciousness; willingness to accept and delegate responsibility; Humility and willpower; simplicity; daring to be different; striving to meet reality; the importance of constantly being on the way.	• Eight values: togetherness; caring for people and planet; cost-consciousness; simplicity; renew and improve; different with a meaning; give and take responsibility; lead by example.
Material resources	• Blue boxes (the big stores) as the backbone). • Flat packages for coproduction. • Showrooms as experience rooms. • Differentiation through control of the value chain. • The IKEA Catalogue. • The IKEA IT platform. • Building up the IKEA industry to create best practice for suppliers.	• The big flagship stores, the blue boxes, outside city centers, are in bigger cities, complemented by new business concepts (started in 2015) and substantial growth of e-commerce. • The IKEA experience supported by a new app which makes the experience "phygital."
Immaterial resources	• A vision with social ambition and a strong value base. • The IKEA business idea explains how to realize the vision. • "A Furniture Dealer's Testament" (Kamprad 1996) (applied in 1976). • Democratic design (three dimensions; applied in 1995). • Knowledge sharing across borders.	• A vision with social ambition and a strong value base (still valid but a broader range of expressions). • Democratic design (five dimensions, with sustainability and quality now added). • The mission still valid with an important transformative change: Democratic design helps create products the company can stand behind and realize its business idea. • IKEA People & Planet Positive 2020 strategy (applied 2012). • IKEA People & Planet Positive 2030 strategy (applied 2018). • The *Circular Product Design Guide* (applied 2019). • Transformation of the business model.

(*continued*)

Table 3.2 Cont.

Time/ transformative change	*IKEA prior to 2010*	*IKEA since 2010*
Sustainability	• Ever since it was founded, IKEA has put effort into *avoiding wasting resources*. • Gradual implementation of IWAY (the IKEA supplier code). • Addressing social and environmental issues in a proactive manner by virtue of the company's vision of everyday business contributing to genuine long-term sustainability.	• Being circular in every aspect of its business and meeting sustainability challenges by: addressing unsustainable consumption; remaining affordable; tackling climate change; sourcing recycled material; improving working conditions; and including vulnerable groups. • Different enablers to make it happen.
Communication	• Market leadership and a balanced market portfolio. • Brand, product, and marketing communication including also the IKEA Catalogue supporting sales in the big stores.	• Continued market leadership and a balanced market portfolio. • More interactive communication in different media. • Inspire and enable people to live a better everyday life within planetary limits.
Steering	• Company controlled by a committed owner with a long-term perspective. • IKEA built as an inaccessible company empire with foundations and two groups: Inter IKEA (which owns the system and the brand) and IKEA Group (including also IKEA Range & Supply and IKEA Industry).	• Company still controlled by a committed owner with a long-term perspective. • The IKEA Range & Supply and production activities were acquired from Ingka Group (formerly IKEA Group) by Inter IKEA in August 2016. • Ambitious goals to *transform the IKEA business*, the industries in the IKEA value chain, and life at home for people around the world. • Global stewardship: the UN SDGs guide IKEA's business and are used as a compass to mobilize change.

could be employed as a driving force, closely linked to ecology and the environment, has now become a reality. The social dimension of sustainability has been further strengthened to create a more societal business. IKEA's interpretation of transcendence is expressed as: "Values-based culture through innovative, circular and societal sustainability strategy."

IKEA Praxis

The above-mentioned ability to reconfigure resource use – inside and outside the company's boundaries (Normann, 2001) – is manifested in IKEA praxis. The legal configuration in which *ownership* and *governance*, along with control over *managing resources* within the IKEA brand, system, design, range, and industry is allocated to Inter IKEA Group, to manage via a franchise system, allows the realization of the ambitious transformative goals. There is a proactive and innovative management – supported by a strong financial situation – of the physical materials infrastructure, and also of a wide range of facilities for production, storage, selling/experience, IT platforms, forestry plantations, solar and wind farms, and so on. The stewardship arrangement for stakeholder interaction is supported by different enablers and guided by the proactive implementation of the People & Planet Positive 2030 strategy. IKEA praxis can be understood as: "IKEA's legal, physical and stakeholder network/ecosystem."

IKEA discourse

This reconfiguration of resource use is also manifested in IKEA discourse. The IKEA vision – "to create a better everyday life for the many people" – has over the last decade led to the company being more interactive and collaborative with its customers and other stakeholders: networking, coproducing, and cocreating for mutual gain. IKEA has acquired a new dimension in its discourse through different types of experience rooms (the "phygital" app, social media, smaller-scale stores in cities, making the "blue boxes" more interactive). The IKEA sustainability mission is part of its discourse. IKEA discourse can be summarized as: "Interactive and collaborative phygital experience and communication."

The interlinkages between IKEA discourse, transcendence, and praxis are summarized in Figure 3.1.

Conclusion/implications

In this chapter, we have shown how a globally integrated enterprise has undergone a vision-driven transformative change process of its entire business concept guided by a dynamic transforming culture and values, in which "full world"(von Weizsäcker and Wijkman, 2018) sustainability thinking played a major role. The chapter has drawn the following inferences:

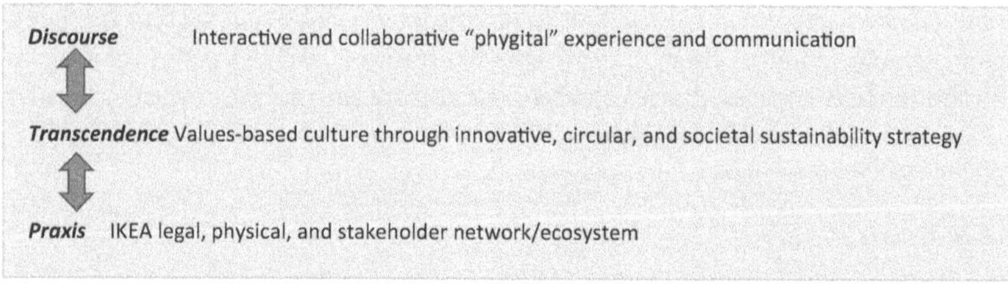

Figure 3.1 The interlinkages between IKEA's discourse, transcendence, and praxis

- A strong vision of reframing the business can be used as the new business mission.
- More effective use of resources inside, and particularly outside, the boundaries of the traditional corporation is a mandatory skill for management.
- Use the network/ecosystem for network collaboration; coproduce and cocreate for mutual gain.
- The time dimension is important for predicting, measuring, and reasoning out the transformative change by coming to terms with the past, understanding the reality of today, and imagining the future.
- Transcendence means going beyond the usual limits and can therefore be seen as a cultural movement in which the physical (materialistic) influences that have dominated the culture are ebbing while the metaphysical (experiential) influences become stronger.
- A values-based culture drives sustainable strategy.
- The circular economy is related to regenerative thinking because it shifts the linear system to a circular one.
- "Sustainability" acquires a more circular and societal meaning when transformative change and innovation takes place based on the logic of the "full world."
- The UN SDGs can be used as a compass to mobilize change for sustainable business practice, and vice versa: sustainable business practice can contribute to fulfilling the aims of the SDGs.

The main purpose of this chapter has been to develop and conceptualize in an explorative way a values-based sustainability practice in a business context embedded in circular-economy thinking, which can be used for challenge-driven transformative change. Using the conceptual and theoretical framework that we have developed to understand IKEA's transformative change, we have searched for a new narrative which has led us to identify four main areas:

- Identify transcendence phenomena in which the usual limits are transcended in order – in the context of a values-based sustainable culture – to create a strong vision or discover a higher purpose (i.e. a reframing of the business), which can be used as the new business mission;

- Go beyond greenwashing, bluewashing, or SDG-washing to invest sustainability thinking with a more circular and societal meaning, leading to transformative change and innovation based on "full world" logic;
- Transform the legal, physical, and stakeholder network/ecosystem to support this transcendence;
- Create a collaborative and stakeholder-oriented discourse of shared values and meanings through interactive experience and communication in different media, both physical and digital.

Notes

1 https://about.ikea.com/en/who-we-are/our-roots/the-ikea-vision-and-business-idea
2 Ibid.
3 https://about.ikea.com/en/life-at-home/how-we-work/democratic-design

References

Asplund, J. (1991). *Essay about Gemeinschaft and Gesellschaft.* Korpen, Göteborg (in Swedish).

Dahlvig, A. (2012). *The IKEA Edge: Building Global Growth and Social Good at the World's Most Iconic Home Store.* New York: McGraw Hill.

Edvardsson, B., and Enquist, B. (2002). "The IKEA Saga": how service culture drives service strategy. *The Service Industries Journal*, 22(4), pp. 153–86.

Edvardsson, B., and Enquist, B. (2009). *Values-Based Service for Sustainable Business: Lessons from IKEA.* London: Routledge.

Edvardsson, B., Enquist, B. and Hay, M. (2006). Values based service brands: narratives from IKEA, *Managing Service Quality*, 16(3), 230–46.

Edvardsson, B., Enquist, B., and Sebhatu, S.P. (2014). The important role of shared values in a sustainable service business. In Raymond P. Fisk, Rebekah Russell-Bennett, and Lloyd C. Harris (Eds.), *Serving Customers: Global Services Marketing Perspectives* (pp. 229–48). Melbourne: Tilde University Press.

Eisenhardt, K.M. (1989). Building theories from case study research. *Academy of Management Review*, 14(4), 532–50.

Ellen MacArthur Foundation. (2013). *Towards the Circular Economy,* Vol. 1, *An Economic and Business Rationale for an Accelerated Transition.* United Kingdom: Cowes, Isle of Wight: Ellen MacArthur Foundation.

Enquist, B., Sebhatu, S. P., and Johnson, M. (2015). Transcendence for business logics in value networks for sustainable service business. *Journal of Service Theory and Practice*, 25(2), 181–97.

Geissdoerfer, M., Savaget, P., Bocken, N., and Hultink, E. (2017). The circular economy: a new sustainability paradigm? *Journal of Cleaner Production*, 143(1), 757–68.

Gummesson, E. (2017). *Case Theory in Business and Management: Reinventing Case Study Research.* London: Sage.

IKEA. (1995). *Democratic Design: A Book about Form, Function and Price – The 3 Dimensions at IKEA.* Booklet. Älmhult, Sweden: IKEA.

IKEA. (2018). *People & Planet Positive: IKEA Sustainability Strategy.* Inter IKEA Systems BV. Retrieved from https://www.ikea.com/ms/ja_JP/pdf/people_planet_positive/IKEA_Sustainability_Strategy_People_Planet_Positive_v3.pdf

IKEA. (2019). *IKEA Facts & Figures FY19.* Inter IKEA Group.

IKEA SR. (2018). *IKEA Sustainability Report FY18.* Inter IKEA Group. Retrieved from https://preview.thenewsmarket.com/Previews/IKEA/DocumentAssets/535135.pdf

IKEA SR. (2019). *IKEA Sustainability Report FY19.* Inter IKEA Group. Retrieved from https://preview.thenewsmarket.com/Previews/IKEA/DocumentAssets/557393.pdf

Ingka Group. (2019). *Annual Summary & Sustainability Report FY19.* INGKA Group. Retrieved from https://www.ingka.com/wp-content/uploads/2020/01/Ingka-Group-Annual-Summary-Sustainability-Report-FY19.pdf?1

Jonsson, A. (2008). *Knowledge Sharing across Borders: A Study in the IKEA World.* Dissertation. Lund Studies in Economics and Management, 97. Lund, Sweden: Lund Business Press.

Kamprad, I. (1976). A furniture dealer's testament. Appendix in B. Torekull, *Leading by Design: The IKEA Story.* New York: Harper Business, 1999.

Kristoffersson, S. (2014). *Design by IKEA: A Cultural History.* London: Bloomsbury Academic.

Lindskog, K. (2020). Soon fossil-free transport around the world. *2038: Understand the Future First* (a magazine from Trivector) (in Swedish).

Lusch, R., and Vargo, S. (2014). *Service Dominant Logic: Premises, Perspectives, Possibilities.* Cambridge: Cambridge University Press.

Normann, R. (2001). *Reframing Business: When the Map Changes the Landscape*, Chichester, UK: John Wiley & Sons.

Pruzan, P. (1998). From control to values-based management and accountability. *Journal of Business Ethics*, 17(13), 1379–94.

Quinn, R.E., and Thakor, A.V. (2019). *The Economics of Higher Purpose: Eight Counterintuitive Steps for Creating a Purpose-Driven Organization.* Oakland, CA: Berrett-Koehler Publishers.

Rockström, J., and Klum, M. (2015). *Big World Small Planet: Abundance within Planetary Boundaries.* Stockholm: Max Ström Publishing.

Salzer, M. (1994). *Identity across Borders: A Study in the "IKEA-World."* Linköping Studies in Management and Economics, Dissertation No. 27.

Torekull, B. (1999). *Leading by Design: The IKEA Story.* New York: Harper Business.

Vince, G. (2019). *Transcendence: How Humans Evolved through Fire, Language, Beauty and Time.* London: Penguin Random House.

von Weizsäcker, E.U., and Wijkman, A. (2018). *Come On! Capitalism, Short-termism, Population and the Destruction of the Planet. A Report to the Club of Rome 50th Anniversary in 2018.* New York: Springer Science + Business Media.

Zink, T., and Geyer, R. (2017). Circular economy rebound. *Journal of Industrial Ecology*, 21(3), 593–602. https://doi.org/10.1111/jiec.12545

4 Sustainable business practices for transformative change

The case of Eataly

Laura Di Pietro, Maria Francesca Renzi, and Bo Edvardsson

Takeaways

- Explaining the role played by value propositions and societal resonance in the development and implementation of sustainable business practice and service innovation.
- Showing how business can contribute to the 17 Sustainable Development Goals of UN Agenda 2030 (UN, 2015) by describing sustainable strategies focusing on "no waste."
- Highlighting the contribution to scaling-up processes made by sustainable business practice in the service ecosystem.
- Contributing to research-based knowledge on services that improve the well-being of individuals, organizations, and societies.

Introduction

Sustainability is the key challenge that modern society faces in order to guarantee the well-being of current and future generations. Contributing to sustainable development has therefore become a key aim for governments, businesses, organizations, and individuals across the world. The United Nations Agenda 2030 (UN, 2015), presented in 2015, with its 17 Sustainable Development Goals (SDGs), is a worldwide call to action, aimed at signposting the right direction for radical positive transformation in the pursuit of global sustainable development. A precursor to these, the UN's eight Millennium Development Goals, established in 2000, largely addressed national governments, whereas the SDGs recognize the crucial role of private organizations and their stakeholders.

This chapter analyzes the role of sustainable practices in enabling and supporting this transformation. The focus is on the dynamics and mechanisms that trigger transformative change, based on the adoption of sustainable practices, throughout a value proposition. In presenting a business case of the company Eataly, we address the following questions: What are the main drivers of transformative change? Who are the main actors involved? What is the relationship between sustainability and transformation? What role does innovation play?

DOI: 10.4324/9781003188773-4

Eataly is a fast-growing innovative Italian food chain offering high-quality fare. Its outlets offer an Italian food experience, which includes both dining and food retail. Its model represents the essential challenge for the kinds of businesses (and other organizations) that can operate only through collaboration with the main stakeholder of a company. Well-being has both an individual and collective relevance (Anderson et al., 2013). And, as recognized by Ostrom et al. (2010, p.10), services can have "a macro, sociocultural impact on the well-being of nations, subcultures, communities, families in addition to individuals." Accordingly, research fields like transformative service research (TSR) can help improve the lives of individuals (customers, employees, citizens), communities, societies, and the global ecosystem more broadly (Anderson and Ostrom, 2015; Anderson et al., 2013). The TSR concept is based on value creation and the understanding that value is cocreated (Vargo & Lusch, 2004) and enabled by collaborations between multiple actors who integrate their skills, knowledge, and other resources (Aal et al., 2016; Wieland et al., 2012). Therefore, to sustain the value co creation processes within a service ecosystem, it is necessary to engage actors by inviting them to join forces in the development of relevant value propositions (Chandler & Lusch, 2014). Thus, a focal point is the explicit inclusion of sustainability features within companies' value propositions in order to arrive at sustainable strategies and practices that provide a compass for collaborating actors in service ecosystems. Indeed, norms, rules, and habits are aspects that govern interactions and integration among the actors and support the scaling-up process (Di Pietro et al., 2018). Strategies and practices to grow and enter new markets need adaptation to the local context by engaging local communities and actors (Di Pietro et al., 2018; Paina & Peters, 2012; Subramanian et al., 2011).

Sustainability has now become a priority in order to maintain long-term success, and it must be embodied in companies' strategies and operations. This implies a definition of sustainable practices strongly linked with an organization's vision and value propositions centered around participation in building a sustainable future. The need to embed sustainable practices as a fundamental pillar of the business requires a transformation in the mindsets of entrepreneurs and management, which represents one of the greatest challenges in the pursuit of transformative change. Organizations must serve their customers while taking into account new moral obligations that are broader than those traditionally considered (Anderson et al., 2013).

Research design

In this chapter, we present a mini-case on Eataly's sustainable practices using a narrative approach. Eataly is a fast-growing, innovative, and sustainable business, and therefore offers valuable insights into the nature of transformative change.

As an innovative and sustainable service ecosystem, the Eataly case offers a useful learning opportunity, as recognized by Aal et al. (2016). In just over a decade, the firm has gone from a startup to one of the world's largest chains in its sector. Its success can be measured in numbers of stores, partners, customers, and countries in which at least one store has opened. And its sustainable practices represent a real and concrete example of business transformation.

To develop the narrative, we adopted an interpretive approach to conceptualize the company's sustainable practices as a form of storytelling, and its business transformation as a form of story-reading (Edvardsson and Enquist, 2002). Following the approach of Gummesson (2017), in-depth interviews were conducted with six Eataly managers in order to collect information to shape the narrative that forms the foundation of the case, and to guarantee a useful and constructive dialogue between researcher and practitioners. To increase the reliability of the data, multiple sources were taken into account (Boyer & McDermott, 1999; Hyer, Brown, & Zimmerman, 1999; Di Pietro et al., 2018). In addition to the in-depth interviews, an analysis of secondary data was conducted and observational activities were undertaken. All data were triangulated to define the narrative by using the lens of societal and business practices and their contribution to transformative change.

Eataly: a business case describing sustainable practices for transformative change

Eataly is an Italian company operating in the food sector with stores in Italy (14), Germany (1), Sweden (1), Turkey (1), Russia (1), USA (8), Canada (1), Brazil (1), South Korea (1), Saudi Arabia (1), United Arab Emirates (2), Kuwait (1), and Japan (2). It is an innovative, high-end Italian food chain which includes high-quality, sustainable food retail, multiple restaurants, food and beverage stations, bakeries, and bookstores, all of which feature a wide range of actors and brands (Di Pietro et al. 2018). Eataly was founded in 2004 by Oscar Farinetti, who opened the first store in Turin, Italy, in 2007. Since then, Eataly (a brand name that combines the two English words *eat* and *Italy*) has scaled up, taking its Italian food, restaurants, and products abroad. Three integrated experiences related to high-quality food are accessible under the Eataly brand: "eat," "shop," and "learn."

Eataly's mission is to disseminate, on a large scale, high-quality agricultural Italian products, following the principles of sustainability, responsibility, and sharing (Table 4.1). To achieve this aim, the Eataly brand has aggregated a large number of small local producers and providers operating throughout Italy.

To emphasize its mission and vision, Farinetti established "FICO Eataly World," a 20-acre park in Bologna dedicated to showcasing the regional diversity of Italian cuisine through fields, workshops, markets, restaurants, and classrooms, all open to the public. FICO opened in 2017 in partnership with over 2,000 companies. It encompasses multiple experiences covering food production and distribution – "from field to fork" – including food education, conscious consumption, and sustainable production.

Table 4.1 How Eataly identifies itself (translated from Italian by the authors)

How Eataly describes itself	"Eataly's brand was born by aggregating a number of small companies operating in the food and wine compartment. It encompasses the famous durum wheat pasta from Gragnano, Piedmont's egg pasta, mineral water from the Maritime Alps, Veneto and Piedmont's wines, Ponente Riviera Ligure oil, Piedmont's fassone meat, and traditional Italian cheese and cold cuts. Since its first opening, Eataly has been able to offer the best artisan products at reasonable prices by creating a direct relation between producers and distributors, and focusing on sustainability, responsibility and sharing." Eataly website: www.eataly.net/it_en/who-we-are/about-eataly
Eataly's slogan	"The Eataly slogan is 'Eat, Shop, and Learn about Italian high-quality food' [...]. Eataly stores are like a small Italian village, where customers can experience the Italian lifestyle and traditions through its restaurants, coffee shops, products, exhibitions, and so on. Eataly stands for high quality and being a part of the narrative of Italian culture" (CEO of Eataly). "This is a store with stories. Here, you won't just discover what you love, you'll also learn about what you love." Eataly website: www.eataly.net/it_it/chi-siamo/manifesto/

Sustainable practices at Eataly

Eataly's strategic view integrates a strong sustainability orientation (see Table 4.2). The company contributes to sustainable development by embodying principles of sustainability into its value proposition, which results in the embedding of environmental and social responsibility within its daily practices. In Eataly, the concept of sustainability is closely linked to the way the company operates, both externally and internally. In contrast to major large-scale food-distribution chains, Eataly shows a stronger commitment to concrete implementation of sustainable practices compared to external communication in pursuit of brand image improvement.

The company is built on sustainable policies and strategies and takes into account the context in which it operates, extending its commitment to its stakeholders (suppliers, customers, partners, employees, etc.). It engages with these stakeholders to foster collaboration and promote sustainability by developing joint projects. As such, Eataly fulfills its sustainable commitments through responsible projects expressing different facets of the company; these include protecting resources and the environmental ecosystem, supporting communities facing hardships, protecting cultural heritage, and promoting sustainable consumer behavior (see Figure 4.1). Through these projects, Eataly pursues its multiple objectives of supporting the community, contributing to its development and protection, and adopting and disseminating sustainable pro-environmental practices. Eataly's stakeholders – customers, employees, partners, providers, and local communities – are made aware of values around food

Table 4.2 Key elements of Eataly's sustainable practices (translated from Italian by the authors)

Element	
Practices	"Eataly includes in its offering the best artisanal products at reasonable prices by creating a direct relationship between producer and distributor and draws its inspiration for its activities through keywords such as 'sustainability,' 'responsibility,' and 'sharing.'" Eataly website: https://www.eataly.net/it_it/chi-siamo/eataly
Responsibility	"Respect, from the Latin 'respicere,' literally 'look again.' Hence the expression 'to have regard' for someone. This is how we understand 'respect': having regard for what surrounds us, taking it to heart, adopting respectful behavior and committing to certain risky scenarios that require projects needing social commitment." Eataly website: www.eataly.net/it_it/eataly-e-il-rispetto
Sustainability	"At Eataly we have always been convinced not only that quality and choice go hand in hand with sustainability, but also that education on nutritional health must include a full understanding of the value of food and its precious cultural function. Food culture is understood not only as excellence, but also as resource valorization and waste reduction. By acting in this way, we teach the youngest generations how to grow, as well as how to eat." Eataly website: https://www.eataly.net/it_it/negozi/milano-smeraldo/archivio-milano-smeraldo/eataly-affianca-cuki-nella-lotta-allo-spreco-alimentare-nasce-la-save-bag-di-cuki/
Sharing	"1. FOOD UNITES US ALL: Good food brings us all together and helps us find a common point of view. […] 6. CO-PRODUCER: We achieve our goal when the consumer understands that he/she is a co-producer, able to determine the quality and quantity of food with his/her choices. Responsible, therefore, not only for the quality of one's own life, but also for those who produce (i.e. farmers, breeders, fishermen, refiners, processors)." Eataly Manifesto, Eataly website: https://www.eataly.net/it_it/chi-siamo/manifesto/
Tangible commitment	"Eataly adopts a pragmatic approach to sustainability. It is largely known for its concrete and effective action; the company prefers to act, work, and have tangible results rather than put lots of effort into communicating an intangible commitment." (interview with Eataly Sustainable Office)

through their daily interactions with the company. For instance, customers are encouraged to buy smaller quantities of healthier sustainable food and to pay attention to seasonality: there is a "seasonal wheel" in-store, and teaching courses are offered within the stores. The learning experiences it provides

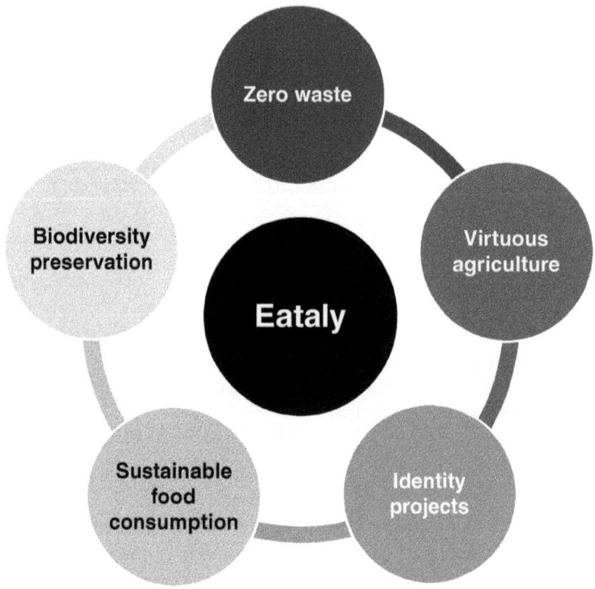

Figure 4.1 Eataly's sustainable development projects.

represent a pivotal element of its value proposition, and are based on a willingness to disseminate the values and the history behind its products and services. Thematic courses are customized for children, students, and the elderly. For example, summer schools, workshops, and lessons on the seasonality and quality of food are provided for beginners; and courses are provided free for pensioners (Aal et al., 2016). With the support of the Slow Food organization, Eataly selects suppliers for small and artisanal products (Venturini, 2009, p. 384), and undertakes to reserve approximately half of the space in its Italian stores for local brands. To promote sustainability in local communities, Eataly has located its main Italian stores in disused buildings that are part of the cities' architectural heritage. In agreement with the local municipalities, Eataly has redeveloped the abandoned train terminal of Ostiense Station in Rome, the old Lingotto factory in Rome, and converted the Smeraldo Theater building in Milan.

A focus on "Zero Waste"

The "Zero Waste" initiative is one of Eataly's most important sustainability projects, highlighting the company's commitment to waste reduction. The initiative includes both internal and external programs integrating the principles of waste reduction, not only within stores but also in relationships with suppliers and customers.

Zero waste means, for example, that any fresh pasta that remains unsold in the store is used in an Eataly restaurant, a conference facility lunch, or during a cooking class. If the pasta cannot be used before it becomes unfit for human consumption, it is used to for animal feed (e.g. for pigs or in poultry production). No pasta is thrown away.

The *external perspective* concerns the supply chain and the process for the selection of producers, suppliers, and partners, which is done under the company's overarching principles of safeguarding environmental resources and respecting traditional and artisan ways of producing. In addition, a shared protocol to reduce over-packaging has been established for strict control over excessive use of plastic and similar wastes (such as polystyrene).

From an *internal perspective*, the "Zero Waste" initiative consists of a policy aimed at maximizing the reuse and recycling of products and packaging, and the exclusion from Eataly stores of all types of disposable plastic cutlery in favor of bioplastic. Its main thrust is a recycling system aimed at eliminating waste, in pursuit of which it has designed a seven-step program (see Figure 4.2).

In the program, seven pivotal environmental aspects – Separate, Communicate, Recycle, Reuse, No Waste, Choose, and Innovate, reflecting the internal and external commitment of Eataly toward the adoption of sustainable practices – are translated into rules of conduct addressed to employees and customers.

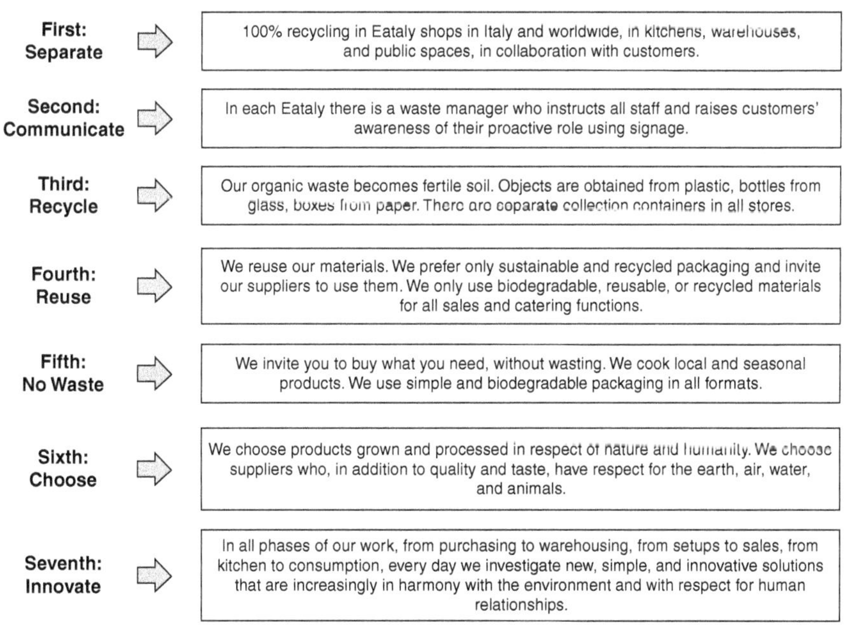

Figure 4.2 The seven-step program to eliminate waste in Eataly stores (from a company infographic translated from Italian by the authors).[1]

The program addresses reuse and recycling of different kinds of materials: organic waste becomes soil, while plastic, glass, and paper are recycled to enter into the production processes for new products. Inside the store, part of the fresh food surplus is "recycled" by the restaurants or used as production input in the small corner factories installed in the stores. In this way, the stores reduce both food waste and costs. The themed restaurants, cookery courses, and conference facilities all use products from Eataly's shelves, shortening the supply chain thereby making it more sustainable (Aal et al., 2016). This process addresses the aims of environmental, economic, and social responsibility by reducing waste and costs and increasing customer satisfaction.

Communication plays a central role in fulfilling the program's aims. The seven steps are disseminated among customers and employees via courses and events and by positioning signage within Eataly stores. Educational activities are also targeted at the external sphere (i.e. to producers and providers) to raise awareness and extend the adoption of a zero-waste strategy across the entire supply chain, with Eataly's suppliers being invited to adopt sustainable and recycled packaging initiatives. Similarly, the stores' servicescapes are designed to help disseminate the values of healthy and traditional food and waste avoidance.

Innovation also has a key role to play in this ambitious goal. Using a sustainable development lens to view its strategies means that Eataly has an ongoing commitment to identify innovative solutions, thanks also to its strong collaboration with partners. For example, the company has been cooperating with Mater-Bi for some years to develop high-quality bioplastic solutions for disposable items, which can be used for dishes, shopping bags, bags for the fruit and vegetable departments, and gloves. Similarly, the company has been working with the Consortium for the Recycling of Waste in Polyethylene (PolieCo) to identify innovative ways to drastically reduce the use of polystyrene in the fish department by adopting polyethylene solutions that can be sanitized and reused. It also monitors the waste levels of its stores. In collaboration with an environmental cooperative, the company has been able to develop reports to track and monitor recycling processes and outcomes, which allows comparisons to be made over time and facilitating a continuous improvement strategy.

With regard to tackling food waste, Eataly has joined Cuki's innovative "Save Bag" project, which promotes responsible consumption and aims to combat food waste. Cuki is a company that provides solutions for the preparation, preservation, cooking, and presentation of food. For a few decades now, it has been focusing attention on environmentally sustainable practices such as recovery of materials, purification of waste, and reduction of negative impacts, while still maintaining the high-quality performance of its products. Eataly's partnership with Cuki has resulted in providing its in-store restaurants with a "Save Bag Kit" for wrapping up and taking away leftover food instead of throwing it away. It promoted this project with the slogan "When you avoid waste, you're being good twice over," and invited exhibitors into its stores to educate customers. Throughout this initiative, Eataly creating opportunities to disseminate

Table 4.3 Key aspects of Eataly projects to reduce food waste (translated from Italian by the authors)

Key words	
Change attitudes	"Breaking down the embarrassment barrier and encouraging the habit of asking to take away any food ordered but not consumed." Eataly website: https://www.eataly.net/it_it/negozi/milano-smeraldo/archivio-milano-smeraldo/eataly-affianca-cuki-nella-lotta-allo-spreco-alimentare-nasce-la-save-bag-di-cuki/
Create opportunities	"To have the choice of 're-consuming' part of the meal later, choosing to take home what has been served up to taste it or share it with others, prolonging its goodness and respecting its value, is an opportunity." Eataly website: https://www.eataly.net/it_it/negozi/milano-smeraldo/archivio-milano-smeraldo/eataly-affianca-cuki-nella-lotta-allo-spreco-alimentare-nasce-la-save-bag-di-cuki/
Disseminate a new culture	"To promote a new culture of responsible consumption of meals and respect for the food, placing the quality, safety, and care of food first and foremost, as evidence and confirmation of the growing attention to the theme of waste reduction." Eataly website: https://www.eataly.net/it_it/negozi/milano-smeraldo/archivio-milano-smeraldo/eataly-affianca-cuki-nella-lotta-allo-spreco-alimentare-nasce-la-save-bag-di-cuki/

sustainable practices and promoted environmentally conscious behavior to its customers (see Table 4.3).

Discussion: lessons learned from Eataly's sustainable practices

Eataly's no-waste narrative shows us a company that is founded on a pragmatic business approach to sustainability. This is no "greenwashing" operation but rather a company holistically committed to integrating sustainable shared principles and practices. The concept is communicated, shared, and accepted by the company's leaders and employees, creating a positive reputation for healthy, nutritious, and environmentally friendly Italian food. The concept is also grounded in traditions and sustainable lifestyles which results in stories embodied in and expressed through value propositions. As Aal et al. (2016, p. 639) have noted, Eataly's service ecosystem resonates with values linked to high-quality, healthy food combined with sustainable principles like "zero waste."

Eataly does not make a direct declaration of commitment to the UN SDGs, but its business model is built on sustainable practices embodied in the company's value propositions which resonate with all the key actors of its service ecosystem (employees, local producers, suppliers, partners, customers, and society). It is, therefore, possible to align the company's aims with certain of the SDGs. Specifically, we have identified Eataly's contribution to Zero Hunger (SDG 2), Quality Education (SDG 4), Sustainable Cities and Communities (SDG 9), Responsible Consumption and Production (SDG 12), Life Below Water (SDG 14), and Life and Land (SDG 15). For each SDG, we have also identified the main stakeholders addressed by Eataly's strategies (see Table 4.4).

Eataly's corporate engagement toward Agenda 2030 (UN, 2015) and its 17 SDGs appears, according to the taxonomy developed by van Tulder (2018), to fall within "Level 3," which is characterized by a strategic and active commitment to corporate social responsibility. A more in-depth exploration of the Eataly approach to sustainability may well conclude that the company belongs at Level 4, a category distinguished by a systemic and proactive attitude to corporate sustainable responsibility which could describe Eataly's entire service ecosystem.

As observed by Aal et al. (2016), values resonance is a pillar of service innovation; in particular, values resonance with a company's stakeholders is a strategic factor in fostering service innovation. In line with this perspective, Lusch and Nambisan (2015) have emphasized that resource integration guided by values resonance acts as an enabler of service innovation.

In Eataly, values resonance takes the form of sharing core values such as sustainability and responsibility among all the components of the service ecosystem (Di Pietro et al., 2018). Eataly's strategies and operations evince a natural orientation toward sustainability and its three facets: social, environmental, and economic. Eataly engages its stakeholders throughout the value creation process: in the recognition and integration of values, traditions, symbols, and sustainability. Stakeholders thus have a sense of belonging to the service ecosystem and feel a connection with the brands represented in that ecosystem.

This is possible because Eataly's sustainable practices are directly integrated into the value propositions that guide the way the business is run. This is a key driver behind Eataly's scaling-up (Di Pietro et al., 2018). Eataly's growth has been supported by the way its founder embodied sustainable practices within the value propositions, in its adaptation to local contexts and in its selection of strategic local partnerships. The design of its integrated experience rooms promotes its customers' awareness of food culture, traditions, and zero waste, thereby enhancing value deployment (Aal et al., 2016, p. 639).

In summary, the case study presented in this chapter has shown a powerful values resonance in which core Eataly values are in line with foundational values within society and among a majority of customers. Eataly's values and the sustainable practices that emerge from them contribute to value creation throughout the relationships that the company establishes and manages with all its stakeholders; together, they form a dynamic and values-driven business that can also be described as a sustainable service ecosystem. These relations are characterized by "push–pull" system dynamics:

Table 4.4 Analysis of Eataly contributions to Agenda 2030 (UN, 2015)

SDGs addressed by Eataly	*Eataly's contribution*	*Stakeholders/actors involved*
Zero Hunger	With its commitment to sharing healthy practices around managing and consuming food, Eataly tries to raise actors' awareness to reduce forms of malnutrition (2.2). Cooperating with small, local, artisanal producers, Eataly fosters the productivity and incomes of small-scale food producers (2.3), promoting the adoption of sustainable food production practices (2.4). Operating in this way, the company attempts to maintain traditional food production (2.5).	• Local producers • Suppliers • Partners • Customers • Employees
Quality Education	Eataly is heavily engaged in the dissemination of knowledge on sustainable food production and consumption practices (4.7) by means of ad hoc educational courses (for students, employees and pensioners), workshops, and informative in-store displays. In this way, Eataly contributes to education and awareness on sustainable development and sustainable lifestyles (4.7), with a particular focus on "zero waste."	• Students • Pensioners • Employees
Sustainable Cities and Communities	With its Identity projects, Eataly contributes to the recovery of cities' cultural heritage (11.4), helping to redevelop abandoned historic buildings and areas (e.g. Ostiense Train Station in Rome, Smeraldo Theater in Milan). In addition, its focus on waste management (not just food waste) attests to a contribution to reducing cities' negative environmental impacts (11.6).	• Society • Citizens • Local government

(*continued*)

Table 4.4 Cont.

SDGs addressed by Eataly		*Eataly's contribution*	*Stakeholders/actors involved*
12 RESPONSIBLE CONSUMPTION AND PRODUCTION	**Responsible Consumption and Production**	Eataly is committed to promoting the sustainable management and use of natural resources (12.2.), reducing food waste throughout the product lifecycle (12.3), and the adoption of recycling and reuse practices (12.5). Similarly, it encourages its stakeholders to adopt sustainable practices (12.6) and, more generally, aims to inspire universal understanding of sustainable principles and lifestyles (12.8).	• Local producers • Suppliers • Partners • Employees • Customers • Society
14 LIFE BELOW WATER	**Life Below Water**	Eataly's aim of protecting and restoring biodiversity is pursued via ad hoc projects concerning habitats and the natural ecosystem as a whole (sea, 14.2; land and freshwater, 15.1; mountains, 15.4).	• Society • Local communities
15 LIFE ON LAND	**Life on Land**		

- Eataly is *pushed* to resonate with the sustainable principles of society, customers, partners, and suppliers. The integration of sustainable principles is a prerequisite for collaboration with these actors in the ecosystem. In that sense, the values resonance impacts the design of the service transformation, by setting rules and guidelines to select suppliers and partners, defining how to collaborate, designing resource integration, and responding to societal and customer values. Aal et al. (2016) posited that, because of values resonance and aligned practices, companies are able to reduce risk through collaboration (Morgan & Hunt, 1994), and facilitate resource integration in ways that enable innovation (Zhao, Ha, & Widdows, 2015).
- Eataly, with its responsible business, *pulls* the same actors toward the adoption of sustainable principles in their daily operations. In this way, the company stimulates a change in existing institutional arrangements by affecting the actors' value creation and facilitating the exchange of knowledge and specialized competences (Aal et al., 2016), thus forming the basis of innovative service (Vargo, Wieland, & Akaka, 2015).

It is clear from the Eataly case that the integration of sustainable principles within the value proposition allows a business to operate in resonance with its stakeholders and, accordingly, foster service innovation and a fast, profitable scaling-up process. Based on this interpretation, we can depict the transformative change as a bidirectional relationship which links sustainable and innovative practices (Figure 4.3). More specifically, sustainable and innovative practices feed off each other, triggering a continuous cycle of transformative change, which begin because of the values resonance of sustainable practices with stakeholders.

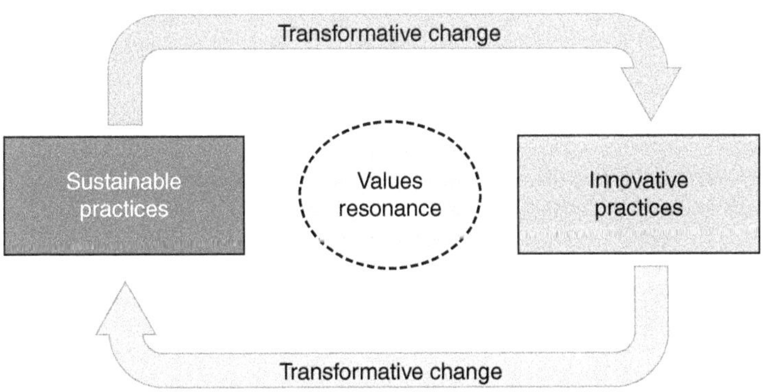

Figure 4.3 The transformative change cycle of values resonance and sustainable and innovative practices.

Conclusion and implications

The Eataly case has shown that sustainable practices rooted in core organizational values can contribute to business transformation. Eataly is an example of transformation that can act as an inspiration for other companies wishing to take the same path. In other words, Eataly's founder has brought about transformation in the company, in its actors, and in society at large. The company's commitment is manifested in its daily activities, in its resource integration practices, and in its partnership development. Eataly shows that, with values resonance, a company can influence society and its component parts, showcasing transformative change, supported by all service ecosystem actors. As the case study shows, this provides energy and direction to push sustainable, transformative change through innovative practices.

The case is a practical demonstration of what is involved in going beyond "greenwashing" or "SDG-washing." Furthermore, it shows how a genuine business commitment by an entrepreneur with core values that resonate with societal values can be a driving force for individuals, other businesses, and communities toward sustainable, transformative change. Embodying a resonance with society's sustainable values in its value proposition has allowed Eataly to scale up around the world (Di Pietro et al., 2018). Companies that want to contribute to this type of sustainable transformative change must develop business strategies grounded in and supported by values shared among customers, employees, and collaborating actors in general. This requires an innovative mindset and a pragmatic strategy, rather than exploiting sustainability and using sustainable transformation as merely a communication and promotional tool.

Note

1 The original Italian infographic is available at: https://www.eataly.net/it_it/mondo-eataly/giornata-mondiale-ambiente-rifiuti-zero

References

Aal, K., Di Pietro, L., Edvardsson, B., Renzi, M.F., and Guglielmetti Mugion, R. (2016). Innovation in service ecosystems: an empirical study of the integration of values, brands, service systems and experience rooms. *Journal of Service Management*, 27(4). https://doi.org/10.1108/JOSM-02-2015-0044

Anderson, L., Ostrom, A.L., Corus, C., Fisk, R.P., Gallan, A.S., Giraldo, M., … and Williams, J.D. (2013). Transformative service research: an agenda for the future. *Journal of Business Research*, 66(8), 1203–10. https://doi.org/10.1016/j.jbusres.2012.08.013

Anderson, L., and Ostrom, A.L. (2015). Transformative service research: advancing our knowledge about service and well-being. *Journal of Service Research*, 18(3), 243–49. https://doi.org/10.1177/1094670515591316

Boyer, K.K., and McDermott, C. (1999). Strategic consensus in operations strategy. *Journal of Operations Management*, 17(3), 289–305.

Chandler, J.D., and Lusch, R.F. (2014). Service systems: a broadened framework and research agenda on value propositions, engagement, and service experience. *Journal of Service Research*, (1) (June), 1–17. https://doi.org/10.1177/1094670514537709

Di Pietro, L., Edvardsson, B., Reynoso, J., Renzi, M.F., Toni, M., and Guglielmetti Mugion, R. (2018). A scaling up framework for innovative service ecosystems: lessons from Eataly and KidZania. *Journal of Service Management*, 29(1), 146–75. https://doi.org/10.1108/JOSM-02-2017-0054.

Edvardsson, B., and Enquist, B. (2002). The IKEA saga: how service culture drives service strategy. *The Service Industries Journal*, 22(4), 153–86.

Gummesson, E. (2017). *Case Theory in Business and Management*. London: SAGE. doi: https://doi.org/10.4135/9781473920811

Hyer, N.L., Brown, K.A., and Zimmerman, S. (1999). A socio-technical systems approach to cell design: case study and analysis. *Journal of Operations Management*, 17(2), 179–203.

Lusch, R., and Nambisan, S. (2015). Service innovation: a service-dominant logic perspective. *MIS Quarterly*, 39(1), 155–75.

Morgan, R., and Hunt, S. (1994). The commitment–trust theory of relationship marketing. *Journal of Marketing*, 58(3), 20.

Ostrom, A.L., Bitner, M.J., Brown, S.W., Burkhard, K.A., Goul, M., Smith-Daniels, V., … and Rabinovich, E. (2010). Moving forward and making a difference: research priorities for the science of service. *Journal of Service Research*, 13(1), 4–36. https://doi.org/10.1177/1094670509357611

Paina, L., and Peters, D.H. (2012). Understanding pathways for scaling up health services through the lens of complex adaptive systems. *Health Policy and Planning*, 27(5), 365–73.

Subramanian, S., Naimoli, J., Matsubayashi, T., and Peters, D.H. (2011). Scaling up and the millennium development goals. *BMC Health Services Research*, 11(336), 1–10.

United Nations (UN) (2015). Transforming our world: the 2030 Agenda for Sustainable Development. 25 September 2015 A/RES/70/1.

Van Tulder, R. (2018). *Business and Sustainable Development Goals: A Framework for the Effective Corporate Involvement*. Rotterdam School of Management, Erasmus University, Rotterdam. Available at: https://www.rsm.nl/fileadmin/Images_NEW/Positive_Change/Business_and_Sustainable_Development_Goals_-_Positive_Change_0_Rob_van_Tulder.pdf (accessed May 31, 2020)

Vargo, S.L., and Lusch, R.F. (2004). Evolving to a new dominant logic for marketing. *Journal of Marketing*, 68(1), 1–17. https://doi.org/10.1509/jmkg.68.1.1.24036

Vargo, S., Wieland, H., and Akaka, M. (2015). Innovation through institutionalization: a service ecosystems perspective. *Industrial Marketing Management*, 44, 63–72.

Venturini, T. (2009). *Il Nostro Pane Quotidiano: Eataly e il Futuro dei Supermercati, Slow Food & Fondazione Cassa di Risparmio di Cuneo*. Available at: http://www.tommasoventurini.it/wp/wp-content/uploads/2013/05/IlNostroPaneQuotidiano.pdf (accessed May 31, 2020).

Wieland, H., Polese, F., Vargo, S.L., and Lusch, R.F. (2012). Toward a service (eco)systems perspective on value creation. *International Journal of Service Science, Management, Engineering, and Technology (IJSSMET)*, 3(3), 12–25. https://doi.org/10.4018/jssmet.2012070102

Zhao, J., Ha, S., and Widdows, R. (2015). The influence of social capital on knowledge creation in online health communities. *Information Technology and Management*, 17, 311–21. https://doi.org/10.1007/s10799-014-0211-3

Part 2

The role of the individual in business and social transformation

5 Designing for transformative collaboration in complex service systems

Lia Patrício, Raymond P. Fisk, and Bo Edvardsson

Takeaways

- The emergence of complex service problems and the role of design in creating service systems for sustainability.
- The concept of transformative collaboration as a foundation for sustainable service systems.
- How service design, with a human-centered, participatory and transformative approach, contributes to the embedding of transformative collaboration in complex service systems.
- How service design contributes to the embedding of transformative collaboration in innovative service systems: from governmental healthcare systems with the Portuguese EHR; to design for sustainability in IKEA, a global company; to a worldwide effort to foster transformative collaboration with ServCollab.

Introduction

The COVID-19 pandemic posed an existential threat to the sustainability of modern human society. Before the crisis, the social and economic service systems of the modern world were based on globalization trends that had been accelerating for decades and had led to unprecedented levels of human interconnectedness. The enabling technologies for this interconnectedness were global transportation and communication systems of high complexity such as air transportation or technology-enabled service platforms such as Airbnb. When the highly contagious COVID-19 virus appeared, it quickly spread across the world via the same global transportation systems. The crisis exposed significant vulnerabilities in modern human service systems and made us desperate for solutions.

Humans are an innately social species, which means that human well-being depends on interaction and collaboration, especially the intimacy of face-to-face interaction. Unfortunately, the COVID-19 virus spread quickly via face-to-face interactions, so people were asked or ordered to "socially distance" themselves from others in virtually every country. At the same time, in an effort

DOI: 10.4324/9781003188773-5

to keep the economy functioning, governments, companies, and civil society discussed how service systems around the world such as tourism and the hospitality industry could be redesigned to become safer in the COVID-19 era.

This chapter presents service design as an approach for embedding transformative collaboration in complex service systems. When transportation systems were severely compromised by COVID-19, we were fortunate that in our modern world we have the ability to communicate and collaborate via telecommunications. Such tools were essential in the face of this existential threat. Transformative collaboration, which allows all participants and other to contribute at the level of their full human potential (Fisk et al., 2019), are a necessary process to transform vulnerable service systems into sustainable and resilient ones.

Given the dramatic challenges the world is facing, service researchers and practitioners should purposefully design service systems for well-being and sustainability. In this chapter, we will argue in favor of transformative collaboration (Fisk et al., 2019) as a means of accelerating human progress toward well-being and sustainability. As a foundation for transformative collaboration, we propose service design, through a human-centered, participatory and transformative approach to creating new service systems. We will first explore how this can take place, and then go on to present three cases from three different contexts: governmental services, business services, and nonprofit services. The first case, in the context of governmental healthcare systems, describes the development of the Portuguese national Electronic Health Record (EHR), which illustrates how service design succeeded in embedding transformative collaboration in the design process as well as in the resulting EHR system. The second investigates how the furniture company IKEA uses collaborative service platforms to design and develop sustainable solutions. Finally, the third case presents ServCollab: a nonprofit collaborative service research initiative that promotes worldwide ventures to foster transformative collaboration.

The need for transformative collaboration to address emerging complex service problems

As modern human societies become increasingly complex, they become subject to new challenges around their service systems. This makes it imperative for service research to rise to the challenge of engaging with these more complex societal problems and innovating to address them: "Society is at a crossroads. Interconnected systems, radical transparency, and rapidly increasing sophistication in skills, communications, and technologies provide a unique context for fostering social innovation at a planetary scale" (Fisk et al., 2019, p. 191). In this chapter, we will follow the van Wijk et al. (2019) definition of social innovation: "the agentic, relational, situated, and multilevel process to develop, promote, and implement novel solutions to social problems in ways that are directed toward producing profound change in institutional contexts" (p. 3).

To enable systemic social innovation, Fisk et al. (2019) propose a new concept, which they name transformative collaboration. "Transformative collaboration occurs when all participants are able to make contributions at their full human potential" (p. 194). Human service systems are nested: from micro, to meso, to macro levels, the most ancient of such a nested system being the family, the tribe, the village, and the city. Therefore, to promote transformative collaboration across our service systems, our efforts need to take nesting into account within the various system levels. In the design phase, we need to assemble research teams that self-organize in pursuit of common social innovation goals. Such teams must share a common service research ethic and a passion for solving complex service system problems. Also, the people affected by design decisions must be involved as cocreators in transformative collaborations.

Interactions and collaboration are central to the concept of service. Indeed, interactions are the lifeblood of human service systems, and they are at their best when participants are engaging willingly and enthusiastically with each other. According to Angus and Newton (2015), such collaboration is distinguished by shared intentionality. Collaboration can be a fragile phenomenon, which is why service systems need to nurture collaboration by means of shared value cocreation.

Service, broadly viewed as the application of competences of one actor for the benefit of another actor (Vargo, Maglio, & Archupru Akaka, 2008), means that these actors interact to cocreate value. Value creation is interactional, meaning that it is always cocreated in interactions among providers, customers, and other actors through the integration of resources and application of competences (Vargo, Maglio, & Archupru Akaka, 2008). Here, the word "interaction" does not refer to face-to-face encounters; it means mutual or reciprocal action or influence (Vargo and Lusch, 2016). For example, a spectator can go to a music concert and physically interact with the band on stage and with the audience and the surrounding environment, cocreating his or her experience and actively influencing how both the band and the other spectators experience the concert. Later on, the same customer, or other customers, can enjoy the video-recorded concert in their homes with their families, listen to a recording of the concert while driving to work, or interact and cocreate value in other ways.

Technology has profoundly changed the service context (Ostrom et al., 2015), by amplifying the ways people, machines, and service providers interact and collaborate, thereby increasing the complexity of service systems. Service systems have traditionally been viewed from an organizational perspective as arrangements of resources including people, shared information, and technology, connected to other service systems by value propositions (Maglio et al., 2009; Spohrer et al., 2007). However, with the rapid expansion of human knowledge and technology, services are now offered through complex service systems and value networks. For example, energy customers can build their own home energy solution, comprising energy production technologies such as photovoltaic panels, energy storage solutions, electric vehicles, and a myriad of smart devices and applications to sense, collect data, and control their energy consumption (Gonçalves et al., 2020).

The increasing complexity of the service environment has broadened the view of service systems from being focused on an organizational level to being multi-actor networks and service ecosystems (Edvardsson et al., 2018). From this perspective, complex service systems are defined as arrangements of multiple entities and stakeholders which interact to cocreate value (Kieliszewski, Maglio, & Cefkin, 2012), moving beyond organizational boundaries to encompass larger concepts such as value constellations (Normann, 2001) or service networks (Tax, McCutcheon, & Wilkinson, 2013). From a more macro service-system perspective, service ecosystems can be defined as "relatively self-contained self-adjusting systems of resource integrating actors connected by shared institutions and logics and mutual value creation through service exchange" (Akaka, Vargo, & Lusch, 2012). In these complex contexts, it is important to look beyond dyadic interactions between the customer and the service provider to understand how the service can enable interactions among multiple actors to cocreate value for each actor and the whole network, so all actors can achieve their goals in a balanced way (Patrício et al., 2018). The following section explores how service design can foster transformative collaboration through its human-centered, participatory, and transformative approach to creating new service systems.

Service design as a human-centered, participatory, and transformative approach to creating new service systems

Service design is a human-centered, holistic, and iterative approach to the creation of new services (Blomkvist, Holmlid, & Segelström, 2010), through a collaborative and creative process of exploration (studying the experience and aspirations of customers and other actors involved); ideation (envisioning new service futures); prototyping (representing the new services and testing them with users); and implementation.

To begin with, service design focused on dyadic service interactions between customers and service providers, designing service interfaces and touchpoints to enhance the customer experience (Sangiorgi, 2009). To this end, service design uses tools such as customer journey mapping to understand the customer experience (Følstad and Kvale, 2018), or service blueprinting to depict how the service system should be designed to support customer activities: namely, the service process, the actors and technologies involved, the frontstage and backstage, and the lines of interaction and visibility (Bitner, Ostrom, & Morgan, 2008; Patrício, Fisk, & Falcão e Cunha, 2008). For example, provision of healthcare services requires a careful design of the physical space, highly trained people, a well-executed healthcare process, and crucial technology support.

Service design has gradually broadened its scope to address more complex service contexts, by designing the organization's value proposition into the value constellation (Patrício et al., 2011) and by designing new services as enablers of value cocreating interactions among multiple actors in value networks and service ecosystems (Patrício et al., 2018). For example, as health service systems move toward people-centered integrated care, it is crucial to design services to empower patients to collaboratively cocreate their health, together with their families and communities, as well as with the network of healthcare providers (Patrício et al., 2020). In these complex service contexts, having multiple actors with different goals, and in which problems are frequently ill-defined, it is important to design service systems for participation, interdependence, and emergence (Sangiorgi, Patrício, & Fisk, 2017). Instead of creating predefined service solutions, service design adopts a facilitator role in a collaborative process to collectively design service systems for transformative collaboration. Two approaches are particularly important when designing new services for interaction and collaboration in these complex service systems: a human-centered and participatory approach; and a transformative approach.

A human-centered and participatory approach to embedding transformative collaboration in the process of creating new service systems

Service design is a collaborative approach to designing for and with people. Service design is human-centered because it entails understanding customers, different actors and their contexts, and translating this understanding into the orchestration of the different service design elements (Evenson, 2008). In being human-centered and designing for people, service design aims to enhance the service users' lives and support organizations in connecting with their existing networks of actors, while discovering new opportunities to cocreate value (Yu & Sangiorgi, 2018).

Service design can also adopt a participatory approach (Meroni & Sangiorgi, 2011), where service designers recognize their role as facilitators of a collaborative effort of cocreating new services with customers and other actors. This participatory approach becomes particularly important for the design of complex service systems such as healthcare, which have loosely defined problems and comprise multiple actors with different perspectives and conflicting goals. This complex context requires a service design approach that is more open and where the different actors collaboratively explore and actively cocreate alternative futures, while the designer takes on a facilitator role (Sanders 2008).

In engaging different actors in participatory processes, service design fosters transformative collaboration by enabling all participants to make contributions to the creation of new service systems at the level of their full human potential (Fisk et al., 2019). For example, in healthcare, these participatory approaches have proved useful in encouraging the participation of patients in vulnerable situations who may not otherwise perceive themselves as suitable participants, as well as mobilizing their hidden resources to innovate healthcare (Patrício et al., 2020). Moreover, not only can the engagement of different system actors in participatory service design processes contribute to the development of new services, but it can also contribute to enduring institutional change toward transformative collaboration. Embedding a transformative collaboration approach into the process of designing new services may foster deep changes of meaning which modify human relationships and explore new ground, generating a virtuous trajectory toward future collaboration and well-being (Blocker & Barrios, 2015).

A transformative approach to creating service systems for transformative collaboration

Service design can also adopt a transformative approach. Design can be viewed as the process of devising courses of action to transform existing situations into preferable ones (Simon, 1969). Service design can, therefore, foster transformative collaboration through this action-oriented approach to tackle service system challenges and build collaborative service futures (Patrício, Teixeira, & Vink, 2019). Moreover, such a transformative service design approach seeks to create not only new service solutions, but also the platforms and capacities for ongoing and lasting change (Sangiorgi et al., 2019). Instead of developing single services to enhance customer experience with a service provider, service design has increasingly been focusing on transforming organizational practices and institutional logics (Kurtmollaiev et al., 2018), as well as on promoting well-being and social change (Alkire et al., 2020). In the same vein, service design can also contribute to service ecosystem transformation by catalyzing institutional change (Vink et al., 2019). This service design approach requires the adoption of a set of transformational principles for collaboration, namely: viewing multiple actors as active cocreators of well-being; intervening at a community scale; building capacities and partnerships; redistributing power; enhancing imagination and hope; building infrastructures and enabling platforms; and evaluating success and impact (Sangiorgi, 2011).

The transformative role of service design can promote the development of service systems that foster transformative collaboration, enabling and encouraging all system actors to contribute to their full potential, and aiming for far-reaching goals for people and the environment (Patrício et al., 2020). For example, design for service inclusion has also been advocated as a way of understanding human needs for inclusion and designing services to properly meet those needs, targeting the highest possible levels of human progress (Fisk et al., 2018). The transformative approach and the well-being focus of service design have also been proposed as a way of unpacking complex and interconnected issues and ensuring an alignment between the mission and strategy of social entrepreneurship organizations (Alkire et al., 2020). Overall, service design has the potential to become a foundation for transformative collaboration and a cornerstone of transformative service research (Patrício, Gustafsson, & Fisk, 2018).

The following three sections present illustrative cases of how service design can foster transformative collaboration toward more sustainable and resilient service systems in three different contexts. The Portuguese national EHR case shows how service design can promote transformative collaboration in public healthcare systems. The IKEA case shows how a multinational company uses service platforms to facilitate collaborative service design to create novel and sustainable value cocreating solutions. The ServCollab case describes a new nonprofit service platform that focuses on enabling transformative collaboration solutions to profound human service system problems.

Service design for transformative collaboration in healthcare systems: the design of the Portuguese Electronic Health Record (EHR)

The complexity of health service systems and the need for transformative collaboration

The increasing complexity of service systems requires us to look beyond dyadic interactions between customer and service provider and consider many-to-many interactions and collaborations among networks of actors. In health service systems, patient well-being and health cocreation can only be achieved through the joint efforts of patient networks (e.g. family and informal caregivers) and health provider networks (e.g. hospitals, primary care units). In complex healthcare service systems, actors may have different goals, which may lead to value co-creation but may also conflict and lead to value co-destruction (Plé & Chumpitaz Cáceres, 2010). As such, it is crucial to foster transformative collaboration in the process through which new health service systems are created and also to purposefully embed transformative collaboration by design.

The vision of healthcare systems has evolved toward people-centered, integrated, and technology-enabled care (WHO, 2016). However, this process has been hindered by traditional practices that view patients as passive receivers of care and a healthcare system that is fragmented and increasingly complex (Lee & Hall, 2010). Electronic Health Records (EHRs) can assist in the move toward this vision, as they offer an integrated view of a patient's clinical history and provide healthcare practitioners with access to the information from different points of care. As such, EHRs can support continuing and integrated healthcare while avoiding duplication of efforts and costs, such as repeated exams (McDonald, Tang, & Hripcsak, 2014). However, the benefits of EHRs have frequently been mitigated by poor user adoption, leading to the failure of EHRs in several countries (Nguyen, Bellucci, & Nguyen, 2014).

The case of the Portuguese national Electronic Health Record

To show how service design can address these challenges, we present a four-year project that applied a service design approach to the development of the Portuguese national EHR, in collaboration with the Portuguese Ministry of Health. Portugal has a national healthcare system, which is public and provides universal coverage. Although the private healthcare sector has been growing, the system remains mostly public. The Portuguese Ministry of Health decided to develop a national, citizen-centered EHR service that would carry clinical information and be accessible from any location and time of healthcare delivery within the public national health system. This project led to the implementation of the Portuguese EHR in 2012, and embedded a transformative collaboration approach in both the design process and the resulting EHR system (Patrício et al., 2018).

Following a human-centered service design approach, the project began with an exploration stage involving an in-depth study of the experience and aspirations of the different healthcare actors. Mapping all healthcare actors and their relationships revealed over 100 actors, which served to highlight the complexity of healthcare service systems (Figure 5.1 shows a simplified version of this network actor map).

Based on this network actor map, 47 interviews were conducted with the four priority groups of actors (citizens, doctors, nurses, and pharmacists). This aimed not only to understand each actor's goals and activities, but also how they interacted with one another, what kind of information they needed to share, and what kinds of potential conflicts might arise among actors' goals. Figure 5.2 shows the interconnected journeys of the citizen, doctor, nurse, and pharmacist, as a citizen is diagnosed with asthma and receives treatment. This example shows how healthcare involves a complex set of interactions and information exchange among citizens, health organizations, and practitioners. This study was key in understanding the interdependencies among network actors, and inspiring the creation of an EHR that promoted collaboration and value co-creation among network actors.

Next, via a participatory approach in the ideation stage, citizens, doctors, and nurses were actively involved in the EHR design process by means of several design meetings and two design workshops involving a total of 87 participants. The workshops began by presenting the study findings and some proposals for the EHR, after which the different groups collaborated to explore future design possibilities for the EHR service concept, as shown in Figure 5.3. For example, doctors, nurses, and citizens analyzed potential conflicts between patient data privacy and data access by healthcare professionals. The discussions in the participatory design sessions led to the different groups of actors jointly arriving at a solution. This involved the inclusion of an access auditing functionality, so that the EHR could enable data access for doctors and nurses in the case of an emergency when the patient might not be in a condition to provide consent, while ensuring that the citizen could later view and control who had access to his or her data. The groups also cast votes on the most important functionalities (the colored dots in Figure 5.3), so that the EHR development priorities were also collaboratively defined.

The service design process of the Portuguese EHR also embedded a transformative approach aiming at fostering collaboration in the system being designed while ensuring a balanced pursuit of societal well-being and health system viability. The EHR is a service platform that cocreates value by enabling

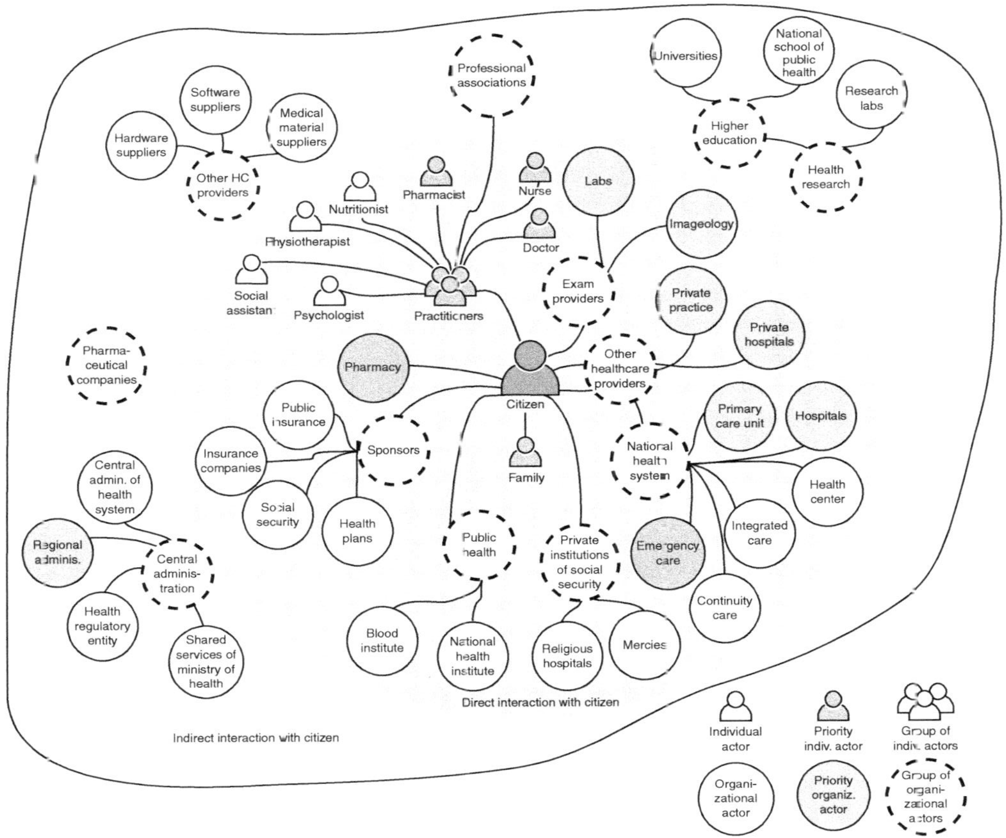

Figure 5.1 Value network actor map for the Portuguese healthcare service (Patrício et al., 2018, p. 8).

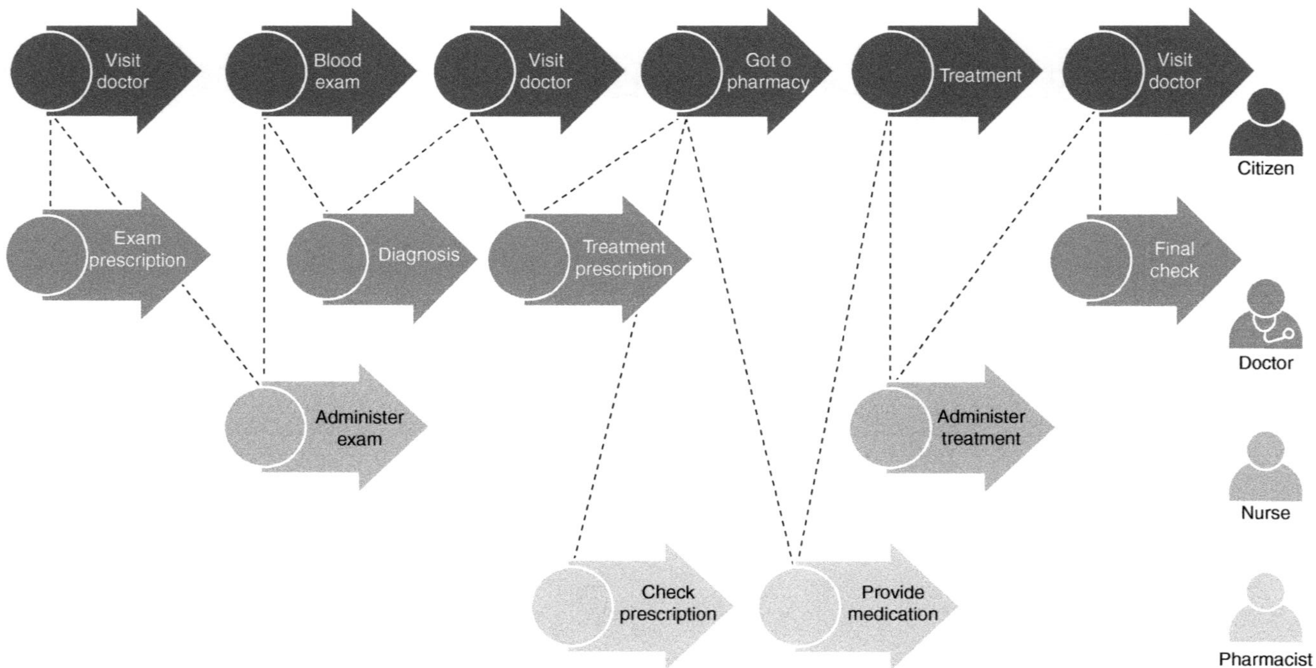

Figure 5.2 Healthcare activities and interactions (citizen, doctor, nurse, and pharmacist) (Patrício et al., 2018, p. 10).

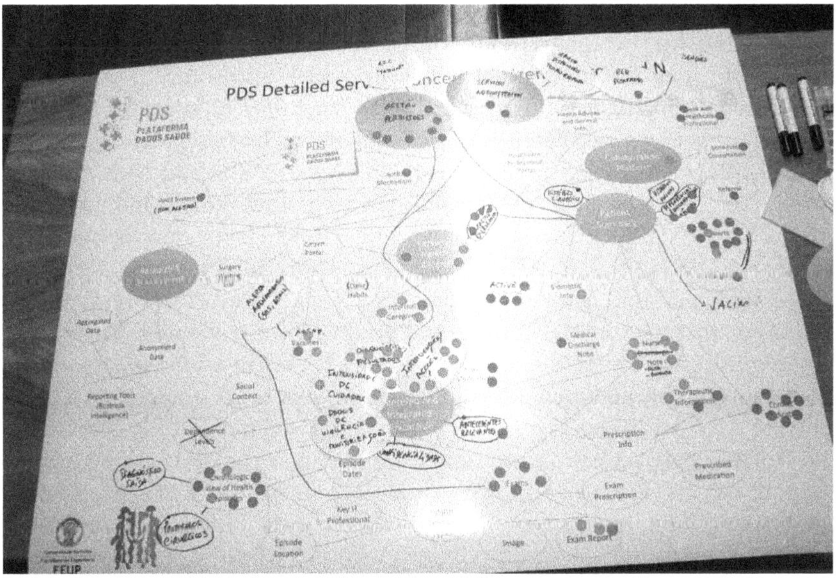

Figure 5.3 The Portuguese EHR value network service concept (Patrício et al., 2018, p. 14).

citizens, doctors, nurses, and other healthcare practitioners to interact and share and access information for better quality of care and improved system efficiency. For example, by accessing a patient's entire clinical history, a doctor can make a more complete and accurate diagnosis while avoiding duplication of medical procedures and exams that are costly and undesirable for the patient. As such, this service design approach also moved the health service system toward transformative collaboration, by creating a platform where citizens, doctors, nurses, and other healthcare actors can share information and collaborate.

Designing collaborative service platforms for sustainability

Platforms are used to coordinate collaborating actors and enable them to design and produce value-creating service (Edvardsson & Tronvoll, 2020). Collaboration is needed because one actor alone neither possesses nor has access to enough resources, knowledge, and skills to design, develop, and produce a sustainable service.

Service denotes a perspective on value creation that is cocreated when goods, services, resources, or other enablers are used by customers in collaboration with other engaged actors to achieve their goals (Edvardsson, Gustafsson, & Roos, 2005; Vargo & Lusch, 2004). Service platforms orchestrate the use of resources among collaborating actors during value creation. They are used in the design and development of new service and in the cocreation of existing service, especially in complex ecosystems.

Meyer and DeTore (2001) define a platform as a set of subsystems and interfaces forming a common structure from which a stream of products can be designed and produced. Robertson and Ulrich (1998) suggest a broader definition of platforms as shared assets, including components, processes, knowledge, people, or relationships. Krishnan and Gupta (2001) and Muffatto and Roveda (2002) use the term "platform" to refer to the subsystems and interfaces forming a common structure that enables a firm to efficiently develop products and services. Perks et al. (2017) present a framework for "network orchestration," where multiple actors collaborate for "value platform development." They argue that the traditional firm- and product-centric view of platforms is changing, as platforms are often developed by a lead firm within a network of collaborating actors and include customers and services as components. This is similar to what Autio and Thomas (2014) argue for when discussing ecosystems with collaborating actors to foster innovations, and in this, they are supported by Fu, Wang, and Zhao (2017), who show that service platforms function as infrastructures in ecosystems to facilitate collaboration among different actors in value co-creation.

Building on earlier research and platforms, we define a service platform as a support structure used by collaborating actors when integrating resources to cocreate a sustainable service. Service platforms provide support in the form of a wide range of resources, including physical and digital technologies configured to foster the design, development, and use of a sustainable service. The collaborating actors are provided with the necessary support to stay focused on attractive and sustainable services. These services need to be designed to fit the guiding institutional arrangements (such as laws, norms, and habits) as well as the company's business model, strategy, and sustainability policy.

Collaborative services are often designed using service platforms in the form of labs or design spaces (see, e.g. "Space10" at IKEA, described below). A design space is a special category of service platform involving collaborating actors with suitable and specific competences. These service platforms build on and orchestrate a wide range of collaborating actors and resources, facilitated by digital technologies to design and test-drive new services, configured to fit service platforms used in ongoing business. Thus, these collaborative service platforms form part of a whole ecosystem of collaborative service platforms for the design and development of ongoing business that is needed to make such businesses sustainable. We will now illustrate the use of collaborative service platforms in practice with an example from IKEA, a furniture company known for a focus on good design for all ("Democratic Design," as IKEA calls it[1]) and sustainability.

The case of IKEA

IKEA has a vision "to create a better everyday life for the many people."[2] This vision goes beyond home furnishings and includes the way products and services are designed, thus helping customers to live more sustainable lives at home. This is facilitated and coordinated by what we have described above as collaborative service platforms, used for both the design and development of new service and for customers' resource integration during value co-creation. "Democratic Design" is a guiding philosophy for all designs and service platforms. It includes form, function, sustainability, quality, and low price. Next, we offer a brief description of "Space10," one of IKEA's collaborative service platforms (focused on design and development), which is used to explore the future of living and solutions to real-life problems in the home.

Space10: a collaborative service platform for the design and development of innovative, sustainable solutions

According to Göran Nilsson, Concept Innovation Manager at Inter IKEA,[3] Space10 was established in 2015 to explore and design new ways of enabling a better and more sustainable life for the many.[4] Acting on identified opportunities, the aim is to design sustainable solutions for people and planet by embracing a holistic mindset. Major societal challenges, such as urbanization, resource scarcity, climate change, food security, and loneliness provide the basis for the research and design projects. In collaboration with experts from around the world, Space10 designs potential solutions to these challenges by prototyping, simulating, and testing, turning good ideas into meaningful designs, products, or services. This is done in a number of development and design projects. One of these projects is SolarVille, developed in collaboration with external partners, including university researchers. In SolarVille, solar panel installations are combined with a solution that enables households to trade energy with one another according to their individual needs. Another project is Future Food Today: a cookbook with a collection of recipes developed in the test kitchen. The focus is on sustainable dishes that help people eat better, both for their bodies and for the planet. Future Food Today inspires people to take sustainable action at affordable cost through their food choices. One example is the veggie hot dog, a plant-based product. Every year, 700 million people buy food at IKEA, thus providing an opportunity and a responsibility to offer food that's good for people's health and the planet, and at affordable prices. Customers are being offered a growing range of plant-based alternatives, including non-dairy soft ice, the veggie balls (which taste like IKEA's original meatballs), and more recently the veggie hot dog. Being plant-based, the veggie hot dog is a more sustainable option than its meat-based cousin. Its main raw ingredients are kale, lentils, quinoa, onions, and wheat protein – all of which need less land and water to grow than animal protein. In fact, the overall climate impact from a veggie hot dog is approximately seven times less than that of a classic hot dog. When Space10 took on the challenge of making an affordable plant-based hot dog, the goal was not to create a meat replacement but rather to offer a healthier, more sustainable snack that everybody could enjoy, regardless of dietary preference. No one will eat something that isn't enjoyable, no matter how sustainable it is.

How is IKEA addressing the challenge of unsustainable consumption?

> Unsustainable consumption is one of our biggest challenges. Tackling it requires changes in behavior and new definitions of what makes a better everyday life. It's about doing more and better with less. Offering solutions, inspiration, knowledge and services that help customers make informed choices and change. We want to lead the way and create circular business models and solutions. But we can't do it alone. We need to work together with governments and other businesses to make the biggest impact.[5]

IKEA's *Annual Summary & Sustainability Report 2019* describes how design, transformation, and circularity are intertwined.

> Circularity includes prolonging the life of products and materials in society and using resources in a smarter way, transitioning to using only recycled or renewable materials, which is a huge task. It also means designing all IKEA products to be repurposed, repaired, reused, resold and recycled, right from the beginning. To make it work we must encourage customers to participate by designing new services and helping customers care for and pass on products. Becoming a circular business is a total transformation, a new business model and it is one important way we will achieve becoming people and planet positive.
>
> (page 22)

According to Inter IKEA Group CFO Martin van Dam:

> Today we're devoting significant resources to make IKEA more affordable, accessible and sustainable for IKEA customers. A part of that is developing new store formats and e-commerce capabilities across the IKEA value chain. This of course impacts short-term results.
>
> (Inka Group, p. 22)

And, according to Jesper Brodin, President and CEO, IKEA:

> As the world keeps changing, our vision to create a better everyday life for the many people is more relevant than ever before. We can make a huge difference for people and the planet, and we're more determined than ever to do it!
>
> (Ingka Group, 2019, p. 6)

We now turn to an example of design for sustainability enabled by collaborative service platforms: the "click system."

A platform for sustainable service: the "click system"

Assembling flat-pack furniture can be a challenge, even if none of the screws is missing. To make toolless assembly a reality, IKEA, in collaboration with different experts, has developed a wedge dowel for wooden products. A table, for instance, will have a small ribbed knob at the top of its leg, which is then inserted into a predrilled hole in the tabletop. It requires no glue and can be taken apart and reassembled multiple times without damaging the dowel.

The traditional assembly technique, using screws and wooden sticks, will become outdated as IKEA products that snap together "like a jigsaw puzzle" supersede it. This quicker and simpler way to assemble products needs no screws, bolts, screwdrivers, or hex keys and is a design driven partly by customers' resistance to the often slow and frustrating experience of putting together IKEA products, and partly as a way of saving resources (both cost and environmental impact), since assembly no longer requires dozens of metal fittings.

Designing for collaborative transformation with ServCollab

ServCollab[6] was created to serve humanity through collaboration. To accomplish its purpose, ServCollab pursues transformative collaboration "through service research projects that reduce violations of human rights and enable more sustainable and satisfying human experiences" (Fisk et al., 2020). Fundamentally, ServCollab seeks to support service research projects that design new and sustainable solutions to significant human service system problems. Making such projects happen will require building operational research capacity by recruiting, training, and collaborating with scholars from the service research field and with scholars from other human-facing disciplines.

ServCollab was designed as a virtual organization that has no physicality beyond its service research members and their resources. As such, the networking and resource integration abilities of the members enable the creation of each service research project. The COVID-19 pandemic has significantly accelerated the need for transformative collaborations. Fortunately, modern communications technology has made global research collaborations possible during the pandemic.

Even before the pandemic hit, global participation in a ServCollab project was achieved by means of electronic collaboration tools such as videoconferencing (e.g. Zoom, Skype, and FaceTime), file sharing (e.g. Dropbox, Google Drive, and iCloud), and collaboration software (e.g. Miro, Slack, and Trello). In the near term, the COVID-19 pandemic will compel ServCollab research teams to conduct most of their work electronically.

Service research designed for human rights goals

ServCollab's service research projects are designed around ServCollab's three human rights goals: "Serve," "Enable," and "Transform." The "Serve" goal concerns essential questions about who is being served by the research project. The "Enable" goal concerns operational issues about how research teams are being served by ServCollab. The "Transform" goal concerns the specific transformations being pursued on behalf of people.

These are the three ServCollab human rights goals:

1. Serve. ServCollab seeks to serve all humans with research that respects their dignity and supports their rights. This includes advocating for fair and inclusive service experiences starting with fair and inclusive access to service, fair and inclusive service encounters, and fair and inclusive ability to exit the service.
2. Enable. ServCollab seeks: (1) to enable collaborations among researchers and organizations that span disciplinary and national boundaries in pursuit of diagnosing and treating humanity's many service system problems; (2) to enable access to the human and financial resources necessary for the success of such collaborations; (3) to enable a deeper understanding of service systems; and (4) to propagate a humane design science for service systems.
3. Transform. ServCollab seeks transformative reductions in human suffering and transformative improvements in human well-being. Further, ServCollab seeks: (1) to measure both the quantities and qualities of service systems; (2) to foster standards of service that are adaptable and measurable across different service systems; and (3) to evolve those service standards to better fulfill human potential.

Designing ServCollab service research projects based on these three human rights goals requires service research teams to be assembled that can self-organize around the pursuit of the three goals. Further, each ServCollab service research team must have a common service research ethic and a shared passion for solving complex service system problems. Also, the people affected by ServCollab service design research decisions must be cocreators of any proposed transformative collaboration on their behalf.

The greatest service design challenges facing ServCollab are those of building sufficient research capacity to tackle large-scale service system problems. The many commonplace large-scale service systems problems, such as hunger, poverty, and inequality, are truly global in nature. Building such global service research teams requires service scholars to be found who share passion and possess complementary skills.

A systems approach to designing ServCollab research projects

Research system inputs

Creating a ServCollab research project requires decisions about the research idea, the participants, the goals, and the research agenda. The selection of ServCollab research project ideas is based on the identification of a key human need that is being neglected or disserved somewhere in the world. Project ideas are discussed vigorously to make sure they seek to significantly reduce human suffering or improve human well-being.

Participants in ServCollab research projects include the individual researchers and the institutions they represent. Diversity of perspective is the essential foundation for any transformative collaboration research team. While empathy is an essential basis on which service research teams can find common purpose, there is no substitute for having a variety of team members who live in different skins. A true understanding of human experience drawn from actually living that experience provides much deeper insights than empathy alone.

While the majority of participants in the early years of ServCollab research projects may self-identify as service researchers, ServCollab is actively seeking research team members from other human facing disciplines with the diversity of skills and perspectives they can provide. Most importantly, ServCollab will assemble research teams that can collaboratively design or redesign solutions to human service system problems.

Modern service research language advocates for cocreation in service systems. In seeking to design or redesign solutions, ServCollab will seek cocreative solutions with those most directly affected by a problem. So, a service design study of refugees would seek to cocreate solutions with refugees. Such an approach is far more likely to create solutions that respect the dignity of refugees and will be quickly adopted.

Participants in ServCollab research projects may include collaboration partnerships with other service organizations. These organizations include the American Marketing Association's Service Special Interest Group (SERVSIG), which is the primary organization serving the service research community. In addition, collaboration will be sought with numerous service research conferences that might encourage ServCollab projects. These include the following well-known service research conferences: Frontiers in Service Conference, the LaLonde Conference, the QUIS Conference, and the SERVSIG Research Conference. There are also numerous well-established university service research centers that are well positioned to help ServCollab raise the visibility of its service research field and expand its service research collaboration networks beyond business disciplines. ServCollab research projects will include sponsoring organizations whenever possible. Such organizations might be a nonprofit organization, corporation, or government agency providing access to their organization and the people they serve. Funding will be sought for these major service system projects from foundations, government agencies, and universities.

More recently, the Responsible Research in Business and Management (RRBM) has emerged as a new nonprofit organization dedicated to inspiring, encouraging, and supporting credible and useful research in the business disciplines.[7] Like ServCollab, RRBM shares an interest in improving human society through research.

Research system throughputs

Collaboration in scientific research has a long history. Many of the hardest problems our species has ever attempted to solve were pursued by large-scale research teams. These include such famous research projects as the Manhattan Project and decoding the human genome. In the first few weeks of the COVID-19 pandemic, unprecedented scientific collaboration emerged to develop tests, treatments, and vaccines.

ServCollab research teams will be coached and mentored by more experienced service researchers to help each team learn to optimize its performance. Learning to create collaborative harmony within a research team requires practice. Collaborative teams in the performing arts are instructive here. Choirs and orchestras practice performing together. As a social species, humans derive profound joy from creating something meaningful together. Musical collaboration was taking place long before scientific collaboration was possible.

Since collaboration is central to human service systems, ServCollab will not only seek to design for transformative collaboration in its own projects, but it will also seek to innovate and share better collaboration practices. ServCollab will always seek programmatic research that enables future research projects to build next-step projects on the foundation of the previous project. Whenever possible, ServCollab will also seek to create new service research tools and new measurement systems for the large-scale service system problems being studied.

Research system outputs

ServCollab seeks to become a trusted source for and strong public advocate for collaborative service research that serves humanity. This includes advocating for and supporting local or global service research that focuses on designing or redesigning service systems to reduce human suffering or improve human well-being.

In the world of scientific research, publishing research in peer-reviewed journals is seen as the gold standard of quality research. Hence, ServCollab research projects will be expected to pursue such publications. Nonetheless, ServCollab will also promote adoption of the recommendations of its research projects. This will entail additional work on the part of the researchers. Press releases, social media sharing, and video interviews with research participants will also be created to raise public awareness and encourage the adoption of research recommendations.

First ServCollab research projects

ServCollab's first project area is service inclusion (Fisk et al., 2020). ServCollab chose inclusion as the first project area because a lack of inclusion is at the core of unjust human service systems. (Earlier in this chapter, we discussed the need to design for service inclusion.) Fisk et al. (2018) define the concept of service inclusion as "an egalitarian system that provides customers with fair access to a service, fair treatment during a service, and fair opportunity to exit a service" (p. 835). Service inclusion is a research theme based on the transformative service research (TSR) paradigm (Anderson et al., 2013). According to Fisk et al. (2018), "Service inclusion should be a moral imperative for service organizations, systems and nation-states" (p. 851).

Unfortunately, across human history, unfair service systems have been common, and they remain common in many modern service experiences. Older systems of unfairness such as slavery or colonialism were quite barbaric. Modern systems of unfairness include preventing access to services and discrimination during service interactions. Such systems are systems of service exclusion. The Black Lives Matter movement arose in the United States in 2013 to prevent exclusion. In the years after, a series of police killings culminated with a videotaped murder of George Floyd by police. That killing led to massive protests against police misconduct across the United States.

Following Fisk et al.'s (2018) building of a logic for service inclusion rather than exclusion, ServCollab has been developing research projects focused on documenting service exclusion and mistreatment, analyzing the experience of victims of these injustices, and designing systems for service inclusion. The first ServCollab service research project was conducted by a multidisciplinary team of academics seeking to assist service scholars, nonprofit service providers, private service providers, and policymakers in transforming refugee lives (Boenigk et al., 2021). Refugees are those involuntarily fleeing their home country because of crises such as persecution, disasters, conflicts, or climate change. Unfortunately, the modern world has unprecedented numbers of refugees fleeing many parts of the world. This project has created a Transformative Refugee Service Framework (based on three dimensions: refugee service journeys, refugee service system levels, and refugee service system experiences) to encourage more refugee service research. Based on the logic of service inclusion, refugees should receive help from hospitable service systems rather than the hostile service systems that occur in many parts of the world.

Conclusion

Globalization and the evolution of technology have led to modern social and economic service systems that are increasingly interconnected and complex. The COVID-19 pandemic has highlighted the need for collaboration to deal with the challenges of creating sustainable and resilient service systems amid this increasing complexity, and the need to purposefully design service systems to foster transformative collaboration.

This chapter has explored service design with a human-centered, participatory, and transformative approach, and how it can be a cornerstone of the creation of transformative collaboration service systems. A human-centered, participatory service design approach can embed transformative collaboration in both the process of cocreating new service systems and in the future service systems being designed, so that all actors contribute to their full potential to the new service systems. An action-oriented, transformative service design approach can help build collaborative service systems and platforms for ongoing and lasting transformative collaboration.

The three cases have illustrated how service design can purposefully embed transformative collaboration in large, complex service systems in government, industrial, and transnational collaboration contexts. The Electronic Health Record (EHR) case has shown how a human-centered and participatory design approach promoted transformative collaboration in the EHR design process, and how a transformative approach enabled the design of the EHR to foster collaboration among healthcare actors and reach a sustainable solution that balances societal well-being and health system viability.

The second case has illustrated how a multinational company (IKEA), known for good design for the many ("Democratic Design"), has used service platforms to facilitate collaborative service design. The platforms orchestrate a wide range of collaborating actors and resources, facilitated by digital technologies to design and test-drive new and sustainable offerings, configured to fit service platforms used in ongoing business. The case zoomed in on how platforms enable the design and realization of value-creating solutions (products and services) in a sustainable way.

The ServCollab case has described a new nonprofit service platform that is designed to support service research collaborations. The contribution of ServCollab is that it seeks to accelerate the pace of human progress by expanding the collaborative power of service researchers through human-centered service design and action research. ServCollab focuses on enabling collaborative solutions to profound human service system problems by training others in participatory design for large-scale service research projects, fostering best practices for designing collaborative teams, and serving as a clearinghouse for collaborative service research resources.

In any era, collaboration is desirable for service design projects as well as for successful careers after graduate school. In a post-pandemic world, knowledge workers will be challenged to adapt and evolve to more resilient structures and processes. Building transformative collaboration systems in your personal and your professional lives will lead to greater career opportunities. A key step in this process is to stretch your mind and your personal human networks to include people who are very different than you. Learn and grow by building personal empathy for those very different than you. We live on the only known planet inhabited by life. Any moral human service system should properly serve the needs of all humans in the service system.

Notes

1 https://www.ikea.com/gb/en/this-is-ikea/about-us/vision-and-business-idea-pub9cd02291
2 https://www.ikea.com/ms/en_JP/about_ikea/the_ikea_way/our_business_idea/index.html
3 https://www.inter.ikea.com/
4 For more information, visit https://space10.com/.
5 "Making healthy and sustainable living a reality for the many." https://about.ikea.com/en/sustainability/healthy-and-sustainable-living/healthy-sustainable-living

6 https://www.servcollab.org
7 https://www.rrbm.network

References

Akaka, M.A., Vargo, S.L., and Lusch, R.F. (2012). An exploration of networks in value cocreation: a service-ecosystems view. In Stephen L. Vargo and Robert F. Lusch (Eds.), *Special Issue: Toward a Better Understanding of the Role of Value in Markets and Marketing* (Vol. 9) (pp. 13–50). Bingley: Emerald Books.

Alkire (née Nasr), L., Mooney, C., Gur, F.A., Kabadayi, S., Renko M., and Vink, J. (2020). Transformative service research, service design, and social entrepreneurship: an interdisciplinary framework advancing wellbeing and social impact. *Journal of Service Management*, 31(1), 24–50. https://doi.org/10.1108/JOSM-05-2019-0139

Anderson, L., Ostrom, A.L., Corus, C., Fisk, R.P., Gallan, A.S., Giraldo, M., Mende, M., Mulder, M., Rayburn, S.W., Rosenbaum, M.S., Shirahada K., and Williams, J.D. (2013). Transformative service research: an agenda for the future. *Journal of Business Research*, 66, 1203–210.

Angus, S.D., and Newton, J. (2015). Emergence of shared intentionality is coupled to the advance of cumulative culture. *PLOS Computation Biology*, 11(10), 1–12.

Autio, E., and Thomas, L.D.W. (2014). Innovation ecosystems: implications for innovation management? In Mark Dodgson, David M. Gann, and Nelson Phillips (Eds.), *The Oxford Handbook of Innovation Management* (pp. 204–88). Oxford: Oxford University Press.

Bitner, M.J., Ostrom, A.L., and Morgan, F.N. (2008). Service blueprinting: a practical technique for service innovation. *California Management Review*, 50(3), 66–94.

Blocker, C.P., and Barrios, A. (2015). The transformative value of a service experience. *Journal of Service Research*, 18(3), 265–83.

Blomkvist, J., Holmlid, S., and Segelström, F. (2010). Service design research: yesterday, today and tomorrow. in Marc Stickdorn and Jakob Schneider (Eds.), *This is Service Design Thinking* (pp 308–15). Amsterdam: BIS Publishers.

Boenigk, S., Fisk, R.P., Kabadayi, S., Alkire, L., Cheung, L., Corus, C., Finsterwalder, J., Kreimer, A.A., Luca, N., Omeira, M., Paul, P., Santos, M.F., and Smidt, N. (2021). Rethinking service systems and public policy: a transformative refugee service framework. *Journal of Public Policy and Marketing*, 2(40), 165–83.

Edvardsson, B., Gustafsson, A., and Roos, I. (2005). Service portraits in service research: a critical review. *International Journal of Service Industry Management*, 16(1), 107–21.

Edvardsson, B., Frow, P., Jaakkola, E., Keiningham, T.L., Koskela-Huotari, K., Mele, C., and Tombs, A. (2018). Examining how context change foster service innovation. *Journal of Service Management*, 29(5), 932–55.

Edvardsson, B., Tronvoll, B. (2020). "How Platforms foster Service Innovation." *Organization Dynamics*, 3(49), 1–8.

Evenson, S. (2008). A designer's view of SSME. In Bill Hefley and Wendy Murphy (Eds.), *Service Science, Management and Engineering: Education for the 21st Century* (pp. 25–30). New York: Springer.

Fisk, R.P., Dean, A.M., Alkire (née Nasr), L., Joubert, A., Previte, J., Robertson, N., and Scott Rosenbaum, M. (2018). Design for service inclusion: creating inclusive service systems by 2050. *Journal of Service Management*, 29(5), 834–58.

Fisk, R., Fuessel, A., Laszlo, C., Struebi, P., Valera, A., and Weiss, C. (2019). Systemic social innovation: co-creating a future where humans and all life thrive. *Humanistic Management Journal*, 4, 191–214.

Fisk, R.P., Alkire (née Nasr), L., Anderson, L., Bowen, D.E., Gruber, T., Ostrom, A.L., and Patrício, L. (2020). Elevating the human experience (HX) through service research collaborations: introducing ServCollab. *Journal of Service Management*, 31(4), 615–35.

Følstad, A., and Kvale, K. (2018). Customer journeys: a systematic literature review. *Journal of Service Theory and Practice*, 28(2), 196–227.

Fu, W., Wang, Q. and Zhao, X. (2017). The influence of platform service innovation on value co-creation activities and the network effect. *Journal of Service Management*, 28(2), 348–88.

Gonçalves, L., Patrício, L., Teixeira, J.G. and Wunderlich, N.V. (2020). Understanding the customer experience with smart services. *Journal of Service Management*, 31(4), 723–44.

Ingka Group. (2019). *Bringing IKEA to More People in New Ways: Annual Summary & Sustainability Report FY19*. Retrieved from https://www.ingka.com/wp-content/uploads/2020/01/Ingka-Group-Annual-Summary-Sustainability-Report-FY19.pdf?1

Kieliszewski, C.A., Maglio, P.P., and Cefkin, M. (2012). On modeling value constellations to understand complex service system interactions. *European Management Journal*, 30(5), 438–50.

Krishnan, V., and Gupta, S. (2001). Appropriateness and impact of platform-based product development. *Management Science*, 47(1), 52.

Kurtmollaiev, S., Fjuk, A., Pedersen, P.E., Clatworthy, S. and Kvale, K. (2018). Organizational transformation through service design: the institutional logics perspective. *Journal of Service Research*, 21(1), 59–74.

Lee, T., and Hall, K.W. (2010). Turning doctors into leaders. *Harvard Business Review*, 88(4), 50–58.

Maglio, P.P., Vargo, S.L., Caswell, N., and Spohrer, J. (2009). The service system is the basic abstraction of service science. *Information Systems and E-Business Management*, 7(4), 395–406.

McDonald, C.J., Tang, P.C., Hripcsak, G. (2014). Electronic health record systems. In Edward H. Shortliffe and James J. Cimino (Eds.), *Biomedical Informatics* (pp. 391–421). London: Springer.

Meroni, A., and Sangiorgi, D. (Eds.). (2011). *Design for Services*. Aldershot: Gower.

Meyer, M.H., and DeTore, A. (2001). Creating platform-based approaches to new services development. *Journal of Product Innovation Management*, 18(1), 188–204.

Muffatto, M., and Roveda, M. (2002). Product architecture and platforms: a conceptual framework. *International Journal of Technology Management*, 24(1), 1–16.

Nguyen, L., Bellucci, E., and Nguyen, L.T. (2014). Electronic health records implementation: an evaluation of information system impact and contingency factors. *International Journal of Medical Informatics*, 83, 779–96.

Normann, R. (2001). *Reframing Business: When the Map Changes the Landscape*. Chichester: John Wiley & Sons.

Ostrom, A.L., Parasuraman, A., Bowen, D.E., Patrício, L., and Voss, C.A. (2015). Service research priorities in a rapidly changing context. *Journal of Service Research*, 18(2), 127–59.

Patrício, L., Fisk, R.P., and Falcão e Cunha, J. (2008). Designing multi-interface service experiences: the service experience blueprint. *Journal of Service Research*, 10(4), 318–34.

Patrício, L., Fisk, R.P., Falcão e Cunha, J., and Constantine, L. (2011). Multilevel service design: from customer value constellation to service experience blueprint. *Journal of Service Research*, 14(2), 180–200.

Patrício, L., Gustafsson, A., and Fisk, R.P. (2018). Upframing service design and innovation for research impact. *Journal of Service Research*, 21(1), 3–16.

Patrício, L., Pinho, N., Teixeira, J., and Fisk, R.P. (2018). Service design for value networks: enabling value cocreation interactions in healthcare. *Service Science*, 10(1), 76–97.

Patrício, L., Teixeira, J.G., and Vink, J. (2019). A service design approach to healthcare innovation: from decision-making to sense-making and institutional change. *Academy of Marketing Science Review*, 9 (1/2), 115–20.

Patrício, L., Sangiorgi, D., Mahr, D., Čaić, M., Kalantari, S., and Sundar, S. (2020). Leveraging service design for healthcare transformation: toward people-centered, integrated, and technology enabled healthcare systems. *Journal of Service Management*, 5(31), 889–909.

Perks, H., Kowalkowski, C., Witell, L., and Gustafsson, A. (2017). Network orchestration for value platform development. *Industrial Marketing Management*, 67(3), 106–21.

Plé, L., and Chumpitaz Cáceres, R. (2010). Not always co-creation: introducing interactional co-destruction of value in service-dominant logic. *Journal of Services Marketing*, 24(6), 430–37.

Robertson, D., and Ulrich, K.T. (1998). Planning for product platforms. *Sloan Management Review*, 39(4), 19–31.

Sanders, E. (2008). An evolving map of design practice and design research. *Interactions*, 15(6), 13–17.

Sangiorgi, D. (2009). Building up a framework for service design research. *8th European Academy of Design Conference*. Aberdeen, Scotland: The Robert Gordon University, 415–20.

Sangiorgi, D. (2011). Transformative services and transformation design. *International Journal of Design*, 5(1), 29–40.

Sangiorgi, D., Patrício, L., and Fisk, R.P. (2017). Designing for interdependence, participation and emergence in complex service systems. in Daniela Sangiorgi and Alison Prediville (Eds.), *Designing for Service: Key Issues and New Directions* (pp. 49–64). London: Bloomsbury Academic.

Sangiorgi, D., Lima, F., Patrício, L., Prestes Joly, M., and Favini, C. (2019). A human-centred, multidisciplinary, and transformative approach to service science: a service design perspective. In Paul P. Maglio, Cheryl A. Kieliszewski, James C. Spohrer, Kelly Lyons, Lia Patrício, and Yuriko Sawatani (Eds.), *Handbook of Service Science* (Vol. II) (pp. 147–81). Cham, Switzerland: Springer.

Simon, H.A. (1969). *The Sciences of the Artificial*. Cambridge, MA: MIT Press.

Spohrer, J.C., Maglio, P.P., Bailey, J.H., and Gruhl, D. (2007). Steps toward a science of service systems. *IEEE Computer*, 40(1), 71–77.

Tax, S.S., McCutcheon, D., and Wilkinson, I.F. (2013). The Service Delivery Network (SDN): a customer-centric perspective of the customer journey. *Journal of Service Research*, 16(4), 454–70.

van Wijk, J., Zietsma, C., Dorado, S., de Bakker, F.G.A., and Martí, I. (2019). Social innovation: integrating micro, meso, and macro level insights from institutional theory. *Business & Society*, 58(5), 887–918.

Vargo, S.L., and Lusch, R.F. (2004). Evolving to a new dominant logic for marketing. *Journal of Marketing*, 68(1), 1–17.

Vargo, S.L., and Lusch, R.F. (2016). Institutions and axioms: an extension and update of service-dominant logic. *Journal of the Academy of Marketing Science*, 44(1), 5–23.

Vargo, S.L., Maglio, P.P., and Archupru Akaka, M. (2008). On value and value co-creation: a service systems and service logic perspective. *European Management Journal*, 26(3), 145–52.

Vink, J., Edvardsson, B., Wetter-Edman, K., and Tronvoll, B. (2019). Reshaping mental models: enabling innovation through service design. *Journal of Service Management*, 30(1), 75–104.

WHO (World Health Organization) (2016). Framework on integrated, people-centred health services. Geneva: World Health Organization.

Yu, E., and Sangiorgi, D. (2018). Service design as an approach to implement the value cocreation perspective in new service development. *Journal of Service Research*, 21(1), 40–58.

6 Steering toward happiness in sustainable travel

Lars E. Olsson and Margareta Friman

Takeaways

- Travel is important for happiness in terms of experience and satisfaction.
- Travel is indirectly important for happiness as means of undertaking daily life activities.
- The benefits of sustainable travel and happiness are wide-ranging and important.

Introduction

Climate change is an acute, ongoing global issue, and an environmentally sustainable lifestyle is seen as part of the solution to this problem (Stern, 2000). Private car use has risen to a level detrimental for the environment, from both a local and global perspective (Gärling & Steg, 2007; van Wee, 2014). At the local level, particle emissions, accidents, and noise are all related to health, and the car infrastructure can be responsible for less habitable urban environments. At the global level, cars emit greenhouse gases contributing to climate change (Sinha, Olsson, & Frostell, 2019). The transformation from cars to public transport and other more sustainable transport solutions is slow, however, and needs to increase if we are to achieve any of the world governments' climate targets. The EU, for instance, has set progressive emission reduction targets for greenhouse gases leading up to 2050 (EC, 2018), which includes reduced private vehicle emissions and the promotion of public transport. The challenge is to transform our car-oriented societies into ones that favor sustainable travel.

Public transport is an important component of sustainable travel, but often remains an unattractive option for many. The market share of public transport is still low, although varying in different parts of the world. The profile of public transport users varies according to country, but it is commonly biased toward women, low-income earners, and young people. In order to attract more users, and appeal to other groups, public transport needs to extend its collaborations with other innovative and sustainable mobility services with the aim of cocreating value and solving users' daily problems and needs. Much research and practice in the area of transport has, to date, focused on dyadic

DOI: 10.4324/9781003188773-6

relationships between service providers and travelers. In contrast to this, a service ecosystem approach (Akaka & Vargo, 2015) would allow transport services, transport providers, and service processes (procedures and servicescapes) to integrate in order to solve mobility needs and pursue happiness in sustainable travel.

This is largely a new way of looking at sustainable transport, but there are already examples in place. We present here a case study on public transport in Finland, in the Helsinki metropolitan area. For several years, Finland has been ranked as the happiest country in the world according to the UN *World Happiness Report* (UN, 2020), which is based on individuals' ratings of their own well-being. Furthermore, the public transport system in the Finnish capital commands a good reputation and is often referred to as being excellent. This chapter begins with an introduction to the theoretical concept of happiness. The following section explains the domain-specific concept of well-being, the domain in this context being daily travel. The case study then shows how domain-specific happiness, which is partly dependent on service quality, is associated with overall well-being among its users.

Why happiness?

A shift in focus in policy and service development in favor of happiness, rather than revenue, GDP, or economic growth, is not just the view of this chapter. In 2011, the United Nations concluded that the pursuit of happiness is a fundamental human goal in their report *Happiness: Towards a Holistic Approach to Development* (UN, 2011). Furthermore, as noted by Easterlin (2019), a 2013 document issued by the UN Secretary-General encouraged governments to use carefully constructed regular, large-scale data on happiness and well-being as a more appropriate indicator for improving macroeconomic policy-making and informing service delivery. Following this, the OECD developed guidelines which included definitions and measures of happiness and subjective well-being (OECD, 2013). Measures of happiness are currently being used in many countries at a national level; however, such metrics are conspicuously absent among service providers as a means of understanding their customers' experiences.

The concept of happiness can be traced back to the philosophers of ancient Greece (McMahon, 2008), as well as more recently to researchers in economics, sociology, and psychology (see, e.g. Diener et al., 1999; Dolan, Peasgood, & White, 2008) who have been studying the concept for some decades now. Happiness can be defined as the subjective experiences of positive and negative affect, and cognitive judgments of satisfaction with life (e.g. Busseri & Sadava, 2011; Diener et al., 1985); the former can be referred to as *affective happiness* and the latter as *evaluative happiness*. In line with this, the OECD defines happiness as "Good mental states, including all of the various evaluations, positive and negative, that people make of their lives and the affective reactions of people to their experiences" (OECD, 2013, p.10). Hence, happiness can be measured both in relation to one's life overall, and also regarding various domains, contexts, and activities in life. There is increasing interest in understanding how domain-specific contexts (e.g. consumption, schools, and public facilities) relate to the perceived quality of life (Diener & Seligman, 2004). And, indeed, research has found support for the importance of general well-being of specific life domains (Schimmack & Oishi, 2005), such as economic, social, work, health, leisure, and family. The paths from domain happiness to overall happiness are identified as being stronger than in the reverse direction (Shimmack, 2008). Thus, changes in happiness in one life domain are likely to lead to changes in happiness more generally.

At a larger scale, happiness has been shown to be correlated with life circumstances both in studies within countries (Lyubomirsky, Sheldon, & Schkade, 2005) and between countries (Helliwell, Huang, & Wang, 2017): in countries with high measures of freedom, social support, and health, people are more satisfied with their life, but less so where corruption is high (Helliwell, Huang, & Wang, 2017). It has been shown that income is positively correlated, although marginally so for those already well-off, and that increases in national levels of income over time correlate with happiness (e.g. Sacks, Stevenson, & Wolfers, 2012). Marriage increases happiness; divorce and the death of a spouse reduces it (Winter et al., 2000); unemployment has a negative effect, especially where there is a lack of social support (Lucas et al., 2004); findings related to gender are mixed (Tesch-Römer, Motel-Klingebiel, & Tomasik, 2008). As regards age, a U-shaped pattern is common (Mroczek & Spiro, 2005), meaning that the young and the elderly are the happiest, although there are contextual variations (e.g. Olsson et al., 2020).

In addition to the life circumstances mentioned above, daily travel, it is argued, is a life domain on which happiness is highly contingent (Ettema et al., 2010). Compared to other disciplines, research into the interaction between sustainable travel, happiness, and life satisfaction is relatively novel, emerging only in the past decade. This now growing body of research was originally triggered by the conceptual models proposed by Ettema et al. (2010), and further developed in relation to children's travel by Waygood et al. (2019). These models include both direct and indirect effects of travel on happiness: direct in terms of experiences and satisfaction with travel itself, and indirect from the instrumental function of travel as means of reaching important activities in our daily lives – out-of-home activities that are important for our well-being (Lyubomirsky, Sheldon, & Schkade, 2005; Jakobsson-Bergstad et al., 2011; Deci & Ryan, 2008). Hence, travel is viewed both as a means to an end, and as an important activity in itself (Mokhtarian & Salomon, 2001). In their book *Quality in Life and Daily Travel*, Friman, Olsson, and Ettema (2018) conclude that there is much research about choice in travel, but less on how to assist people in switching to sustainable alternatives, and the consequences this may have for happiness. Efforts to address this discrepancy have gained momentum over the past decade, with new research streams offering improved conceptual models and novel empirical research on travel and happiness (e.g. Chatterjee et al., 2020; Delbosc & Currie, 2011; De Vos et al., 2013; Ettema et al., 2016; Nordbakke & Schwanen, 2014; Singleton, 2019; Waygood et al., 2017).

Travel as a domain-specific happiness

Having defined happiness as consisting of cognitive and affective evaluations that people make of their experiences and their own lives, it is important to develop and validate self-reporting measures if we are to capture these evaluations. Several such metrics have been used by international panels over the years, such as the Eurobarometer, the Social Values Survey, Gallup, and many others, in order to measure life happiness, with subscales also constructed for various life domains (e.g. Friman, Westman, & Olsson, 2019; Shimmack & Oishi, 2005). Self-report scales specifically addressing happiness related to the transport domain are only a recent development, however. One such measure is the validated and widely used Satisfaction with Travel Scale (STS), specifically designed to measure the affective and cognitive dimensions of travel happiness (e.g. Ettema et al., 2011; Friman et al., 2013; Westman et al., 2017).

The STS is a multi-item scale that was initially developed to measure evaluations and experiences of any form of travel. With slight refinements over the years to apply to different modes, languages, and age groups, the scale has been extensively applied to travel in general, for specific modes, or combinations of them (see, e.g. Singleton, 2019 for a review of studies applying the STS). The STS combines one dimension, a cognitive evaluation of satisfaction with quality, with two orthogonal dimensions of affect associated with travel. The nine items in the STS are shown in Table 6.1. The affective dimensions are based on validated adjectives from the Swedish Core Affect Scale (Västfjäll et al., 2002) which were originally derived from the much earlier Circumplex Model of Affect (see, e.g. Gärling et al., 2020; Yik, Russell, & Steiger, 2011). All the items in the STS are usually answered on seven-point scales (either from −3 to

Table 6.1 The Satisfaction with Travel Scale (STS)

Three dimensions of travel satisfaction		
Cognitive evaluation		
Travel was worst (−3)	–	best I can think of (3)
Travel had low(−3)	–	high standard (3)
Travel worked well (−3)	–	worked poorly (3)
Positive activation–negative deactivation		
I felt tired (−3)	–	alert (3)
I felt bored (−3)	–	enthusiastic (3)
I felt fed up (−3)	–	engaged (3)
Positive deactivation–negative activation		
I felt hurried (−3)	–	relaxed (3)
I felt worried (−3)	–	confident (3)
I felt stressed (−3)	–	calm (3)

+3, or from 1 to 7) ranging from negative experiences and evaluations to positive ones. To assure high content validity, the scales of the STS include affective components that are frequently experienced during travel, such as alertness, boredom, relaxation, and stress (which correspond to the valence and activation dimensions of the circumplex), and cognitive quality evaluations related to the level of standard and functionality. It has been suggested that the STS may be equally applicable to other service offering settings, such as healthcare, retail, and hospitality (Olsson et al., 2012), as it captures the essential aspects related to domain-specific happiness. This assumption is yet to be tested in practice, however, which is something we urge future research to do.

Analyses of the psychometric properties of STS have shown that the three dimensions are distinct constructs positively correlated with one another, but which can also be combined to a latent higher-order overall measure of satisfaction with travel (Friman et al., 2013). The STS has been validated in other contexts, supporting claims for its dimensionality (e.g. Glasgow et al., 2018), although slight modifications of the vocabulary may be warranted in some contexts (Singleton, 2019). Research from Belgium suggests that the STS is best used as a single overall construct (De Vos et al., 2015), and a recent validation study of the STS in an US context (Singleton, 2019) concluded that the scale is indeed an effective summary measure.

The path in steering toward happiness in public transport seems to follow the logic – introduced by Ettema et al. (2010) – that changes in the attributes related to quality of travel have an influence on domain-specific happiness (measured by the STS, for instance), which in turn relates to overall happiness in life (see Figure 6.1). Creating a transport system in which people are satisfied with their daily travel may therefore be one key to creating a society of happy citizens.

If one aim is to create a sustainable transport system, and another aim is to improve or sustain well-being, it is therefore important to understand both what would make a traveler choose public transport and also what would make that traveler satisfied with the experience. In the next section, we will use Helsinki as a case study to illustrate the relationships among quality attributes, domain-specific happiness, and overall happiness, as shown in Figure 6.1.

Figure 6.1 The relationship between quality attributes, domain-specific happiness, and overall happiness.

Daily travel and happiness: the case of Helsinki

Helsinki has approximately 650,000 inhabitants in its inner-city area, and 1.4 million in its wider metropolitan district. The residents of Helsinki can claim to live in the happiest country in the world (UN, 2020). Understanding how Helsinki is dealing with a transition to sustainable travel, and how this links to life happiness, can provide a benchmark for other regions. In the case of Helsinki, we discuss how sustainable travel has been prioritized by government and regional decision-makers. We also present data on how residents in Helsinki are experiencing their daily travel.

Strategic plans and governance play an important role in a transition to sustainable travel. Helsinki's mobility plan has, since 2015, strongly favored public transport: the Helsinki Regional Transport Authority's vision for 2025 states that public transport should be the number one choice for all travel. As a result, more journeys are made by public transport than by car; a breakdown of all journeys in Helsinki by mode (2018) is: 11% cycle, 19% car, 33% public transport, and 36% walking. The total number of public transport journeys has increased from 276 million (2017) to 296 million (2018), mainly due to an expanded metro. Public transport in these figures includes bus, metro, trams, commuter trains, and ferry services.

Karjalainen and Juhola (2019) describe how Helsinki is strongly linked with its surrounding regions through public transport services. Financing comes from a joint tax-based funding structure among seven municipalities in the region and from ticket revenues. This joint financing arrangement has, according to Karjalainen and Juhola (2019), been instrumental in the system's success, engendering cooperation and financial stability.

Helsinki's transport planning follows the TOD (transit-oriented development) method, which revolves around a mixed and dense urban structure in pursuit of sustainable development. Land use and development take into consideration proximity to transit facilities, as well as walking and cycling distances. The TOD method favors public transport, leading to the prioritization in Helsinki of light rail transit, tram routes, and metro. Finland has been a pioneer in the development of the "Mobility as a Service" (MaaS) concept, which allows commuters to plan and pay for trips across multiple transportation modes via a single access point (e.g. the Whim app, with its 8,500 active users in Helsinki, according to Huhtala-Jenks [2019]). Within a MaaS system, digital platforms offer "all transport in one app," whereby a user can choose from various subscriptions which include city bikes, e-scooters, taxis, public transport, and on-demand rental cars. Although public transport is the backbone of Helsinki's transport system, innovative new mobility services such as these offer an additional attractive and sustainable alternative to the car. MaaS solutions have the potential to attract a different customer segment than those who would have traditionally chosen public transport.

In summary, public transport in Helsinki is embedded within a complex ecosystem that has political, technical, and social dimensions. The political dimension is about tearing down silos and working together across boundaries in order to achieve a common vision. Here, Helsinki's vision of public transport being everybody's first choice plays an important function. The technical dimension is about including the needs of current and potential travelers in all infrastructure-related projects, while the social dimension is about offering value and attracting users to sustainable transport. The application of the TOD method, along with strategic work linking regional land use, housing, and transport (HLJ, 2015), has created opportunities for collaboration across several different domains that would not normally combine in pursuit of innovative solutions. In the social dimension, user experiences are especially important. Since this chapter's focus is on happiness, in the following discussion we will present data on the social dimension, including customer experiences.

In order to gauge how Helsinki's residents experience their daily travel, in 2018, we conducted an STS study, which had a total of 1,616 respondents. The respondents were asked to reflect on all of their routine journeys and answer the questions in the STS. Rather than using all the STS's nine questions as separate items, for simplicity's sake, the scale was collapsed into three questions capturing all nine items and all three dimensions. The results are reported in Table 6.2.

The results show that the quality of daily travel is generally perceived as high, with people to a high extent reporting feeling enthusiastic and relaxed during travel. In the same survey, respondents were also asked to estimate their general life satisfaction, and the results confirm the findings of the UN *World Happiness Survey*, showing that the respondents are very happy in life (a mean of 5.71 on a seven-point scale). The correlation between the STS index and general life satisfaction was high and significant (.337, $p < .001$), indicating that

Table 6.2 The Satisfaction with Travel Scale (STS) among Helsinki's residents in 2018 (on a scale of 1–7, with 4 being the neutral midpoint)

	STS per dimension	*STS in total*
	Mean (SD)	*Mean (SD)*
Cognitive evaluation The trips work poorly, are of low standard, worst imaginable – The trips work well, are of high standard, best imaginable	5.12 (1.29)	
Positive activation–negative deactivation I feel very bored, fed up, tired – I feel very enthusiastic, alert, engaged	4.77 (1.37)	
Positive deactivation–negative activation I feel very stressed, worried, hurried – I feel very relaxed, confident, calm	5.27 (1.38)	
Satisfaction with travel (index mean of the three dimensions)		5.05 (1.15)

experiences of daily travel in Helsinki are positively correlated with general satisfaction with life.

Domain-specific satisfaction depends on satisfaction with quality attributes (as illustrated in Figure 6.1). In the 2018 survey, respondents were asked to rate their experiences of public transport on a number of quality attributes on a five-point scale. These were subsequently transformed into service quality indexes building on previous knowledge of important service quality dimensions in public transport. Four dimensions were established: functionality (capturing travel time, reliability, frequency, transfers, and closeness); information (during critical incidents and at stops); comfort (comfortable, modern, clean, seat availability); and cost (value for money and reasonable price). An analysis of these four dimensions shows that the residents in Helsinki, in general, are very happy with the quality of their public transport (see Figure 6.2.).

The functionality of the system is very good and is appreciated by the users. They rate comfort as being very high; they think that public transport is providing value for money; and the information is satisfactory. In 2018, over 75% would partly or fully recommend public transport to others.

Our concluding message from this case study is that happiness in life is associated with satisfaction with daily travel. The quality of the system, in this case public transport, contributes to an explanation of why people feel happy with their daily travel. Political, technical, and social dimensions all need to be addressed in order to generate happiness in daily travel.

Although we have chosen Helsinki as a case study, the findings presented here are not necessarily specific to Finland. In other empirical studies, we have provided similar evidence of a relationship between daily travel and well-being: among children in Canada, Japan, and Sweden (Waygood et al., 2019); among adult commuters (Olsson et al., 2013); and among different segments of elderly populations (Lättman et al., 2019). Hence, the relationship between quality attributes, domain-specific happiness, and overall happiness, as described in Figure 6.1, is not uniquely applicable to Helsinki; it is apparent across a

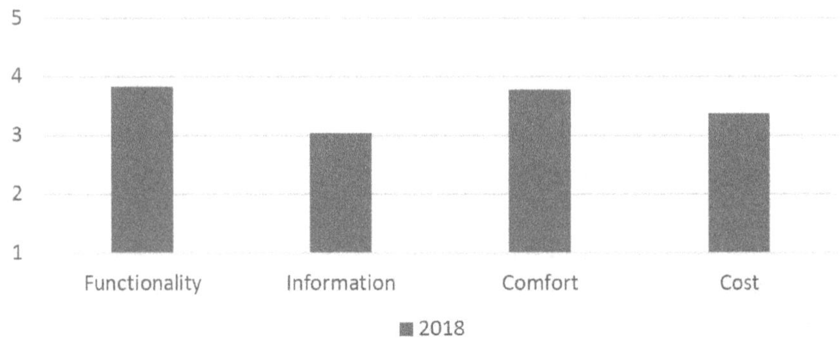

Figure 6.2 Ratings of service quality in public transport.

variety of contexts. Nonetheless, the Helsinki case is especially interesting, with its high-quality transport system and citizens who can claim to be the happiest in the world.

Concluding remarks

In this chapter, we have discussed the need to shift toward happiness in order to facilitate the transition to sustainable transport. National governments can enact various programs and measures that enhance well-being. The Finnish government has achieved success in this regard, with Finland being named the world's happiest country for the third year in a row (2018, 2019, 2020). The 2020 UN report, for the first time, also ranked individual cities according to residents' subjective perceptions of their own well-being. Not unexpectedly, Finland's capital Helsinki came top. There are a number of causes underlying Helsinki's happiness. Research points, on an aggregated level, to social relationships and the potential to achieve one's life goals as contributing factors. In this regard it is vital to discuss the role of daily travel.

Transport is often a necessity in order to participate in desirable activities. This is one explanation for why daily travel has been shown to influence our happiness in life. It can thus also have a negative influence, such as when the journey time is long, cutting into family and friends time, or when crowding or congestion make us stressed or worried. Some may have the opportunity to choose their mode of travel, whereas others may be restricted to one specific mode, undermining their sense of autonomy. Hence, travel can influence happiness in many different ways.

In many countries, it is difficult to travel in a sustainable way. Perhaps public transport is not well developed, there are insufficient bike lines, or none at all, or there is a stigma attached to use of sustainable modes. But the transition to sustainable travel must continue if we are to meet our commitments to reducing emissions and averting the worst of the climate predictions. In this chapter, we have argued that change can be effected by putting people's happiness at the heart of policy and strategic thinking. The pioneering psychologist Ed Diener explains that the benefits of sustainable happiness are important and wide-ranging (Diener et al., 2009), just a few being better health and longevity, superior work performance, more supportive social relationships, and being more likely to help others, volunteer, or donate money to charity.

The Helsinki case has shown that active support for an ecosystem consisting of a plurality of sustainable transport modes has a positive effect on users' experiences. High quality in combination with a well-integrated ecosystem provides value in daily life which has a positive influence on happiness. Public transport is the backbone of Helsinki's sustainable transport system, but it also relies on the support of various innovative mobility services, which are starting to be integrated and serve to increase a sense of autonomy in relation to sustainable travel. Helsinki has also benefited from a strategic land use policy that encourages cycling and walking. The result of all this is a city with residents who are not only happy with their lives, but also experience a general satisfaction with their daily travel. Those who choose sustainable travel modes are also happy. This represents a welcome rebalancing of the transport system. Among the benefits of an extended sustainable transport system are reduced emissions and less congestion, which can also be appreciated by those who continue to travel by car.

A shift from car to public transport will depend on personal preferences and attitudes, and on instrumental factors related to needs and the functionality of the transport system. We propose that aiming also to steer toward happiness in public transport, by adding measures of domain-specific and overall happiness to the equation, will aid decision-making by providing a better picture of choices and causes of mode use. We believe that measuring and understanding these factors are necessary if we want to achieve a sustainable future with happy citizens. A focus on happiness will facilitate the transition by making the alternatives more attractive and less burdensome for the user. A happy user is a loyal user, happy users are happier in life, and happy citizens are more productive and contribute to safety and trust in society. There are thus many benefits in steering toward happiness in public transport.

References

Akaka, M.A., and Vargo, S.L. (2015). Extending the context of service: from encounters to ecosystems. *Journal of Services Marketing*, 29(6–7), 453–62.

Busseri, M.A., and Sadava, S.W. (2011). A review of the tripartite structure of subjective well-being: implications for conceptualization, operationalization, analysis, and synthesis. *Personality and Social Psychology Review*, 15, 290–314.

Chatterjee, K., Chng, S., Clark, B., Davis, A., De Vos, J., Ettema, D., … and Reardon, L. (2020). Commuting and wellbeing: a critical overview of the literature with implications for policy and future research. *Transport Reviews*, 40(1), 5–34.

De Vos, J., Schwanen, T., van Acker, V., and Witlox, F. (2013). Travel and subjective well-being: a focus on findings, methods and future research needs. *Transport Reviews*, 33, 421–42.

De Vos, J., Schwanen, T., van Acker, V., and Witlox, F. (2015). How satisfying is the scale for travel satisfaction? *Transportation Research Part F: Traffic Psychology and Behaviour*, 27, 121–30.

Deci, E.L., and Ryan, R.M. (2008). Facilitating optimal motivation and psychological well-being across life's domains. *Canadian Psychology/Psychologie Canadienne*, 49(1), 14.

Delbosc, A., and Currie, G. (2011). Exploring the relative influences of transport disadvantage and social exclusion on well-being. *Transport Policy*, 18(4), 555–62.

Diener, E., and Seligman, M.E. (2004). Beyond money: toward an economy of well-being. *Psychological Science in the Public Interest*, 5(1), 1–31.

Diener, E.D., Emmons, R.A., Larsen, R.J., and Griffin, S. (1985). The satisfaction with life scale. *Journal of Personality Assessment*, 49(1), 71–75.

Diener, E., Suh, E.M., Lucas, R.E., and Smith, H.L. (1999). Subjective well-being: three decades of progress. *Psychological Bulletin*, 125(2), 276.

Diener, E., Lucas, R., Schimmack, U., and Helliwell, J. (2009). *Well-being for Public Policy*. Oxford series in Positive Psychology. Oxford: Oxford University Press.

Dolan, P., Peasgood, T., and White, M. (2008). Do we really know what makes us happy? A review of the economic literature on the factors associated with subjective well-being. *Journal of Economic Psychology*, 29(1), 94–122.

Easterlin, R.A. (2019). Three revolutions of the modern era. *Comparative Economic Studies*, 61(4), 521–30.

EC (European Commission) (2018). Communication from the Commission to the European Parliament and the Council. A clean planet for all: a European strategic long-term vision for a prosperous, modern, competitive and climate neutral economy, COM(2018) 773 final (November 28).

Ettema, D., Gärling, T., Olsson, L.E., and Friman, M. (2010). Out-of-home activities daily travel and subjective well-being. *Transportation Research Part A: Policy and Practice*, 44, 723–32.

Ettema, D., Gärling, T., Erikson, L., Friman, M., Olsson, L.E., and Fujii, S. (2011). Satisfaction with travel and subjective well-being (SWB): development and tests of a measurement tool. *Transportation Research Part F: Traffic Psychology and Behaviour*, 14, 167–75.

Ettema, D., Gärling, T., Friman, M., and Olsson, L.E. (2016). Travel mode use, travel mode shift and subjective well-being: overview of theories, empirical findings and policy implications. In D. Wang and S. He (Eds.), *Mobility, Sociability and Wellbeing of Urban Living* (pp. 125–50). New York: Springer.

Friman, M., Ettema, D., and Olsson, L.E. (Eds.). (2018). *Quality of Life and Daily Travel*. New York: Springer.

Friman, M., Westman, J., and Olsson, L.E. (2019). Children's life satisfaction and satisfaction with school travel. *Child Indicators Research*, 12(4), 1319–32.

Friman, M., Fujii, S., Ettema, D., Gärling, T., and Olsson, L.E. (2013). Psychometric analysis of the satisfaction with travel scale. *Transportation Research Part A: Policy and Practice*, 48, 132–45.

Gärling, T., and Steg, L. (Eds.). (2007). *Threats from Car Traffic to the Quality of Urban Life: Problems, Causes, and Solutions*. Amsterdam: Elsevier.

Gärling, T., Ettema, D., Connolly, F.F., Friman, M., and Olsson, L.E. (2020). Review and assessment of self-reports of travel-related emotional wellbeing. *Journal of Transport and Health*, 17, 100843.

Glasgow, T.E., Geller, E.S., Le, H.T., and Hankey, S. (2018). Travel mood scale: development and validation of a survey to measure mood during transportation. *Transportation Research Part F: Traffic Psychology and Behaviour*, 59, 318–29.

Helliwell, J.F., Huang, H., and Wang, S. (2017). The social foundations of world happiness. In J.F. Helliwell, R. Layard, and J. Sachs (Eds.), *World Happiness Report 2017*. New York: Sustainable Development Solutions Network.

HLJ (Helsinki Region Transport System Plan) (2015). Retrieved May 20, 2020 from https://www.hsl.fi/en/hlj-helsinki-region-transport-system-plan/hlj-materials

Huhtala-Jenks, K. (2019). *MaaS of the Month: Whim. Insights from the World's First Mobility as a Service (MaaS) Operator*. Maas Alliance Report. Brussels: Maas Global.

Jakobsson Bergstad, C., Gamble, A., Hagman, O., Polk, M., Gärling, T., Ettema, D., Friman, M., and Olsson, L.E. (2011). Subjective well-being related to satisfaction with daily travel. *Transportation*, 38, 1–15.

Karjalainen, L.E., and Juhola, S. (2019). Framework for assessing public transportation sustainability in planning and policy-making. *Sustainability*, 11(4), 1028.

Lättman, K., Olsson, L.E., Friman, M., and Fujii, S. (2019). Perceived accessibility, satisfaction with daily travel, and life satisfaction among the elderly. *International Journal of Environmental Research and Public Health*, 16(22), 4498.

Lucas, R.E., Clark, A.E., Georgellis, Y., and Diener, E. (2004). Unemployment alters the set point for life satisfaction. *Psychological Science*, 15, 8–13.

Lyubomirsky, S., Sheldon, K.M., and Schkade, D. (2005). Pursuing happiness: the architecture of sustainable change. *Review of General Psychology*, 9(2), 111–31.

McMahon, D.M. (2008). The pursuit of happiness in history. In M. Eid & R.J. Larsen (Eds.), *The Science of Subjective Well-being* (pp. 80–93). New York: Guilford Press.

Mokhtarian, P.L., and Salomon, I. (2001). How derived is the demand for travel? Some conceptual and measurement considerations. *Transportation Research Part A: Policy and Practice*, 35(8), 695–719.

Mroczek, D.K., and Spiro III, A. (2005). Change in life satisfaction during adulthood: findings from the veterans affairs normative aging study. *Journal of Personality and Social Psychology*, 88(1), 189.

Nordbakke, S., and Schwanen, T. (2014). Well-being and mobility: a theoretical framework and literature review focusing on older people. *Mobilities*, 9(1), 104–29.

OECD (2013). *OECD Guidelines on Measuring Subjective Well-being*. OECD Publishing. http://dx.doi.org/10.1787/9789264191655-en

Olsson, L.E., Friman, M., Pareigis, J., and Edvardsson, B. (2012). Measuring service experience: applying the satisfaction with travel scale in public transport. *Journal of Retailing and Consumer Services*, 19(4), 413–18.

Olsson, L.E., Gärling, T., Ettema, D., Friman, M., and Fujii, S. (2013). Happiness and satisfaction with work commute. *Social Indicators Research*, 111, 255–63.

Olsson, L.E., Friman, M., Lättman, K., and Fujii, S. (2020). Travel and life satisfaction: from Gen Z to the silent generation. *Journal of Transport and Health*, 18.

Sacks, D.W., Stevenson, B., and Wolfers, J. (2012). The new stylized facts about income and subjective well-being. *Emotion,* 12, 1181–87.

Schimmack, U. (2008). The structure of subjective well-being. In M. Eid and R.J. Larsen (Eds.), *The Science of Subjective Well-being* (pp. 97–123). New York: Guilford Press.

Schimmack, U., and Oishi, S. (2005). The influence of chronically and temporarily accessible information on life satisfaction judgments. *Journal of Personality and Social Psychology*, 89(3), 395–406.

Singleton, P.A. (2019). Validating the Satisfaction with Travel Scale as a measure of hedonic subjective well-being for commuting in a US city. *Transportation Research Part F: Traffic Psychology and Behaviour*, 60, 399–414.

Sinha, R., Olsson, L.E., and Frostell, B. (2019). Sustainable personal transport modes in a life cycle perspective: public or private? *Sustainability*, 11(24), 7092.

Stern, P.C. (2000). New environmental theories: toward a coherent theory of environmentally significant behavior. *Journal of Social Issues*, 56(3), 407–24.

Tesch-Römer, C., Motel-Klingebiel, A., and Tomasik, M.J. (2008). Gender differences in subjective well-being: comparing societies with respect to gender equality. *Social Indicators Research*, 85(2), 329–49.

UN (United Nations) (2011). *Happiness: Towards a Holistic Approach to Development*. RES/65/309. Retrieved June 1, 2020 from https://digitallibrary.un.org/record/715187

UN (United Nations) (2020). World Happiness Report. Ed. John F. Helliwell, Richard Layard, Jeffrey D. Sachs, and Jan-Emmanuel De Neve. Retrieved October 9, 2020 from https://happiness-report.s3.amazonaws.com/2020/WHR20.pdf

van Wee, B. (2014). The unsustainability of car use. In T. Gärling, D. Ettema, and M. Friman (Eds.), *Handbook of Sustainable Travel*. Dordrecht: Springer.

Västfjäll, D., Friman, M., Gärling, T., and Kleiner, M. (2002). The measurement of core affect: a Swedish self-report measure. *Scandinavian Journal of Psychology*, 43, 19–31.

Waygood, E.O., Friman, M., Olsson, L.E., and Taniguchi, A. (2017). Transport and child well-being: an integrative review. *Travel Behavior and Society*, 9, 32–49.

Waygood, E.O., Friman, M., Taniguchi, A., and Olsson, L.E. (2019). Children's life satisfaction and travel satisfaction: evidence from Canada, Japan, and Sweden. *Travel Behaviour and Society*, 16, 214–23.

Winter, L., Lawton, M.P., Casten, R.J., and Sando, R.L. (2000). The relationship between external events and affect states in older people. *International Journal of Aging and Human Development*, 50(2), 85–96.

Westman, J., Olsson, L.E., Gärling, T., and Friman, M. (2017). Children's travel to school: satisfaction, current mood, and cognitive performance. *Transportation*, 44(6), 1365–82.

Yik, M., Russell, J.A., and Steiger, J.H. (2011). A 12-point circumplex structure of core affect. *Emotion*, 11, 705–31.

7 Transforming people's lives and world for the better

The new purpose of marketing

Per Kristensson

Takeaways

- Groups and individuals need to "break the story" in order to view their surrounding world in a more beneficial way.
- Marketing has long been understood as a field that uses its techniques and frameworks to persuade people to increase their consumption. Now is the time for marketing to become a field that transforms people's lives and world for the better.
- A number of psychological concepts, theories, and techniques are readily available to policymakers and changemakers who are eager to improve people's lives.
- This chapter identifies psychological theories that can aid in creating a better life and a better world. Examples from a high-school context are used.

"Break the story"

"Break the story" is a phrase commonly used in journalism when something vital and new makes the news, or when a deeper truth about something is revealed – something that has previously been misunderstood, understood differently, or simply not reported. "Breaking the story" is therefore usually a "scoop" that transforms how people view and think about something. Solnit (2018) describes breaking news as people receiving information from the media finding their understanding of reality transformed, enabling them to think in a way that sets them free to a greater extent than before.

As an example, during the Hurricane Katrina catastrophe in New Orleans in 2005, the media reported alarming stories about black people looting, raping, and robbing each other as a result of the catastrophe. However, the truth behind that story, which the majority of the media failed to report, was one of governmental failure to plan and implement the infrastructure that could have saved thousands of lives. When the story of black people committing crimes against each other was disrupted – or "broken" in a different sense – the underlying truth of how governmental executive leadership had failed, despite years of

DOI: 10.4324/9781003188773-7

warnings about the risks that this part of the country was facing, became the new story, thus absolving poor black people from blame and instead giving them some hope of being redeemed from the negative publicity of the previous story. Another powerful example of a story that has been "broken" in this new sense concerns Galileo and his message to an unprepared 17th-century world that the earth revolves around the sun, which started a 400-year-long movement gradually moving the church away from its hegemonic position. However, "broken" stories do not need to be as monumental as that; a small piece of information can transform how someone views and understands something – a small change, but one that leads to a meaningful and large effect for the person concerned.

This chapter does not focus on the groundbreaking stories of investigative journalism, nor does it give an account of breakthroughs of the past, like Galileo's paradigm-changing heliocentrism. Rather, in this chapter, I focus on what happens when a new story is on the brink of being accepted: namely, the behavioral change that occurs in individuals or groups of people when they have a new story to guide themselves in their lives. Some stories, like those described above, can function as a prison. "Breaking" those stories enables people to "break out" of their prison and act in ways that they previously could not. It is a form of liberation; in some cases, it can change lives or change the world. In this chapter, I draw on research from many different streams to describe what I call the transformation effect. This effect, I contend, is driven by stories that people have internalized over time and which, mostly subconsciously, function as a compass for how people act, think, and perform.

How stories are made: the scientific basis

Every person has a story in their head. It is a narrative about something that functions as a guide for future behavior, feelings, or thoughts. All stories are highly personal and differ among people to a great extent. For example, some people have stories that tell them that they are highly moral; others' stories inform them that they are criminals. Regardless of the story an individual might have, it is going to affect them in certain life situations. Stories can also be shared among groups: if you are born and raised in Silicon Valley, or in Gnosjö in Sweden, entrepreneurism is most likely to loom larger than if you are born in Compton or Husby (suburbs in Los Angeles and Stockholm, respectively, where socioeconomic status is significantly lower than elsewhere).

A story is a mental shortcut – to a non-negligible extent an unconscious one – that we use when we think about something. It contains assumptions about how things function and how X will affect Y. In psychology, attribution is the name given to the theory that is concerned with how most people explain the causes of behavior and events. Fiske and Taylor (1991, p. 23) explain that "attribution theory deals with how the social perceiver uses information to arrive at causal explanations for events. It examines what information is gathered and how it is combined to form a causal judgment." Stories, like the ones described above, function as attributions that tell us what we are capable of and who we are. If an individual has a story that informs them that entrepreneurship is the default choice for a future job, putting forward a sales pitch for future investment is a normal and expected activity.

A story is a form of schema that organizes categories of information and the relationships among them. Schemas function automatically and provide a framework through which an understanding of future events is formed (Nadkarni & Narayanan, 2007). As an example, if I hear my math teacher in school say "on Wednesday there is a big exam on everything we have done this semester," my schema, and attribution, will immediately be activated. If I've performed poorly in math up to now, the story I carry is that "I suck at math" – this is going to prove that "I'm a disaster in school" and I will expect this "to turn out bad."

Self-perception theory (Bem, 1972) helps to describe how and why people construe various justifications for their behavior. Self-perception theory states that people infer their attitudes from their own behavior, which means that if someone gets low scores in math, they will believe that they hate math. Bem revolutionized social psychology by showing that, contrary to the general hypothesis about attitude formation – that attitudes determine behavior – often our attitudes are in fact formed by our behavior. People interpret their own overt behaviors rationally in the same way that they try to explain others' behaviors. This means that if individuals see themselves behaving as if they don't care about their school grades, they might form a story along the lines of "school is not something I like."

The need for a transformative approach that offers a way of "breaking" bad stories

Given the fact that people, at both a group and individual level, retain stories that have a negative impact on themselves and on society, the question is how might it be possible to disrupt or "break" them. The question might seem self-evident at first, because the usual approach in today's society is to provide knowledge and information to change how people are thinking in order to move them toward a desired goal (e.g. attending school). But there is clearly a need for a transformative approach that offers new ways of "breaking" the bad stories in our society.

To illustrate, let's say you get a bad grade in school. Most of us have experienced this – some more than others – the feeling of "Oops, I really flunked out on this test." How did you explain it to yourself at the time? One way of attributing the reason for your poor performance would be to think "I'm just not smart enough so I better give up math." Another way would be to see the poor performance as an indicator that you need to work harder. It's obvious which of the two stories would be most beneficial for your future performance, as well as for society as a whole. This is why we need a transformative approach that can edit bad stories and turn them into good ones.

The intention of the term *story editing* is to attempt to change people's attributions about the cause and effect of their behavior and its performance. In terms of the above example, it would mean helping the student to choose the second explanation for their failure in the test. The story-editing approach means changing the story, not only in terms of breaking with the previous one, but also helping to create a new one, one that is more beneficial for the individual and/or society.

But how do people edit their stories when they don't find their stories adaptive? Aren't all types of negative thinking (e.g. "everyone expects me to fail") typically quite robust? A reasonable response to this is that it would take much effort and many years to change such negative patterns of thought. However, in fact it might not be so difficult after all. Recent research in psychology provides several examples of how to edit and break stories. Let's have a look at them.

Four story-editing approaches

The four story-editing approaches presented below are called *Social Norm, Story Prompting, Do Good – Be Good,* and *Metaphoric Framing*. Each approach is accompanied by references to research giving evidence of its effectiveness.

Social Norm

The first story editing approach is the *Social Norm*. Social Norms imply that other people's behavior can serve as a guide for my own correct behavior. This approach to editing stories implies getting information about other people that have been in the same situation and then find a new story allowing them to discard the problematic one. Take, for example, juvenile delinquency. The information is made known that, of those having been condemned for a felony, "32% of them have taken the opportunity of finishing high school while at a detention center and thereby finding a job once released." By acquiring this information, about how other people have been dealing with the same situation, those finding themselves in detention are invited to edit their own story about how to react to the situation. Social Norms have been shown to be an effective way of editing people's stories, as many individuals faced with new and difficult tasks desire to do as other people around them have done.

In Hamm et al. (2020), achievement setbacks were reframed in the way outlined above. Their study had a two-step approach, in which the participants, university students in the US, were first asked to watch a social exchange between two students discussing how they improved their subsequent performance on a university course after experiencing initial failure (note: how they improved served as the Social Norm). In the second stage, the participant students were asked to process what had been said in the exchange and to apply whatever they found applicable to themselves. In this second phase, the students were also instructed to participate in a group discussion and disclose their own attributions for their previous poor performance (i.e. their existing story) and discuss how a new attributional model (i.e. a new story) might make a difference. The results showed, among other things, that students with low high-school grades differed significantly in terms of future performance in comparison to a control group who had not taken part in story-editing.

Story Prompting

The second story-editing approach is called *Story Prompting* (Wilson, 2011). It functions like a switch, whereby a person is redirected onto a more positive track. The easiest way to do this is to simply give a label to a person, which is the story you want them to use. In this way you can label a person "math-clever" and thereby encourage them to internalize a new story about themselves as pro-math or pro-hard-working in school. In Story Prompting you label people in a way that enhances the likelihood of their using that story to attribute their future behavior. As in the example here, Story Prompting is a way to reframe achievement in a more positive way.

One of the premier research results regarding Story Prompting comes from Carol Dweck's (2006) research on growth and fixed mindsets. A growth mindset is one where students expect better results if they practice a lot, whereas a fixed mindset is where individuals believe the truth of their performance in perpetuity which, regardless of training, will remain the same.

Another similar approach is found in Tybout and Yalch's (1980) research, in which they introduced the term "labeling." Labeling entails classifying, or giving someone a describing characteristic, with the intention that the individual's actions will be consistent with that classification or characterization. Using labeling as a technique implies a heightened self-perception of a certain behavior, which enhances the likelihood that label-consistent behavior will be displayed later. Research shows that activation of cognitive and perceptual representations often leads to corresponding overt behavior (Dijksterhuis & Van Knippenberg, 1998). For example, Dijksterhuis and Van Knippenberg (1998) found that activating the mental representation of a certain social group (for example, professors) led to behaviors corresponding with specific attributes of that social group (such as intelligence) being displayed. Tybout and Yalch (1980) found that citizens labeled as having an "above-average probability of voting" were more likely to actually vote in an election a week later than those citizens labeled as having an "average probability of voting."

Do Good – Be Good

The third method is a story-editing approach that implies letting people do something good to begin with, with the result that they will later infer that this is their true nature. Wilson (2011) calls this the "Do Good – Be Good" approach. It means that an individual's behavior will guide them in shaping the story they later develop. So, if someone is acting in an environmentally friendly way, they will start to view themselves as environmentally friendly, and the more likely they are to behave in such a way subsequently, thus strengthening their new story.

An important piece of research that represents the underlying mechanism behind the "Do Good – Be Good" story-editing approach is self-perception theory (Bem, 1972), which was alluded to earlier. Self-perception is an account of attitude formation that asserts that people can develop an attitude when no previous attitude existed. Bem reasoned that attitudes are inferred from more or less unconscious observations of individuals' own behavior. The theory is valuable as it suggests the importance of getting individuals to behave in a desired way in areas in which they have no previous experience as this is likely to guide their future attitudes and behavior.

Metaphoric Framing

A final story-editing method is Metaphoric Framing. Research makes it clear that the metaphors we use to describe complex concepts shape the way we think about them. For example, if people read about crime being referred to as either a beast or a virus, it affects the way they think society should be dealing with it (Thibodeau & Boroditsky, 2013). People who read that crime was a beast saw law enforcement and punishment as viable solutions to a greater extent than those who read that crime was a virus. Similarly, thinking about one's relationship as a single unit can result in feelings of threat when interpersonal conflicts arise, in contrast to thinking about the relationship as a journey that is more likely to naturally have its ups and downs (Lee & Schwarz, 2014). Thus, story-editing one's own performance in school in terms of an ant building a big anthill over the years should result in a positive mindset about knowledge being constructed longitudinally in an accumulative way (i.e. the ant is a metaphor for being everywhere; necessary for others' existence; working hard in teams; never giving up; small things leading to something big; and so forth). Finally, in line with the above, metaphorically framing school as a journey increased academic engagement among primary school students. Landau, Barrera, and Keefer (2017) tested whether it was possible to motivate primary school students in an economically disadvantaged school setting. Their results revealed that pupils framing their school experience as part of a journey reported higher academic engagement than pupils who were not provided with a metaphor. More importantly, their findings also extended metaphor-priming effects to low-income and minority adolescents, a crucial population in educational research worldwide.

Transforming people's lives and world for the better

To transform someone from one state to another that is perceived as being more beneficial should be the new purpose of marketing. Historically, marketing has only partially taken that as its purpose, and has largely been a means of transforming potential consumers into actual ones (as quickly as possible). The idea has been to collect the maximum amount of knowledge about buying behavior so companies can use the right mix to promote a product in a certain place and at a certain price, so that as few customers as possible can say no. For sure, this implies a transformation – and, after all, some customers actually do need the offerings they buy – but it has also led to serious over-consumption with well-known adverse consequences. Few would argue that this era of consumption is drawing to a close any time soon, which is why the aim of this chapter is to extend the purpose of marketing to embrace other types of transformations – transformations where people live better and feel better. Therefore, the final part of this chapter assembles some thoughts on how we can use the behavior-changing theories presented above to move people from one state (doing not so well in school) to another (doing better and staying in school).

Get more students to do better and stay longer in school

How can we persuade students at all levels of school not to drop out early? Keeping students at all levels alert and knowledge-active as long as possible would imply a decrease in early forms of juvenile delinquency, drug abuse, and youth mental illnesses, not to mention the advantages they would accrue in the future job market. It seems clear that getting students to stay in school longer and aim for educational achievement would dramatically improve societies' well-being.

In Rosenthal and Jacobson's classic 1966 study (Rosenthal & Jacobson, 1992), a psychological phenomenon, called the Pygmalion effect, was observed where high expectations lead to improved performance in a given area for school students in primary school. In summary, their study showed that teachers' expectations of their students affected the students' subsequent performance. The lessons learned from Rosenthal and Jacobson's seminal study informed psychologists that there is a power of construal: how we interpret things that surround us forms subjective views and thoughts which, in turn, influence our subsequent behavior. In fact, research shows that subjective views tend to be more important than objective facts in shaping our behavior (Ross, 1977).

Recent developments in social-psychological research show that people's behavior stems from their construals – empirical evidence that Dweck (2006) picked up in her studies of how mindsets affect primary and secondary school students. As explained earlier, Dweck's research shows that students who viewed their abilities as a fixed trait were at disadvantage, especially when they encountered difficulties and challenges. Even worse, when they confronted these knowledge hurdles, they took them as evidence that they lacked inherent ability: there was no point in trying since their ability was not subject to improvement. On the contrary, students who more or less unconsciously employed a growth mindset viewed their own abilities as something that could be improved with practice – and this made these students improve in those instances where they faced a setback in terms of results.

The story-editing approaches presented earlier in this chapter can serve the purpose of "breaking" stories for students, and in fact younger adults too, such as college students, who suffer from a negative (fixed) mindset which is to their disadvantage. For example, research shows that for students at risk of internalizing negative stereotypes about themselves as a result of group identity (e.g. a geographic area with a poor reputation, social class, or ethnicity), self-affirmation writing exercises can help. In one study, school students were asked to write about things they valued, such as their family and friends or their favorite activities. For low-performing African American students, this simple intervention produced better grades over the next two years (Cohen et al., 2009).

In addition, consider the low interest in many Westernized countries in science education (typically abbreviated STEM: Science, Technology, Engineering, and Math), which is declining in both Scandinavia and the US, among others. A notable study discovered that freshmen science students who were given the task of writing about the relevance as they perceived it of the science curriculum not only increased their interest in STEM, but also improved their achievements in terms of grades. What was particularly interesting about this study was that students with the lowest expectations were those who improved the most (Hulleman & Harackiewicz, 2009).

To find that a new way of editing one's story changes one's behavior is, perhaps, not so surprising. The surprise is rather that most of us tend to be unaware of exactly how much it affects both behavior and cognition. Consider a study where schoolteachers are asking fifth-graders to not turn the classroom, or the corridors, into a mess. Both janitors and teachers kept telling the students not to throw trash, to tidy their desks, and to be neater in general. This conforms to how adult people generally behave when they want someone to follow their advice: we tend to believe that guidance in the form of information is enough to change other people's behavior. However, consider how a type of Story Prompting persuades pupils to do what they are being asked by giving them a framing label instead (Wilson, 2011). In the first experimental group, school students were asked to be tidy, pick up their trash, and so on, as usual. This group represents the traditional way people behave when they wish to shape behavior. In the second group, a framing label was given to the fifth-graders: instead of being asked to be tidy, they were praised for their tidiness and how neat their classroom was. In fact, the children were told that their classroom and corridor were among the tidiest that the janitors and teachers had ever seen. In the experiment, a third control group was created that received no information. The results were unmistakable. The second group was by far the tidiest. Merely assigning a positive frame to people helps them to start a positive spiral of behavior editing; it helped young pupils engage in a behavior that was prosocial and pro-environmental (Miller, Brickman, & Bolen, 1975). The framing label has been used in other types of research, with similar effects. For example, consumers were asked if they thought environmentally friendly consumption was important or not, which resulted in them buying more pro-environment labeled food (Kristensson, Wästlund, & Söderlund, 2017).

Conclusion

This chapter has argued that people, groups, and other factions of society on certain occasions need to "break" their stories. Breaking a story implies a new way of thinking about something, with the implication that this new perspective leads to well-being, pro-social behavior, and other beneficial forms of psychological states that are positive for our society and planet. Individuals edit the stories they have about something, for the benefit of that individual and for the benefit of society.

The historical purpose of marketing, viewed from a helicopter perspective and in its most simplified way, has been to get people to buy things. It is time for a new era, one where marketing assists in creating societies where people live better, feel better, and take care of our society and planet. In this chapter, several theoretical concepts have been presented that are not only evidence-based, backed up by careful research, but also present themselves as available tools for changemakers, policymakers, and other types of agents that want to help our world to become a better place.

References

Bem, D.J. (1972). Self-perception theory. In L. Berkowitz (Ed.), *Advances in Experimental Social Psychology*. Vol. 6 (pp. 1–62). New York: Academic Press.

Cohen, G.L., Garcia, J., Purdie-Vaughns, V., Apfel, N., & Brzustoski, P. (2009). Recursive processes in self- affirmation: intervening to close the achievement gap. *Science*, 324, 400–403.

Dijksterhuis, A., & Van Knippenberg, A. (1998). The relation between perception and behavior, or how to win a game of Trivial Pursuit. *Journal of Personality and Social Psychology*, 74(4), 865.

Dweck, C.S. (2006). *Mindset: The New Psychology of Success*. New York: Random House.

Fiske, S.T., & Taylor, S.E. (1991). *Social Cognition*. New York: McGraw-Hill.

Hamm, J.M., Perry, R.P., Chipperfield, J.G., Hladkyj, S., Parker, P.C., & Weiner, B. (2020). Reframing achievement setbacks: a motivation intervention to improve 8-year graduation rates for students in Science, Technology, Engineering, and Mathematics (STEM) fields. *Psychological Science*, 31(6), 623–33.

Hulleman, C.S., & Harackiewicz, J.M. (2009). Promoting interest and performance in high school science classes. *Science*, 326, 1410–12.

Kristensson, P., Wästlund, E., & Söderlund, M. (2017). Influencing consumers to choose environment friendly offerings: evidence from field experiments. *Journal of Business Research*, 76, 89–97.

Landau, M.J., Barrera, J., & Keefer, L.A. (2017). On the road: combining possible identities and metaphor to motivate disadvantaged middle-school students. *Metaphor and Symbol*, 32(4), 276–90.

Lee, S.W.S., & Schwarz, N. (2014). Metaphor in judgment and decision making. In M. Landau, M.D. Robinson & B.P. Meier (Eds.), *The Power of Metaphor: Examining its Influence on Social Life* (pp. 85–108). Washington, DC: American Psychological Association.

Miller, R.L., Brickman, P., & Bolen, D. (1975). Attribution versus persuasion as a means for modifying behavior. *Journal of Personality and Social Psychology*, 31(3), 430–41.

Nadkarni, S., & Narayanan, V.K. (2007). Strategic schemas, strategic flexibility, and firm performance: the moderating role of industry clock speed. *Strategic Management Journal*, 28(3), 243–70.

Rosenthal, R., & Jacobson, L. (1992). *Pygmalion in the Classroom: Teacher Expectation and Pupils' Intellectual Development*. Newly expanded ed. Bancyfelin, Carmarthen, Wales: Crown House Pub.

Ross, L. (1977). The intuitive psychologist and his shortcomings: distortions in the attribution process. In L. Berkowitz (Ed.), *Advances in Experimental Social Psychology*. Vol. 10 (pp. 173–220). Orlando, FL: Academic Press.

Solnit, R. (2018). *Call Them by Their True Names: American Crises (and Essays)*. Chicago: Haymarket Books.

Thibodeau, P.H., & Boroditsky, L. (2013). Natural language metaphors covertly influence reasoning. *PloS one*, 8(1).

Tybout, A.M., & Yalch, R.F. (1980). The effect of experience: a matter of salience? *Journal of Consumer Research*, 6(4), 406–13.

Wilson, T.D. (2011). *Redirect: Changing the Stories We Live By*. London: Hachette UK.

Part 3

Base of the Pyramid thinking for transforming business-societal practice

8 Advancing service research at the Base of the Pyramid

A service ecosystems perspective

Ana Valdés-Loyola, Javier Reynoso, and Bo Edvardsson

Takeaways

- Answers the multiple calls for further service research into new perspectives on poverty alleviation.
- Brings a service ecosystems framework into the Base of the Pyramid (BoP) context.
- Highlights the key role of actors' social embeddedness, private resources, and informal institutions in enabling value co-creation in the service ecosystem.
- Provides insights for the ongoing collaboration in, refinement of, and development of a framework for BoP service ecosystems.

Introduction

Two-thirds of the world's population live in poverty, earning the equivalent of less than US$9 per day (Arnold & Valentin, 2013), while over 730 million people live in conditions of extreme poverty and earn less than US$1.90 a day (World Bank, n.d.). People who live in such conditions have limited access to basic services such as healthcare, education, and transportation, among others (Fisk et al., 2016). They also live with inadequate service systems which trap them in a self-perpetuating cycle of poverty consisting of self-reinforcing mechanisms that promote further poverty. As a result, unless there is outside intervention, current poverty will be itself a direct cause of future poverty (Azariadis & Stachurski, 2005).

This global problem has been studied for many years from various theoretical perspectives, creating a large body of knowledge built by researchers from areas such as policy development, economics, and sociology, among others (Reynoso, Valdés, & Cabrera, 2015). The focus of these perspectives has centered on the idea of improving social and economic conditions through aid, creating the perception that poverty alleviation should mainly be the domain of governments, nonprofits, and NGOs. However, over the past 15 years the "Base of the Pyramid" (BoP) approach to poverty alleviation (Prahalad & Hammond, 2002; Prahalad & Hart, 2002) has emerged and quickly garnered much interest

DOI: 10.4324/9781003188773-8

from both the business and academic community (Kolk, Rivera-Santos, & Rufin, 2014). It is an approach that proposes that for-profit businesses can play a key part in bringing prosperity to the poor by breaking poverty cycles while simultaneously tapping into new sources of profit (Prahalad & Hart, 2002). Its premise centers on reducing poverty through inclusive business strategies that aim to create gains for both provider and customer.

In recent years, the BoP approach has evolved from its initial focus on *selling to the poor* to *engaging with the poor* through the cocreation of goods and services (Follman, 2012). In this regard, Prahalad and Hart (2002) stated that opportunities at the BoP cannot be unlocked unless large and small firms, governments, civil society organizations, development agencies, and the poor themselves work together with a shared agenda. Furthermore, this approach argues that businesses should not merely sell to the poor; rather, they should engage with them in *cocreation* (Simanis, Hart, & Duke, 2008). Under this approach, those at the BoP are active partners rather than passive consumers, which can lead to the generation of greater shared value for all (Simanis, Hart, & Duke, 2008). Nonetheless, previous research has found that such engagement can involve multiple challenges, particularly in terms of the venture's sustainability (e.g. London & Hart, 2004; Karnani, 2007). In response, in recent years the BoP approach has expanded its focus from singular poverty alleviation solutions to developing innovation ecosystems that generate sustainable solutions cocreated together with and for BoP communities (Casado Cañeque & Hart, 2015).

In parallel with the increasing popularity of the concept in business research, the BoP approach has been gaining momentum in recent years within service research. Gebauer and Reynoso (2013) presented an initial research agenda with theoretical perspectives, empirical fields, and research approaches that can enrich service research at the BoP. Reynoso, Valdés, and Cabrera (2015) further advanced this agenda by proposing five BoP service research streams that emerge from the intersection of BoP literature and service research priorities. Additionally, there have been numerous articles calling for further BoP service research that provides a new perspective on service research phenomena while contributing to solutions to this global problem (Fisk et al., 2016; Gummerus et al., 2013; Ivanovich & Fuxman, 2012; Reynoso, 1999).

This chapter aims to respond to these calls and to contribute to the *BoP networks in service ecosystems* research stream (Reynoso, Valdés, & Cabrera, 2015) by providing a new perspective on the service ecosystems framework. To do so, we must contextualize the service ecosystems framework for the BoP. This chapter, therefore, clarifies how the characteristics of the BoP environment influence service ecosystems with regard to *actors*, *institutions*, and *resources*. We will highlight the key roles of actors' social embeddedness, informal institutions, and private resources in enabling value co creation at the BoP. The chapter thus aims to provide insights that contribute to the ongoing collaboration in, refinement of, and development of the framework for BoP service ecosystems.

The remainder of the chapter is organized as follows. First, there is a review of the origin and evolution of the BoP concept in business research, from its initial focus on "selling to the poor" to its current emphasis on sustainable development and ecosystems. This section also discusses recent developments in BoP service research as well as BoP service research streams. Second, we discuss the definition and concepts of the service ecosystems framework, grounded in service research. Third, we bring the key concepts of service ecosystems into the BoP context, expanding on the framework's current assumptions about the characteristics of actors, institutions, and resources in BoP service ecosystems. Fourth, we present our conclusions, which discuss the main benefits of adopting a service ecosystems perspective within the BoP context.

A Base of the Pyramid (BoP) approach to poverty alleviation

From "selling to the poor" to sustainable development

The "Base of the Pyramid" (BoP) refers to the largest and poorest socioeconomic group in the world (Prahalad & Hart, 2002). It includes the 4 billion worldwide who live on less than US$9 a day (Arnold & Valentin, 2013; Prahalad & Hart, 2002). These people lack basic services such as healthcare, energy, sanitation and water; and the services they do have, in many cases, will cost them more than people in middle- or high-income segments pay (Hammond et al., 2007). This is called the "poverty penalty" and it creates a cycle in which current poverty leads to future poverty (De Soto, 2000).

Traditionally, the main approach to help improve the lives of people living in poverty has been aid-based programs run by governments, charities, and nonprofit organizations. Despite the large efforts and investments, it has been questioned whether these programs actually have any positive long-lasting effect in alleviating poverty (Banae & Yandell, 2006; Riddell, 2008). One of the biggest issues is that philanthropic programs generate large financial burdens for themselves which increase their risk of failure, particularly if funding is constrained. In an effort to solve this problem, it has been suggested that an improved approach to poverty alleviation would combine the efforts of government, nonprofit organizations, and social and commercial enterprises to generate self-sustaining programs (e.g. Prahalad & Hart, 2002; Viswanathan & Rosa, 2007).

It was this line of thinking that spurred Prahalad and Hart (2002) to introduce what they called at the time the "Bottom of the Pyramid" approach, as a call for multinational enterprises (MNEs) to "seek their fortunes and bring prosperity to the aspiring poor" (Prahalad & Hart, 2002) – thus advocating for market-based solutions that can service the BoP profitably. The BoP approach encouraged organizations to develop new business strategies aimed at poverty alleviation that contribute to solving this global problem while making a profit (Prahalad & Hart, 2002). This idea is based on two premises: *inclusive capitalism* and *mutual value*. Inclusive capitalism aims to bring markets into the BoP and enable the participation of the poor in these markets; mutual value proposes that businesses generate value for themselves as well as simultaneously for the local BoP community (Simanis, Hart, & Duke, 2008). The approach, therefore, encourages organizations to stop conceptualizing the BoP as a passive recipient of aid from philanthropic organizations (Gebauer & Reynoso, 2013) but instead view it as an attractive new market, particularly for two types of organizations: *for-profit corporations* who help the poor by bringing in their much-needed services while obtaining profits (London, Anupindi, & Sheth, 2010) and *social businesses* who seek to achieve a social objective while recovering their full costs (Yunus, 2010).

Despite the increasing popularity of the BoP approach in business research and its appeal to MNEs and large local firms, some authors have denounced it, considering it to be "at best, a harmless illusion and potentially a dangerous delusion" (Karnani, 2007). Other critics have questioned whether it can deliver on the promise of mutual profit creation and poverty alleviation (Simanis, 2012). For instance, Hart (2015) discovered that "most BoP ventures and corporate initiatives over the past decade have either failed outright or achieved only moderate success at great cost."

In response, the BoP discourse evolved from presenting the poor as potential consumers of goods and services (BoP 1.0) to integrating them as partners in cocreation or "business co-venturing" (BoP 2.0) (Prahalad & Hart, 2002). This second iteration of the BoP perspective kept inclusive capitalism and mutual value creation as core elements, while encouraging organizations to additionally incorporate BoP partners into their business models as distributors or suppliers (Simanis, Hart, & Duke, 2008; Simanis & Hart, 2009). Thus, whereas BoP 1.0 centered on "finding a fortune at the BoP," and was characterized by MNEs selling cheaper versions of their products in developing markets, BoP 2.0 centered on the *development of new markets and the engagement in cocreation with people living in poverty* (Simanis, Hart, & Duke, 2008). This new approach emphasized the importance of cocreating with the poor in a way that creates value for all partners in terms important to each (Dembek, Sivasubramaniam, & Chmielewski, 2019; Simanis, Hart, & Duke, 2008).

However, some critics have argued that the BoP 2.0 approach still fails to provide lasting employment opportunities, while promoting unsustainable consumption patterns (Karnani, 2009). They have thus called for organizations to broaden their perspective, arguing that their responsibilities should not be limited to shareholders but rather to a multitude of stakeholders (Davidson, 2009; Dembek, Sivasubramaniam, & Chmielewski, 2019). Additionally, they have called on BoP ventures to extend their limits beyond a focus on generating profits, and act instead as members of a larger society.

In response to this criticism, a third iteration of the BoP approach has recently emerged: BoP 3.0. Although BoP 3.0 maintains the core elements of inclusiveness and cocreation, it also includes sustainability objectives with a triple-bottom-line perspective (Casado Cañeque & Hart, 2015). This iteration shifts from a promotion of singular poverty alleviation solutions and aims instead at achieving greater levels of well-being that consider the social,

Table 8.1 The evolution of the BoP concept: from "selling to the poor" to sustainable development

Authors	*BoP 1.0*	*BoP 2.0*	*BoP 3.0*
	Prahalad and Hart (2002)	*Simanis, Hart, and Duke (2008)*	*Casado-Cañeque and Hart (2015)*
Focus	"Selling to the poor"	"Business co-venturing"	"Sustainable development, bottom-up model"
BoP role	Consumer	Business partner	Small producer
Engagement	Deep listening	Deep dialogue	Ad hoc process, cross-sector partnerships, and networks
Relationship	Arm's length relationships *mediated* by NGOs	Direct, personal relationships *facilitated* by NGOs	*Direct relationships with stakeholders* by the BoP small producers' initiative

Adapted from Dembek, Sivasubramaniam, & Chmielewski, 2019.

economic, and ecological impacts of the BoP ventures (London, 2016). In order to achieve this, BoP 3.0 calls for the development of innovation ecosystems and cross-sector partnerships. It encourages organizations to integrate different local actors that play multiple roles through ad hoc processes, and these include: local firms, NGOs, and the members of the local community (Follman, 2012). Table 8.1 summarizes the evolution of the BoP approach, from BoP 1.0 to BoP 3.0.

In summary, in the last 18 years, the BoP approach to poverty alleviation has emerged and been popularized in business research. It was initially proposed by Prahalad and Hart (2002) and it urged for-profit organizations to engage in direct cocreating relationships with the poor in order to generate mutual benefits and help improve their lives (Neghina et al., 2015). It is an approach that represents an alternative to the traditional perspective which considers these markets the exclusive domain of governments, aid agencies, and nonprofits. It frames the needs of people living in poverty as available market opportunities for private companies, who can become agents of change through market-based solutions that help alleviate poverty (London, Anupindi, & Sheth, 2010). Most recently, this approach has shifted its focus from the development of singular ventures to the construction of socially embedded ecosystems that integrate local actors into BoP ventures, and these include: local firms, NGOs, and the local community (Dembek, Sivasubramaniam, & Chmielewski, 2019). In recent years, the BoP approach has also seen its presence increase within service research, generating a growing literature stream that aims at expanding service knowledge at the BoP and producing service research that can help improve the well-being of people living in poverty. The evolution of BoP service research is discussed further in the next section.

BoP service research

Although the BoP concept has been increasingly popular in business research since the early 2000s, the stream of BoP service research has advanced mostly in the last decade (e.g. Fisk et al., 2016; Gebauer & Reynoso, 2013; Joncourt et al., 2019; Reynoso, Valdés, & Cabrera, 2015; Reynoso & Cabrera, 2019).

Gebauer and Reynoso (2013) were responsible for one of the initial instances of integration of the BoP approach into service research. Their article introduced a research agenda that proposed multiple theoretical perspectives, empirical fields, and research approaches that could help further advance service research within the BoP environment. These authors posited that exploring service at the BoP could help expand service theories and concepts by bringing them into a context in which they don't apply, or at least not in the same way (Gebauer & Reynoso, 2013).

Further, Reynoso, Valdés, and Cabrera (2015) combined BoP research perspectives with "service research priorities" (Ostrom et al., 2015). As a result, these authors proposed five research streams that could help further develop BoP service research. The first, *socially inclusive service innovation and sustainable development,* aims to clarify how organizations can involve the BoP in service innovation processes. The second, *cocreation of service experiences in low-income markets,* focuses on understanding how to develop services that match needs with the local economic and infrastructure conditions. The third, *service design in social entrepreneurship,* seeks to apply the concepts and frameworks of service design research to enable social entrepreneurs. The fourth, *transformative services for poverty alleviation,* aims to increase the understanding of the social and ecological impacts of service at the BoP. Finally, the fifth, *BoP networks in service ecosystems,* proposes the use of the service ecosystems framework to further understand service in this context.

The purpose of this chapter is to contribute to the fifth BoP service research stream (i.e. *BoP networks in service ecosystems*) (Reynoso, Valdés, & Cabrera, 2015). We aim to extend this line of research by contextualizing the service ecosystems framework in the BoP environment, thus providing insights into the ways in which BoP service ecosystems are different to those in a non-BoP context. This is developed further in the next section.

Contextualizing service ecosystems at the BoP

Service ecosystems: definition and concepts

The ecosystems lens has been proposed by multiple strategy and marketing researchers as a theoretical framing that can help understand complex and changing environments (e.g. Alderson, 1965; Ben Letaifa, Edvardsson, & Tronvoll, 2016; Moore, 1996; Wieland et al., 2012). Ecosystems refer to networks of actors (Moore, 1996) or communities that cocreate value by integrating complementary resources (Ben Letaifa & Reynoso, 2015). This perspective has become increasingly relevant to service research because it enables a broader social and institutional framework with which to understand business and nonbusiness relationships (Wieland et al., 2012).

Vargo and Lusch (2011; 2016) introduced the service ecosystems concept, which is based on S-D logic. They defined the service ecosystem as "a relatively *self-contained*, *self-adjusting* system of *resource-integrating* actors, connected by *shared institutional logics* and their *mutual value creation practices*, which *benefit engaged actors* through their service exchange [emphasis added]" (Vargo & Lusch, 2016). Five elements constitute this definition. First, the definition proposes that ecosystems are relatively *self-contained*, meaning that they have fuzzy or unclear boundaries. Second, actors are *relatively self-adjusting*, which means they exhibit adaptive behavior. Third, all actors in the ecosystem are considered to be *resource integrators*. Fourth, actors in service ecosystems are connected by *institutions and institutional logics*, meaning that formal and informal norms influence their behavior. Fifth, service exchange in service ecosystems *results in mutual value creation*, but this only happens when equitable and balanced interaction among actors occurs.

Ben Letaifa and Reynoso (2015) presented an initial effort to conceptualize service ecosystems at the BoP. First, they identified three main challenges in BoP literature: BoP services are designed with a top-down approach; BoP users are regarded as passive consumers; and solutions are disconnected from the local context. To address these challenges, the authors connected S-D logic with key concepts of service ecosystems literature. As a result, they posited four theoretical propositions for designing sustainable service ecosystems within a BoP environment. First, for BoP service ecosystems a *multi-actor* approach is required, in which individuals are considered active operant resources. Second, *social embeddedness* of actors and resources is necessary in order to design relevant services with a local focus. Third, services are *cocreated with and for* local communities, and BoP actors play *multiple social roles*. Fourth, value at the BoP is determined as *multilevel* (for all beneficiaries) and *multidimensional* (social, economic, ecological, and cultural) *value* (Ben Letaifa & Reynoso, 2015).

Against this theoretical background, this chapter aims to further advance the development of the BoP service ecosystems framework by exploring the main characteristics of its actors, institutions, and resources, as well where they differ from those in non-BoP environments. Previous research has found that there are significant differences in BoP markets compared to traditional non-BoP markets, something that has important implications for business research and practice (e.g. Nielsen & Samia, 2008; Rivera-Santos & Rufin, 2010; Reficco & Márquez, 2012). Contextualizing current service theories and concepts at the BoP is important because the complexity of the social and economic environment can invalidate service theories and concepts, or at least render them not applicable in the same way (Gebauer & Reynoso, 2013).

The importance of considering context in the development of theory has been increasingly acknowledged in business research (e.g. Bamberger, 2008; Johns, 2001; Rousseau & Fried, 2001; Whetten, 2009). Johns (2006) defines context as "situational opportunities and constraints that affect the occurrence and meaning of organizational behavior as well as functional relationships between variables." Contextual effects are defined as "the set of factors surrounding a phenomenon that exert some direct or indirect influence on it – also characterized as explanatory factors associated with higher levels of analysis than those expressly under investigation" (Whetten, 2009, p. 31). Alvesson and Kärreman's (2007) discussion of theory development also emphasizes the importance of context in theorizing, positing that "no theory is always wrong or always right – all are more or less relevant and helpful in different situations" (p. 1272). Contextualization enables creative and novel analysis and explanations by situating theories into their natural setting. Given its acknowledgment and integration of the environment, contextualization has the capacity to enrich theoretical perspectives that have guided thinking about service at the BoP by providing an opportunity to advance the current theoretical frameworks.

The following sections discuss each of the three key concepts of service ecosystems in the BoP context: institutions, resources, and actors. Each section first looks at current assumptions, then the characteristics of the BoP environment, and, finally, the implications for BoP service ecosystems.

Institutions: informal institutions prevail at the BoP

The service ecosystems framework currently highlights the influence of institutions in value co creation. They are considered to be the key to understanding the structure and functioning of the ecosystem, or the glue that enables and constrains value co creation within these social systems (Vargo & Akaka, 2012; Vargo & Lusch, 2016). Institutions are defined as rules, norms, and meanings that enable and constrain human action (Scott, 2001); they represent the embodiment of the set of expectations in society and define socially acceptable actions and outcomes (Suchman, 1995). Thus, they have the power to influence people's actions by encouraging them to act in a socially acceptable manner, thereby regulating human behavior and establishing the framework within which social life takes place.

Institutions can take various forms, ranging from an individual's attitudes and beliefs to the legal system. Thus, they can be classified into two distinct categories: *formal institutions* and *informal institutions*. First, *formal institutions* include the political, legal, and economic systems that are established by the government to regulate people's behaviors and reduce transaction costs (North, 1990). They represent the laws and regulations that define and enforce social acceptability from a legal standpoint: for example, constitutions, contracts, and forms of government (North, 1990; Lowndes, 1996). Formal institutions help regulate the distribution of power, land tenure, and ownership rights, among other things. Second, *informal institutions* are behavioral regularities based on socially shared rules, usually unwritten (North, 1990). They are created, communicated, and enforced outside of officially sanctioned channels (Helmke & Levitsky, 2004).

They consist of norms, customs, traditions, religion, and other forms of behavior that emerge spontaneously (not designed or enforced by the government) and pass the test of time (North, 1990). While formal institutions are enforced by official entities, such as courts, judges, police, etc., informal institutions are self-enforcing through mechanisms of obligation, such as expectations of reciprocity, standard operating procedures, shunning, boycotting, and public shaming, among others (De Soysa & Jütting, 2007). Informal institutions define the legitimacy of behaviors and outcomes, and are characterized by their long durability (Williamson, 2000). Together, formal and informal institutions encourage people to engage in desirable actions through rewards (e.g. reduced transaction costs) and enforcement (e.g. fines and/or termination of contract), enabling expectations regarding other people's behaviors, which reduce risk and transaction costs (DiMaggio & Powell, 1983).

Multiple studies have found that the characteristics of institutions vary widely across societies and social environments (e.g. Hofstede, 1980; House et al., 2004). For instance, institutions in developed markets are very different than institutions in BoP markets (Rivera-Santos & Rufin, 2010). At the BoP, formal institutions tend to be weaker than in developed markets (Webb et al., 2010). Consequently, in this environment, informal institutions become stronger than formal institutions, replacing the role of formal institutions (London & Hart, 2004) even when they are contradictory (Arnould & Mohr, 2005). For example, given the lack of law enforcement and regulations, and the absence of well-defined property rights, any issues will lead to informal resolutions because little to no protection is available in the event of violations (De Soto, 1989; Ricart et al., 2004; Webb et al., 2010). Because people lack access to formal capital markets (such as banks), when a credit is needed people rely on their friends, family, and neighbors for a personal loan (De Soto, 1989). In rural areas, since public infrastructure is undependable and inadequate, what infrastructure exists is largely supported by private communities rather than public funds (Webb et al., 2010).

Because of the weakness of formal institutions, people have found alternative ways to subsist at the BoP by relying on their personal relationships and social networks which provide them with access to the needed resources and services (Rivera-Santos & Rufin, 2010). This is possible given the strength of informal institutions at the BoP (London & Hart, 2004). Thus, in a BoP context, having access to a strong collaborative network of friends and family is the primary source of safety, insurance, and livelihood (Narayan, 2002).

Thus, given that formal institutions are weaker than in a non-BoP context, informal institutions play a key role in BoP service ecosystems. They do so by providing actors with access to necessary and scarce tangible and intangible resources through their social relations. Thus, social embeddedness in informal networks is key for the ecosystem's success and survival in the BoP context.

Table 8.2 summarizes the key differences in formal institutions in developed markets and BoP markets.

Table 8.2 Formal institutions in developed markets vs. BoP markets

Formal institutions	*Developed markets*	*BoP markets*
Capital markets	Multiple formally established sources of funding, including equity markets, banks, venture capitalists, business angels, etc.	No formal capital markets. No access to banks, equity markets, etc. Actors must rely on friends and family ties, limited personal savings and "loan sharks" for capital.
Infrastructure	Organizations rely on public transportation (paved highways and roads), communication systems, and utilities.	Public infrastructure in highly populated areas is undependable and inadequate. In rural areas, private communities rather than public funds mostly support infrastructure.
Contracts and enforcement	Formal contract law and regulatory and court systems for enforcing contracts.	Scarce or no enforcement of formal contracts. Trust is based on informal governance mechanisms related to group norms, reputation, and power.
Property rights	Established property rights defining one's property, the means through which one can increase one's property, and the means through which to enforce one's rights.	Lack of property rights. Notions of ownership exist but are only informally recognized: "barking dogs" effect. Little to no property rights protection available in the event of violations.

Source: Webb et al., 2010.

Resources in BoP service ecosystems

The service ecosystems framework recognizes that actors integrate resources from multiple sources through service-for-service exchange (Vargo & Lusch, 2011). Thus, value co creation resides in the intersections of all actors and resources that are integrated, including those that influence value co creation indirectly (Lusch & Vargo, 2014).

Resources are classified in terms of the market venue: *market-facing*, *private* or *public* resources (Vargo and Lusch, 2011; 2018). First, *market-facing* resources refer to those that can be obtained through the market: for example, buying a car. Second, *private resources* are non-market-facing and include resources that are exchanged through social networks such as a personal loan provided by a close friend. Third, *public resources* are shared, communal, non-market-facing resources generally provided through government or quasi-governmental actors: for example, police protection, parks and recreation areas, or public health services.

Although these three types of resources exist in all markets, in contrast to non-BoP environments people at the BoP have limited access to *market-facing* and *public resources*. For example, they don't have access to reliable government services such as healthcare or transportation services (Rivera-Santos & Rufin, 2010). Consequently, *private resources* in BoP service ecosystems have a larger role than in non-BoP ecosystems (Ben Letaifa & Reynoso, 2015). As mentioned in the section above, given that governments at the BoP don't provide the support that is necessary for survival, people have found ways to survive through their strong personal relationships and social relations (Rivera-Santos & Rufin, 2010). Thus, the development of a strong network of collaboration between friends and family is the primary source for resources that enable safety, insurance, and livelihood (Narayan, 2002). For example, the self-provision of sanitation services and water is the norm at the BoP because many people have no access to these commodities any other way. Informal credit mechanisms and saving strategies based on family or friends are prevalent in this context because of a lack of access to formal capital markets. Informal childcare arrangements commonly occur between neighbors and family members because of a lack of access to affordable childcare services.

In summary, BoP environments are characterized by the scarcity of *market-facing* (e.g. retail store products) and *public resources* (e.g. technology, infrastructure), and, therefore, access to *private resources* (e.g. products or services given by a friend or family member) is key. Thus, in BoP service ecosystems, private resources, accessed via informal relationships, play a key role in enabling resource integration.

Table 8.3 summarizes the differences in resources in developed and BoP markets.

Table 8.3 Resources in developed markets vs. BoP markets

Resources	*Developed markets*	*BoP markets*
Market-facing resources	Obtained through the market. E.g. buying a car.	Can be difficult to obtain because of scarcity. E.g. no money to buy car, no access to bank loans.
Private resources	Obtained through social networks. E.g. childcare arrangement with family or friends.	Play a key role given the lack of other resources. E.g. informal childcare arrangements with family or friends.
Public resources	Obtained through government or quasi-governmental actors. E.g. government-provided water and sanitation services.	Government services are generally undependable and inadequate. E.g. self-provision of water and sanitation services.

Source: Ben Letaifa & Reynoso, 2015; Rivera-Santos & Rufin, 2010; Vargo and Lusch, 2011; 2018.

Actors in BoP service ecosystems

Instead of having a "single-actor" centricity (e.g. customer or company centricity), the service ecosystems perspective is characterized by a balanced centricity (Gummesson, 2008) and a more generic actor conceptualization (Lusch & Vargo, 2014). Value in service ecosystems is cocreated by *multiple actors* through processes of exchanging and interchanging public, private, and market-facing resources in an effort to increase the well-being of all actors engaged in the ecosystem (Wieland et al., 2012). And, in this multi-actor environment, value is uniquely and phenomenologically determined by the different participating actors (Ben Letaifa & Reynoso, 2015). The ecosystems perspective removes the simplistic notion of actors as either consumers or producers, and instead conceptualizes all actors as resource-integrating actors. This allows for the inclusion and mapping of different types of actors that engage in the exchange, such as direct and indirect stakeholders and other influencers.

This multilevel and multi-actor perspective of value, value creation, and value capture that differentiates the ecosystems framework (Gummesson, 2008; Vargo & Lusch, 2016) is highly relevant for BoP service ecosystems. This is because, in this environment, multiple actors must interact and play different social roles, as this diversity of actors allows the integration of complementary resources that are naturally scarce. Thus, shifting toward a multiple-actor BoP ecosystem represents a more inclusive perspective, in which all socioeconomic actors can draw on their resources and capabilities to build sustainable service innovations (Reficco & Márquez, 2012; Rivera-Santos & Rufín, 2010). This is in line with calls for "total wealth maximization" (Zahra et al., 2009) in which networks of profit and nonprofit organizations collaborate to generate value within a BoP environment (Weerawardena & Mort, 2006).

There is an increasing recognition in BoP research of the significant role of BoP actors' social embeddedness: this is what allows them to easily adapt to the conditions of their environment (e.g. London & Hart, 2004; Rivera-Santos & Rufín, 2010). Social embeddedness can help individual actors and organizations build their capacity to "create a web of trusted connections with a diversity of organizations and institutions, generate bottom-up development, and understand, leverage, and build on the existing social infrastructure" (London & Hart, 2004). Hart (2005) further argues that social embeddedness is necessary to engage in market transactions. He, therefore, discourages the disruption of the prevalent culture and lifestyle and instead recommends building on the existing resources and capabilities naturally available in this environment (Hart, 2005). Gibb and Adhikary (2000) found that social embeddedness lifts the psychological and cultural barriers that can exist between organizations and the BoP environment. Other benefits include helping reduce transaction costs, enabling last-mile connectivity and reach by leveraging existing market channels, and helping gain social acceptance among the people (Putnam, 1995).

In summary, diverse actors interact with one another and play different social roles as services are cocreated with and for local communities. Actor diversity

Table 8.4 Key concepts of BoP service ecosystems

Key concept	*BoP characteristics*	*Implications for BoP service ecosystems*	*Authors*
Resources	Market-facing and public resources are scarce or unreliable; thus, actors rely primarily on private resources.	Private resources are key for value cocreation in BoP service ecosystems.	Rivera-Santos & Rufin, 2010; Vargo & Lusch, 2011, 2018;
Institutions	Formal institutions are weaker than in non-BoP markets, while informal institutions are stronger. Thus, informal institutions substitute the role that formal institutions play in non-BoP markets.	Informal institutions, rather than formal institutions, enable value cocreation in service ecosystems.	Baron et al., 2018, Reficco & Márquez, 2012; Rivera-Santos and Rufin, 2010; Webb et al., 2010
Actors	Actor social embeddedness is key in a context with scarce or unavailable resources and capabilities.	Diverse actors interact with each other and play different social roles as services are cocreated with and for local communities.	Ben Letaifa & Reynoso, 2015; Reficco & Márquez, 2012; Rivera-Santos & Rufin, 2010; Wieland et al., 2012

is very important for BoP service ecosystems because it allows the integration of different capabilities and resources, which are naturally scarce in this environment. Thus, actors' social embeddedness is key for BoP service ecosystems.

Table 8.4 presents a summary of the key concepts of BoP service ecosystems.

Conclusions

For service research, the BoP represents an opportunity both to help the billions of impoverished people across the world as well as to contextualize service theories and frameworks into a very different and challenging institutional context (Reynoso, Valdés, & Cabrera, 2015). Thus, contextualizing service concepts and frameworks at the BoP can help expand service knowledge and research by actively learning from and with the poor (Fisk et al., 2016). The BoP context represents an opportunity to further understand the different manifestations of service in this specific context, which can enrich established theories and frameworks while responding to the call to action for service research that can have a positive impact on the well-being of the world's poor (Fisk et al., 2016; Reynoso, Valdés, & Cabrera, 2015).

Applying a service ecosystems perspective to service in a BoP context can provide multiple benefits to service research and practice, as well as generating new lines of research. First, the service ecosystems framework can help further understand and solve sustainability and scalability challenges at the BoP because of its wider scope (Ben Letaifa & Reynoso, 2015; London & Hart, 2004), which allows for an inclusive perspective in which all socioeconomic actors can draw on their resources and capabilities to contribute to sustainable services (Reficco & Márquez, 2012; Rivera-Santos & Rufin, 2010). Future research could use this framework to map the social, economic, and ecological impacts of service on the local community.

Second, building on the idea that nothing happens in isolation, this framework provides a systemic and dynamic vision of the socioeconomic exchanges that occur between multiple actors. It reinforces the point that service occurs within a network environment, something that sociologists (Granovetter, 1973; Burt, 2017) and other marketing scholars (e.g. Achrol & Kotler, 1999) have been discussing for some time (Vargo & Lusch, 2016). Further research could explore how network characteristics enable or hinder BoP service ecosystems.

Third, the ecosystems view can broaden the focus beyond a dyadic view of customer and service provider. Thus, it allows for a wider view that includes the multiple actors that play important roles in service at the BoP (Ben Letaifa & Reynoso, 2015). Further research along these lines could explore the elements of the social context that influence the interactions between the actors in service ecosystems (e.g. governments, universities, nonprofit organizations, or local citizens) (Ben Letaifa, Edvardsson, & Tronvoll, 2016; Follman, 2012).

Fourth, the ecosystems perspective frames value creation in terms of a network of actors rather than a single actor, thereby drawing attention to the multiple levels of interaction as well as the role of institutions (i.e. Social Norms, collective meanings, and other coordinating heuristics) as drivers of value co creation (Akaka et al., 2013; Chandler & Vargo, 2011). This perspective provides a systemic view that shows how all actors coordinate and integrate resources with the purpose of creating value for themselves and others. This is highly relevant in attempting to grasp the various socioeconomic processes that influence value co creation in multiple levels of aggregation (e.g. micro, meso, macro) (Edvardsson, Tronvoll, & Gruber, 2011; Vargo & Lusch, 2016).

References

Achrol, R.S., and Kotler, P. (1999). Marketing in the network economy. *Journal of Marketing*, 63, 146–63.

Akaka, M.A., Vargo, S.L., and Lusch, R.F. (2013). The complexity of context: a service ecosystems approach for international marketing. *Journal of International Marketing*, 21(4), 1–20.

Alderson, W. (1965). *Dynamic Marketing Behavior: A Functionalist Theory of Marketing*. Homewood, IL: Richard D. Irwin.

Alvesson, M., and Kärreman, D. (2007). Constructing mystery: empirical matters in theory development. *Academy of Management Review*, 32(4), 1265–81.

Arnould, E.J., and Mohr, J.J. (2005). Dynamic transformations for base-of-the-pyramid market clusters. *Journal of the Academy of Marketing Science*, 33(3), 254–74.

Arnold, D.G., and Valentin, A. (2013). Corporate social responsibility at the base of the pyramid. *Journal of Business Research*, 66(10), 1904–14.

Azariadis, C., and Stachurski, J. (2005). Poverty traps. *Handbook of Economic Growth*, 1, 295–384.

Bamberger, P. (2008). Beyond contextualization: using context theories to narrow the micro–macro gap in management research. *Academy of Management Journal*, 51, 839–46.

Banae, M.E., and Yandell, D. (2006). Development strategies and opportunities: the case of Africa. *Review of Human Factor Studies*, 12(1), 114–33.

Baron, S., Patterson, A., Maull, R., and Warnaby, G. (2018). Feed people first: a service ecosystem perspective on innovative food waste reduction. *Journal of Service Research*, 21(1), 135–50.

Ben Letaifa, S., and Reynoso, J. (2015). Toward a service ecosystem perspective at the base of the pyramid. *Journal of Service Management*, 26(5), 684–705.

Ben Letaifa, S., Edvardsson, B., and Tronvoll, B. (2016). The role of social platforms in transforming service ecosystems. *Journal of Business Research*, 69(5), 1933–38.

Burt, R.S. (2017). Structural holes versus network closure as social capital. In N. Lin, K. Cook, and R.S. Burt (Eds.), *Social Capital Theory and Research* (pp. 31–56). London: Routledge.

Casado Cañeque, F., and Hart, S L. (2015). *Base of the Pyramid 3.0: Sustainable Development through Innovation and Entrepreneurship*. London: Routledge.

Chandler, J.D., and Vargo, S.L. (2011). Contextualization and value-in-context: how context frames exchange. *Marketing Theory*, 11(1), 35–49.

Davidson, P. (2009). *The Keynes Solution: The Path to Global Economic Prosperity*. New York: St. Martin's Press.

De Soto, H. (1989). *The Other Path: The Invisible Revolution in the Third World*. New York: HarperCollins.

De Soto, H. (2000). *The Mystery of Capital: Why Capitalism Triumphs in the West and Fails Everywhere Else*. New York: Basic Books.

De Soysa, I., and J. Jütting (2007). Informal institutions and development: how they matter and what makes them change. In J. Jütting, D. Drechsler, S. Bartsch, and I. de Soysa (Eds.), *Informal Institutions: How Social Norms Help or Hinder Development* (pp. 29–43). OECD Development Centre.

Dembek, K., Sivasubramaniam, N., and Chmielewski, D.A. (2019). A systematic review of the bottom/base of the pyramid literature: cumulative evidence and future directions. *Journal of Business Ethics*, 165, 365–82.

DiMaggio, P.J., and Powell, W.W. (1983). The iron cage revisited: institutional isomorphism and collective rationality in organizational fields. *American Sociological Review*, 48(2), 147–60.

Edvardsson, B., Tronvoll, B., and Gruber, T. (2011). Expanding understanding of service exchange and value co-creation: a social construction approach. *Journal of the Academy of Marketing Science*, 39(2), 327–39.

Fisk, R.P.P., Anderson, L., Bowen, D.E., Gruber, T., Ostrom, A., Patrício, L., and Sebastiani, R. (2016). Billions of impoverished people deserve to be better served. *Journal of Service Management*, 27(1), 43–55.

Follman, J. (2012). BoP at ten: evolution and a new lens. *South Asian Journal of Global Business Research*, 1(2), 293–310.

Gebauer, H., and Reynoso, J. (2013). An agenda for service research at the base of the pyramid (BoP). *Journal of Service Management*, 24(5), 482–502

Gibb, A., and Adhikary, D. (2000). Strategies for local and regional NGO development: combining sustainable outcomes with sustainable organizations. *Entrepreneurship & Regional Development*, 12(2), 137–61.

Granovetter, M.S. (1973). The strength of weak ties. *American Journal of Sociology,* 78(6), 1360–80.

Gummesson, E. (2008). Extending the service-dominant logic: from customer centricity to balanced centricity. *Journal of the Academy of Marketing Science*, 36(1), 15–17.

Gummerus, J., Lefebvre, C., Liljander, V., Martin, C., McColl-Kennedy, J., Nicholls, R., and Wilson, A. (2013). Global perspectives on service. In R. Fisk, R. Russell-Bennet, and L. Harris (Eds.), *Serving Customers: Global Services Marketing Perspectives* (pp. 298–322). Melbourne: Tilde University Press.

Hammond, A.L., Kramer, W.J., Katz, R.S., Tran, J.T., and Walker, C. (2007). The next 4 billion. *Innovations: Technology, Governance, Globalization*, 2(1–2), 147–58.

Hart, S.L. (2005). *Capitalism at the Crossroads: The Unlimited Business Opportunities in Solving the World's Most Difficult Problems.* Upper Saddle River, NJ: Pearson Education.

Hart, S.L. (2015). BoP 2.0: The next generation of strategy for the Base of the Pyramid. In S.A. Mohrman, J. O'Toole, & E.E. Lawler II (Eds.), *Corporate stewardship: Achieving sustainable effectiveness* (pp. 190–204). Sheffield, UK: Greenleaf Publishing.

Helmke, G., and Levitsky, S. (2004). Informal institutions and comparative politics: a research agenda. *Perspectives on Politics*, 2(4), 725–40.

Hofstede, G. (1980). Motivation, leadership, and organization: do American theories apply abroad? *Organizational Dynamics*, 9(1), 42–63.

House, R.J., Hanges, P.J., Javidan, M., Dorfman, P.W., and Gupta, V. (Eds.). (2004). *Culture, Leadership, and Organizations: The GLOBE Study of 62 Societies.* London: Sage Publications.

Ivanovic, A., and Fuxman, L. (2012). Productivity and innovation in service: the multidisciplinary perspective offered by service science. In J.G. Hernández, M.J. García, and G.J. Hernández (Eds.), *Service Science Research, Strategy, and Innovation: Dynamic Knowledge Management Methods* (pp. 170–84). Hershey, PA: IGI Global.

Johns, G. (2001). In praise of context. *Journal of Organizational Behavior: The International Journal of Industrial, Occupational and Organizational Psychology and Behavior,* 22(1), 31–42.

Johns, G. (2006). The essential impact of context on organizational behavior. *Academy of Management Review*, 31(2), 386–408.

Joncourt, S., Gebauer, H., Reynoso, J., Cabrera, K., Valdes, A., and Greve, K. (2019). Extending the base-of-the-pyramid concept. *Service Science*, 11(3), 241–61.

Karnani, A. (2007). The mirage of marketing to the Bottom of the Pyramid: how the private sector can alleviate poverty. *California Management Review,* 49(4), 90–111

Karnani, A. (2009). Romanticising the poor harms the poor. *Journal of International Development,* 21(1), 76–86.

Kolk, A., Rivera-Santos, M., and Rufin, C. (2014). Reviewing a decade of research on the "base/bottom of the pyramid" (BOP) concept. *Business & Society,* 53(3), 338–77.

London, T., (2016). *The Base of the Pyramid Promise: Building Businesses with Impact and Scale.* Stanford, CA: Stanford University Press.

London, T., and Hart, S.L. (2004). Reinventing strategies for emerging markets: Beyond the transnational model. *Journal of International Business Studies,* 35(5), 350–70.

London, T., Anupindi, R., and Sheth, S. (2010). Creating mutual value: lessons learned from ventures serving base of the pyramid producers. *Journal of Business Research*, 66(3), 582–94.

Lowndes, V. (1996). Varieties of new institutionalism: a critical appraisal. *Public Administration*, 74(2), 181–97.

Lusch, R.F., and Vargo, S.L. (2014). *Service-Dominant Logic: Premises, Perspectives, Possibilities*. Cambridge: Cambridge University Press.

Moore, J.F. (1996). *The Death of Competition: Leadership and Strategy in the Age of Business Ecosystems*. New York: Harper Business.

Narayan, D. (2002). *Bonds and Bridges: Social Capital and Poverty*. Geneva: World Bank Publications.

Neghina, C., Caniëls, M.C., Bloemer, J.M., and van Birgelen, M.J. (2015). Value co-creation in service interactions: dimensions and antecedents. *Marketing Theory*, 15(2), 221–42.

Nielsen, C., and Samia, P. (2008). Understanding key factors in social enterprise development of the BOP: a systems approach applied to case studies in the Philippines. *Journal of Consumer Marketing*, 25(7), 446–54.

North, Douglass C. (1990). *Institutions, Institutional Change and Economic Performance*. Cambridge: Cambridge University Press.

Ostrom, A., Parasuraman, A., Bowen, E., Patrício, L., and Voss, C. (2015). Service research priorities in a rapidly changing context. *Journal of Service Research*, 18(2), 127–59

Prahalad, C.K., and Hammond, A. (2002). Serving the world's poor, profitably. *Harvard Business Review*, 80(9), 48–59.

Prahalad, C.K., and Hart, S. (2002). The fortune at the bottom of the pyramid. *Strategy and Business*, 26, 54–67.

Putnam, R.D. (1995). Tuning in, tuning out: the strange disappearance of social capital in America. *PS: Political Science & Politics*, 28(4), 664–83.

Reficco, E., and Márquez, P. (2012). Inclusive networks for building BOP markets. *Business & Society*, 51(3), 512–56.

Reynoso, J. (1999). Progress and prospects of services management in Latin America. *International Journal of Service Industry Management*, 10(5), 401–408.

Reynoso, J., and Cabrera, K. (2019). Managing informal service organizations at the base of the pyramid (BoP). *Journal of Services Marketing*, 33(1), 112–24.

Reynoso, J., Valdés, A., and Cabrera, K. (2015). Breaking new ground: base-of-pyramid service research. *The Service Industries Journal*, 35(13), 695–709.

Ricart, J.E., Enright, M.J., Ghemawat, P., Hart, S.L., and Khanna, T. (2004). New frontiers in international strategy. *Journal of International Business Studies*, 35(3), 175–200.

Riddell, R.C. (2008). *Does Foreign Aid Really Work?* Oxford: Oxford University Press.

Rivera-Santos, M., and Rufin, C. (2010). Global village vs. small town: understanding networks at the base of the pyramid. *International Business Review*, 19, 126–39.

Rousseau, D.M., and Fried, Y. (2001). Location, location, location: contextualizing organizational research. *Journal of Organizational Behavior: The International Journal of Industrial, Occupational and Organizational Psychology and Behavior*, 22(1), 1–13.

Scott, W.R. (2001). *Institutions and Organizations*. Thousand Oaks, CA: Sage.

Simanis, E. (2012). Reality check at the bottom of the pyramid. *Harvard Business Review*, 90(6), 2–6.

Simanis, E., and Hart, S. (2009). Innovation from the inside out. *MIT Sloan Management Review*, 50(4), 77–86.

Simanis, E., Hart, S., and Duke, D. (2008). The base of the pyramid protocol: beyond "basic needs" business strategies. *Innovations: Technology, Governance, Globalization,* 3(1), 57–84.

Suchman, M.C. (1995). Managing legitimacy: strategic and institutional approaches. *Academy of Management Review*, 20(3), 571–610.

Vargo, S.L., and Akaka, M.A. (2012). Value cocreation and service systems (re)formation: a service ecosystems view. *Service Science*, 4(3), 207–17.

Vargo, S.L., and Lusch, R.F. (2011). It's all B2B... and beyond: toward a systems perspective of the market. *Industrial Marketing Management*, 40(2), 181–87.

Vargo, S.L., and Lusch, R.F. (2016). Institutions and axioms: an extension and update of service-dominant logic. *Journal of the Academy of Marketing Science*, 44(1), 5–23.

Vargo, S.L., and Lusch, R.F. (Eds.). (2018). *The SAGE Handbook of Service-dominant Logic.* London: Sage Publications.

Viswanathan, M., and Rosa, J.A. (2007). Product and market development for subsistence marketplaces: consumption and entrepreneurship beyond literacy and resource barriers. *Advances in International Management*, 20, 1–17.

Webb, J.W., Kistruck, G.M., Ireland, R.D., and Ketchen, Jr., D.J. (2010). The entrepreneurship process in base of the pyramid markets: the case of multinational enterprise/nongovernment organization alliances. *Entrepreneurship Theory and Practice,* 34(3), 555–81.

Weerawardena, J., and Mort, G.S. (2006). Investigating social entrepreneurship: A multidimensional model. *Journal of World Business*, 41(1), 21–35.

Whetten, D.A. (2009). An examination of the interface between context and theory applied to the study of Chinese organizations. *Management and Organization Review,* 5(1), 29–56.

Wieland, H., Polese, F., Vargo, S.L., and Lusch, R.F. (2012). Toward a service (eco)systems perspective on value creation. *International Journal of Service Science, Management, Engineering, and Technology (IJSSMET)*, 3(3), 12–25.

Williamson, O.E. (2000). The new institutional economics: taking stock, looking ahead. *Journal of Economic Literature*, 38(3), 595–613.

World Bank (n.d.). *Poverty & Equity Data Portal.* Retrieved April 15, 2020, from http://povertydata.worldbank.org/poverty/home/.

Yunus, M. (2010). *Building Social Business: The New Kind of Capitalism That Serves Humanity's Most Pressing Needs.* New York: PublicAffairs.

Zahra, S.A., Gedajlovic, E., Neubaum, D.O., and Shulman, J.M. (2009). A typology of social entrepreneurs: motives, search processes and ethical challenges. *Journal of Business Venturing*, 24(5), 519–32.

Further reading

Cañeque, F.C., and Hart, S.L. (Eds.). (2017). *Base of the Pyramid 3.0: Sustainable Development through Innovation and Entrepreneurship.* London: Routledge.

London, T., and Hart, S.L. (2010). *Next Generation Business Strategies for the Base of the Pyramid: New Approaches for Building Mutual Value.* London: FT Press.

Prahalad, C.K. (2009). *The Fortune at the Bottom of the Pyramid: Eradicating Poverty through Profits* (revised and updated 5th anniversary edition). London: FT Press.

Yunus, M. (2009). *Creating a World without Poverty: Social Business and the Future of Capitalism.* New York: PublicAffairs.

9 The Integrative Justice Model as a challenge-driven normative framework for sustainable and just business practice

Nicholas J. C. Santos and Gene R. Laczniak

Takeaways

- Authentic engagement is based on mutual trust between sellers and buyers.
- It falls to the partner with greater power (normally the seller) to audit transactional outcomes so that they are mutually and socially beneficial.
- Long-term sustainable partnerships, particularly with disadvantaged consumer segments, require investment in those consumers to develop their future buying power and their ability to participate in and analyze market dynamics.
- Interest representation requires that potential sellers cultivate an empathy with their impoverished customers (or other stakeholders) if a genuine awareness helpful to creating sustainable transactions is to occur.
- Business case history seems to indicate that taking a long-term perspective is superior to short-run profit maximization as a financially advantageous and sustainable strategy.
- Just, fair, and sustainable markets for disadvantaged consumers are more likely to come about when the organization intends and plans for such outcomes from the beginning.

Introduction

As the novel SARS virus causing COVID-19 reached the pandemic stage in 2020, the United Nations Global Compact (UNGC) made a special appeal to global businesses. In this appeal, the UNGC (2020) encouraged businesses everywhere, in a spirit of responsibility, solidarity, and international cooperation, to take immediate action to support disproportionately affected communities and enterprises in their time of need. For example, Vesoulis (2020), writing in *Time*, points out that the coronavirus especially hurts the poor, with societal after-effects that reverberate for all. The Vesoulis commentary reiterated the conventional COVID-19 advice of public health experts: avoid crowds, stockpile groceries, work from home, and contact a doctor if ill. The key problem with such advice, however, according to Vesoulis, is that many low-income people

DOI: 10.4324/9781003188773-9

cannot afford to follow it due to their lack of economic resources, deprived locations, employment demands, or the absence of reliable healthcare.

Similarly, as universities and schools move to online methods of course delivery, and as employees work at home and major sports and entertainment events are canceled, there is minimal conversation about the significant impact of such decisions on the poor and vulnerable. Such disadvantaged groups are typically less likely to have online access and more likely to be in employment that requires their in-person presence and/or service jobs that previously supported the now eliminated community events. In short, the poor bear a disproportionate burden of the pandemic and this social outcome is "unjust and unfair." The question is: How can business operate in challenging situations (such as a pandemic) and still execute its operations in a socially responsible and sustainable manner? Answering this question is basically what the UNGC and its Sustainable Development Goals (SDGs) are designed for (i.e. to enhance sustainable development via innovative thinking), despite a challenging external environment. Such innovative thinking creates transformational change by questioning traditional assumptions about business and creating a mind shift that is oriented toward sustainability.

In this chapter, we present a normative ethical framework labeled the "Integrative Justice Model" (IJM) for impoverished markets (see Figure 9.1). The IJM was developed in the context of marketing to poor and disadvantaged consumers and was inspired by writings in moral philosophy, marketing theory, and corporate social responsibility (CSR) frameworks, as well as religious traditions (Santos & Laczniak, 2009). We hold that the tenets of the IJM are also applicable to the pandemic and post-pandemic context in which we find ourselves. Within the context of the UNGC SDGs, the IJM framework particularly helps vitalize SDG #12, which requires responsible organizations to "ensure sustainable consumption and production patterns" (United Nations, 2015).

The IJM postulates five interrelated components that we argue are essential for treating impoverished populations in a fair and just manner. These five components are: (1) authentic engagement without exploitative intent; (2) cocreation of value with customers; (3) investment in future consumption; (4) genuine interest representation; and (5) a focus on long-term profit management. It is expected that the *outcomes* for business firms that adhere to these five characteristics will be long-term relationships, customer empowerment, sustainable business initiatives, and the creation of a fairer marketplace. The aim of the IJM is to enhance *fairness* and *equity* in economic transactions involving impoverished consumers. Without these qualities, market transactions with disadvantaged markets are unlikely ever to be sustainable or positively transformative. Below, we introduce the IJM and describe how it has been systematically developed, as well as how it has been applied in a variety of contexts. Included are examples of how IJM thinking might manifest itself in Base-of-the-Pyramid (BoP) settings.

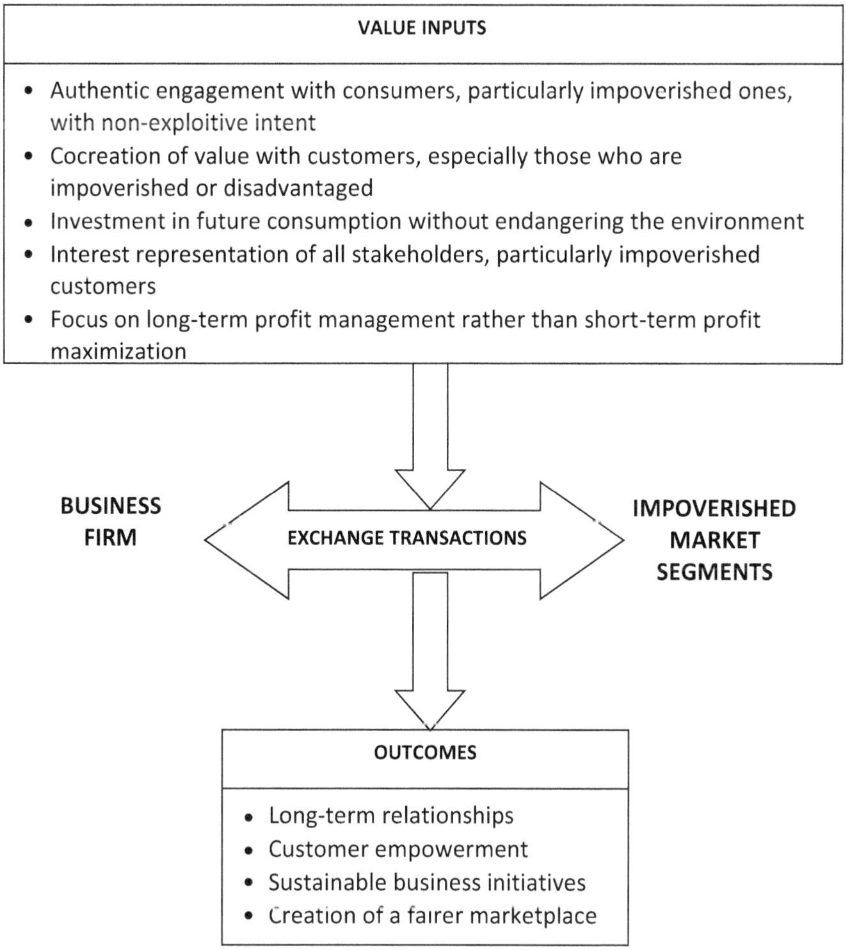

Figure 9.1 An Integrative Justice Model for impoverished markets (Santos & Laczniak, 2009).

Derivation of the model

The IJM has been developed following the guidelines for normative theory construction proposed by the philosopher J.D. Bishop (2000). Bishop proposes that every normative theory ought to address seven issues: (1) recommended values; (2) the grounds for accepting those values; (3) a decision principle that business people who accept the theory can use; (4) who the normative theory applies to (i.e. the agents); (5) whose interests need to be considered (i.e. the decision principle's scope); (6) in what contexts it applies; and (7) what legal and regulatory structures it assumes. In terms of derivation of the model, the IJM does *not* blend different theories or types of justice such as procedural, legal, or restorative justice. Instead, it *integrates* the notion of "fairness" or "equity" in marketing transactions as developed from an examination of different moral and managerial perspectives. These perspectives were: (1) Catholic social teaching; (2) Habermas's discourse theory; (3) Kant's categorical imperative; (4) Rawls's difference principle; (5) Ross's theory of duties; (6) Sen's capability approach; (7) virtue ethics; (8) classical utilitarianism; (9) the S-D logic of marketing; (10) socially responsible investing; (11) stakeholder theory; (12) sustainability; and (13) the triple bottom line. The five key principles of the IJM that were mentioned earlier emerged from an examination of these different thought streams. Readers interested in further particulars about the derivation process are encouraged to consult Santos and Laczniak (2009) or Laczniak and Santos (2016).

As an illustration, the theories that provide a normative foundation for the first IJM principle, which is an *authentic engagement* without intending to exploit the disadvantaged consumer, are Catholic social teaching (CST), Immanuel Kant's categorical imperative (second formulation), Ross's theory of duties (beneficence), S-D logic, and virtue ethics. For instance, CST emphasizes the inherent and inviolable dignity of the human person. The second formulation of Kant's categorical imperative decrees that people should never be treated as merely a means to an end. One of Ross's *prima facie* duties is *beneficence*, which suggests rendering aid to those in need whenever reasonable. S-D logic places a considerable focus on the centrality of the customer as an active coparticipant in the exchange process. And virtue ethics emphasizes the role that values play in shaping behavior. All of these frameworks are suggestive of the treatment of customers, particularly impoverished and vulnerable ones, with fairness and without exploitation (Santos & Laczniak, 2012). Likewise, an important theory that provides the normative foundation for the third IJM principle, namely an investment in future consumption, is Amartya Sen's "capability approach" (Sen, 1999, 2009; Enderle, 2013). Sen's approach views those living in poverty not only in terms of minimal income, but also as "capability-deprived": that is, lacking entitlement and freedom, whereby the poor are unable to make choices to achieve what they truly value being and doing.

Elaborating on the key elements of the IJM

While the key elements of the IJM are not intended to be an exhaustive list of "just" market situations, they can be seen as both distinct and symbiotic dimensions of what constitutes a just marketplace. These dimensions are not fragmented, isolated ones, but rather are to be considered in their entirety, as *interdependent* and related characteristics. The five defining features of the IJM are meant to guide the relationship between the business corporations and the impoverished market segment so as to achieve fairness in the marketplace, thereby leading to a sustainable, and perhaps even more profitable, business enterprise. We elaborate on each of the IJM elements below.

Authentic, non-exploitative engagement

An authentic engagement is one that should possess the intrinsic quality of being trustworthy as well as being a process that aims to win the trust of the constituents engaged. The corporate scandals at the beginning of the new millennium, the subprime mortgage crisis, and the 2008 meltdown of the financial markets all contributed to a fundamental breakdown of trust. This is unfortunate, as the value of trust in business functioning cannot be overemphasized. Thomas (2002) points out that trust is crucial in a stakeholder society. Murphy (1999) argues that trust is one of the five core virtues that an ethical business organization should possess. In the context of relationship marketing, Murphy, Laczniak, and Wood (2007) see trust as a primary virtue. One important means of developing trust with impoverished customers is by engaging them authentically and without trying to exploit them unfairly.

Samli (2008) makes a distinction between greed and ambition. A company that is motivated merely by greed will attempt to win at any cost, in any way possible, trying to get as much for themselves as possible, as fast as they can, without any concern for the external environment. In contrast, an ambitious company realizes that working and collaborating with other stakeholders increases opportunities for progress and benefits a larger number of people. Such a firm takes a long-term perspective and holds that improving the quality of society and the environment is to the benefit of all.

> **Proposition 1**: Authentic engagement is based on mutual trust between sellers and buyers.

Co-creation of value

Co-creation of value is an approach in marketing which holds that, instead of autonomously positing what constitutes value for consumers, a firm ought to involve such consumers in the value-creation process itself since value is ultimately determined by the beneficiary (Vargo & Lusch, 2004, 2006, 2008). As Prahalad and Ramaswamy (2002, 2004a, 2004b) indicate, this value creation does not just take place at the point of exchange but at all points of interaction between the firm and the consumer. It should be noted that Prahalad and Ramaswamy's position on "joint value creation" is based on their perception of consumers being well informed, empowered, connected, and actively engaged. However, this perception is not necessarily true of the BoP segment where there is often lack of education, information asymmetries, and economic, cultural, and social deprivations (Karnani, 2007). Therefore, in the case of value co-creation with impoverished consumers, a higher social responsibility falls to the more informed and more powerful market participant, namely the business firm (Laczniak, 2006).

In co-creating value with impoverished customers, a firm should not make the assumption that just because the customer is involved in the co-creation process there is going to be resultant value or benefit for the customer. It is incumbent upon the firm to ensure that there is resultant value for the impoverished customer by engaging in a co-creation process that fosters partnership and develops mutual trust that extends beyond the consumption of the product or service (Murphy, Laczniak, & Wood, 2007).

> **Proposition 2:** It falls to the co-creating partner with greater power (normally the seller) to audit transactional outcomes so that they are mutually and socially beneficial.

Investment in future consumption

At first glance, an investment in future consumption might seem to imply the promotion of increased consumption. However, this particular element is influenced by the capabilities approach of the Nobel laureate in economics Amartya Sen (1999). In line with Sen's idea of expanding people's capabilities and freedoms, an investment in future consumption is an attempt at procuring better participation of the impoverished in the market system. This participation can be as producers, innovators, employees, distributors, customers, consultants, etc. In order to enhance such participation, it is important that the capabilities of the impoverished population be developed and the freedoms they enjoy be expanded. Strategies aimed at increasing the capabilities of impoverished segments create enabling conditions that contribute to the long-term functioning of the business enterprise.

> **Proposition 3**: Long-term sustainable partnerships, particularly with disadvantaged consumer segments, require investment in those consumers to develop their future buying power and their ability to participate in and analyze market dynamics.

Interest representation of all stakeholders

This IJM element implies that a business firm should consider in its functioning what matters to its stakeholders and what is to their advantage or benefit. By "stakeholder," we mean *any group or individual who can affect or is affected by the firm's functioning* (Freeman, 1984). As such categorization is rather broad, Freeman, Harrison, and Wicks (2007) distinguish between *primary* stakeholders, who are vital to the survival and growth of the business, and *secondary* stakeholders, who can affect the relationship with the primary stakeholders. In order that the interests of the stakeholders are better served, Freeman, Harrison, and Wicks (2007) recommend that managers put themselves in the place of the stakeholder and see things from that perspective. This can be a challenge in the case of impoverished stakeholders. For example, a manager who has lived an affluent lifestyle and faced few disadvantages has little idea about the situation of an impoverished consumer. Thus, such a manager might misrepresent what she or he perceives to be the interests of such a stakeholder. It is important, then, that managers familiarize themselves with the situation of impoverished stakeholders by either immersing themselves for a short while in that context or making greater effort to learn about them.

> **Proposition 4**: Interest representation requires that potential sellers cultivate an empathy with their impoverished customers (or other stakeholders) if a genuine awareness helpful to creating sustainable transactions is to occur.

Focus on long-term profit management

Financial returns undoubtedly play an important role in the functioning of a business enterprise and are a central indicator of whether the company is performing efficiently. However, an obsession with immediate financial rewards can, ironically, act against the long-term interests of the business firm and its stakeholders. The examples of Enron and WorldCom's accounting manipulations at the turn of the century are cases in point. More recently, Volkswagen's "Dieselgate" scandal and Wells Fargo's "account churning" indicate how executives keen on maximizing short-term gains can put not only their company, but also the entire market at risk (Murphy, Laczniak, & Harris, 2017). Instead of profit maximization, a firm ought to concentrate on long-term profit management. This element is intended as a better long-view strategy because, if impoverished segments are developed for their sustainability, their eventual profit stream might also prove to be superior.

If a business organization considers itself to be only a money-making enterprise, it is likely to base all its decisions in terms of financial value. However, a business firm is more than just a money-spinning endeavor. It is an economic institution that plays a social function. While profit maximization aims at increasing financial returns, often in the short run, profit management strives at increasing long-term business success. The notion of long-run profit management is consistent with the *triple bottom line* (TBL): namely, that the measure of business success is based on social, environmental, and financial returns (Elkington, 1998). While many companies accept that they have a responsibility toward social and environmental issues, this responsibility is often looked at as a "cost" or "strategy constraint." Instead, Porter and Kramer (2006) advise that these should be viewed as sources of opportunity, innovation, and competitive advantage.

> **Proposition 5**: Business case history seems to indicate that taking a long-term perspective is superior to short-run profit maximization as a financially advantageous and sustainable strategy.

Connecting the IJM with the "basic perspectives" framework of Laczniak and Murphy[1]

Additional theoretical support for the IJM framework can be garnered by anchoring it in the normative perspectives about marketing ethics developed by Laczniak and Murphy ("L&M") (2006). If the IJM can be shown to be theoretically robust, it can give practitioners greater confidence in utilizing the IJM elements in their decision-making regarding BoP markets and enhanced sustainability.

L&M construct a comprehensive normative approach to marketing ethics based on eight essential "basic perspectives" (BPs) (see Figure 9.2). Each BP is linked to aspects of moral theory or to normative managerial frameworks. The BPs are meant to be viewed as dynamic, interactive, and connected in order to create a broad-based aspirational ideal for ethical behavior in marketing. The BPs have a *micro* dimension, in that they can be seen as providing ethical norms for marketing firms. But they are also *macro*, in that they should be universally advocated for all marketing organizations. This is because they are grounded in an understanding of the role that marketing firms play in society, along with an explicit recognition of the social contract that exists between business and society. In addition, at its core, the L&M approach also pervasively recognizes the fundamental dignity of all persons.

The IJM in focus in this chapter is highly consistent with L&M's broader normative theory of marketing ethics. Understanding that close connection

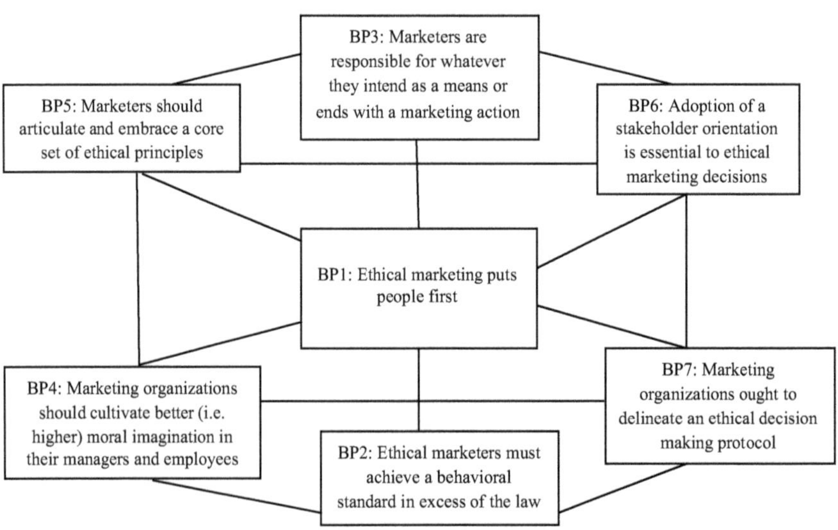

Figure 9.2 A summary of the essential Basic Perspectives (BPs) for evaluating and improving marketing ethics (Laczniak & Murphy, 2006).

provides the reader with a perspective about the derivation and robustness of the IJM and how it fits into the larger marketing ethics literature. Both L&M and the IJM are derived from the theory development protocol of Bishop (2000). The IJM also operates on a similar, albeit more targeted, level than L&M. Specifically, the IJM is grounded in a macro understanding of what constitutes a just market for impoverished consumers and, from such vantage points, ethical prescriptions for *all* firms that market to the poor consumers are deduced. The consistency of the IJM with L&M adds to its concurrent and face validity. Below the specific connections between the elements of the IJM and dimensions of the L&M approach are laid out, albeit briefly.

The "authentic engagement... with non-exploitative intent," the initial element of the IJM, can be seen as an extension of L&M's first BP in which "ethical marketing puts people first." As L&M (2006) write, "ethically concerned marketers should seek to fully comprehend their societal influence and to ensure their marketing operations create a perceived and real benefit" (p. 157). It is also a direct reflection of BP5, in which L&M (2006) articulate that "marketers who aspire to operate on a higher ethical plane should embrace a core set of ethical principles" (p. 164), including "the principle of protecting vulnerable market segments," of which the poor are clearly a primary constituent. For example, the American Marketing Association (2020) in its Statement of Ethics reminds its members (academics and practitioners) that they have a special commitment to vulnerable market segments.

"Co-creation of value with customers," the second element of the IJM, can be viewed as being embedded in BP3 of the L&M (2006) frame work, which suggests that "marketers are responsible for their intent as well as the means and ends of their marketing actions" (p. 161). Surely one of the easiest ways to generate creative (and ethical) symbiosis – and avoid negative outcomes – is to partner with impoverished customers from the beginning. For example, Amanz' Abantu, a South African provider of water and sanitation services, involves consumers from the beginning of the innovation process (Krämer & Belz, 2008, p. 227; Sprague, 2007). A direct inquiry process conducted during the incubation phase enabled customers to select the design of the sanitation structure. Additionally, rural-community-based village groups called project steering committees were set up to enable the villagers to play an active role in the project's design and implementation, thereby leading to greater ownership. Such an open innovation paradigm grants consumers "the role of a 'prosumer,' integrating him/her actively and deeply in one or – ideally – all stages of the innovation process (invention, incubation, market introduction and diffusion)" (Krämer & Belz, 2008, p. 218).

"Investment in future consumption without endangering the environment," element three of the IJM approach, is reflective of BP5 of the general L&M (2006) approach. In particular, this BP, which advocates the adoption of a core set of ethical principles, includes "distributive justice," whereby "[t]here is an obligation on the part of all marketing organizations to assess the fairness of marketplace consequences flowing from their collective marketing practices" (p. 166). An example of an organization following this dictum in the context of the IJM is the Sekeem Group, an Egyptian conglomerate attempting to expand organic farming in the desert northeast of Cairo (Hamm, 2008, p. 53). When done right, the "organic approach" is not only healthier for consumers, but it can also be conducted with less water and without pesticides and, hence, can flourish in harsher terrain. In order to maintain the Sekeem network of 800 independent farmers cultivating 50,000 acres, the company has invested, through its corporate foundation, in a school, medical center, and various social support programs for the villages that have sprung up around the desolate area.

"Interest representation of all stakeholders, particularly impoverished ones" is the fourth element of the IJM. It is in close consonance with L&M (2006) BP6, which states that "The adoption of a stakeholder orientation is essential to the advancement and maintenance of ethical decision-making in all marketing organizations" (p. 167). Such attention to the unique needs of impoverished consumers was shown when the Grameen Family of Enterprises entered into a partnership with Danone Foods of France to develop and distribute affordable "single serving" yogurt portions that were also nutrition-enhanced (Hamm, 2008, p. 51). This particular combination of attributes would not have been required in the developed markets that Danone typically served.

The fifth element of the IJM calls for "focus on long-term profit management rather than short term profit maximization." This evokes BP4 of L&M (2006), which calls for the cultivation of managers with moral imagination "who are such moral exemplars that they will always try to do what is morally right in their marketing decisions" (p. 164). In other words, the ethical organization, when engaging with impoverished market segments, desires to train managers capable of creating strategies that will generate future sustainability. An excellent example of this sentiment would be the Belgian organization Apopo (Hamm, 2008, p. 52). Established as a purely altruistic endeavor, the firm creatively trained giant African pouch rats to sniff out land mines in Tanzania so that these killing fields might be safely cleared. When donations flagged, the company contracted with consultants from Oxford Business School to help expand its service applications to Middle Eastern markets and to suggest training the rodents to detect disease in refugee camps and elsewhere. In this manner, Apopo's investment in product development expertise enhanced its likelihood of staying the course in its market of origin.

Application of the IJM

The IJM is a model of ethical innovation in marketing to the poor in at least two respects (Laczniak & Santos, 2016). First, in contrast to descriptive-explicative models, the IJM is a normative-ethical model which comprises five key components that *ought to be* present when marketing to the poor. As such, unlike most of the mainstream marketing models that do not articulate their implied ethical or unethical values, the IJM makes the ethical dimension explicit. Second, the IJM is also different in substantive ethical terms: it is about *justice* (not exploitation), *honesty* (not deception), and *sustainability* (not short-term operations). While the IJM is a normative model, and admittedly aspirational, attempts have been made to apply it in varied contexts, and thus demonstrate its practicality.

Santos and Laczniak (2012) lay out over four dozen actional, mid-range decision guidelines for dealing ethically with impoverished customers which are matched to the five elements of the IJM. These were arrived at via an examination of numerous case studies from global settings where MNCs engaged with the BoP market. Facca-Miess and Santos (2016) used these decision guidelines to assess marketers' and managers' perceptions regarding the tenets of the IJM. Statistical analysis in this study indicated strong support for the IJM elements. While individual managers and marketers might be supportive of the IJM elements, the importance of endogenous corporate culture – as an institutional force – in assuring that the poor are treated with dignity and fairness, cannot be overemphasized (Santos, Laczniak, & Facca-Miess, 2015). Additionally, exogenous forces of various kinds, such as the government or regulatory agencies such as the United Nations, must exercise their power to ensure that the consumer rights of the poor are being recognized.

As a separate thrust, the IJM has been connected to social entrepreneurship (Santos, 2013) and to the context of subsistence marketplaces (Facca-Miess & Santos, 2014). The charter of social entrepreneurial firms frequently involves a mission-driven purpose to more directly serve impoverished segments and as such can easily relate to the IJM. This is not necessarily so in the case of MNCs, where the *realpolitik* of their profit pressures could likely result in many firms not easily embracing the socially responsible approach advocated by the IJM. The IJM has also been applied to the context of social marketing and to develop a macro-social marketing ethical framework (Kennedy & Santos, 2019).

The case of Jesuit Worldwide Learning: higher education at the margins

Jesuit Worldwide Learning (JWL) is an initiative that aims to provide higher education to refugees, internally displaced people, and others living at the margins (Habash, 2020). It was founded in 2010 and currently serves students in 14 countries (Habash, 2020). JWL uses a blended learning model, in which online instruction is provided to all the sites while allowing each site to form cohorts of students aided by on-site tutors or coordinators.

The IJM was used to analyze the JWL initiative with a special focus on transformation in quality of life (TQL) (Facca-Miess & Santos, 2019). While tertiary education clearly facilitates employment opportunities, JWL focuses on developing leaders who will stay in or return to their communities as transformative leaders and change agents. Using an online survey tool, distributed to varied JWL stakeholders, the tenets of the IJM were measured using items based on the decision principles outlined by Santos and Laczniak (2012) and later statistically vetted by Facca-Miess and Santos (2016). Items were adapted slightly to the context of the people at the margins: namely, refugee camps and post-conflict settings. Each of the tenets of the IJM was subjected to multiple regression analysis to identify the overall rating for each tenet with regard to the tenet's significant predictors of beneficiaries. Then, each IJM predictor was regressed on TQL using the stepwise method. Overall predictors included understanding responsibility to contribute to the good of the community, value alignment, relevance of programs and services, and challenges viewed as opportunities for innovation. One commonality of all the predictors is that they flow from a commitment to shape positive social outcomes for the focus community. The IJM, applied in this way, yields ample statistical evidence measuring JWL's outcomes and their impact on its beneficiaries.

> **Proposition 6:** Just, fair, and sustainable markets for disadvantaged consumers are more likely to come about when the organization intends and plans for such outcomes from the beginning.

Conclusion

The COVID-19 pandemic and post-pandemic situation means a likely increase in the number of business organizations that will necessarily be engaged with impoverished populations. One reason for this is that the number of people at the BoP is unfortunately going to increase. Oxfam (2020) estimates that at least half a billion people could be pushed into poverty by COVID-19. These impoverished BoP consumers will lack purchasing options and economic leverage and, therefore, will easily invite exploitation by unscrupulous entities. However, such exploitation could be mitigated by enlightened business practitioners willing to thoughtfully consider their ethical and professional obligations to vulnerable consumers. The IJM approach provides a defensible set of general ethical values, grounded in theory, which can help steer a course that is fair, just, and sustainable when marketing to vulnerable populations.

Note

1 This section is excerpted in part from Laczniak and Santos (2016).

References

American Marketing Association. (2020). Statement of ethics. Retrieved June 21, 2020 from https://www.ama.org/codes-of-conduct/

Bishop, J.D. (2000). A framework for discussing normative theories of business ethics. *Business Ethics Quarterly*, 10(3), 563–92.

Elkington, J. (1998). *Cannibals with Forks: The Triple Bottom Line of 21st Century Business*. Oxford, UK: Capstone.

Enderle, G. (2013). The capability approach as guidance for corporate ethics. In G. Luetge (Ed.), *Handbook of the Philosophical Foundations of Business Ethics* (pp. 675–90). New York: Springer.

Facca-Miess, T.M., and Santos, N.J.C. (2014). Fostering fair and sustainable marketing for social entrepreneurs in the context of subsistence marketplaces. *Journal of Marketing Management*, 30(5–6), 501–18.

Facca-Miess, T.M., and Santos, N.J.C. (2016). Assessing perceptions of the Integrative Justice Model propositions: a critical step toward operationalizing a macro model. *Journal of Macromarketing*, 36(1), 68–77.

Facca-Miess, T.M., and Santos, N.J.C. (2019). Applying the Integrative Justice Model to predict transformative impact. the case of Jesuit Worldwide Learning, Higher Education at the Margins. *Proceedings of the Annual Macromarketing Conference*. Macromarketing Society. Retrieved from http://society.macromarketing.org/assets/proceedings/2019-macromarketing-proceedings.pdf

Freeman, R.E. (1984). *Strategic Management: A Stakeholder Approach*. Boston, MA: Pitman.

Freeman, R.E., Harrison, J.S., and Wicks, A.C. (2007). *Managing for Stakeholders: Survival, Reputation, and Success*. New Haven, CT: Yale University Press.

Habash, M. (2020). Learning with students at the margins: Creighton University's pilot program with Jesuit Worldwide Learning 2017–2018. *Jesuit Higher Education: A Journal*, 9(1): Article 3.

Hamm, S. (2008). Capitalism with a human face. *BusinessWeek*, December 8, 49–53.

Karnani, A. (2007). The mirage of marketing to the bottom of the pyramid: how the private sector can help alleviate poverty. *California Management Review*, 49(4), 90–111.

Kennedy, A., and Santos, N.J.C. (2019). Social fairness and social marketing, *Journal of Social Marketing*, 9(4), 522–39

Krämer, A., and Belz, F. (2008). Consumer integration into innovation processes: a new approach for creating and enhancing innovations for the base of the pyramid? In P. Kandachar and M. Halme (Eds.), *Sustainability Challenges and Solutions at the Base of the Pyramid: Business, Technology and the Poor* (pp. 214–41). Sheffield, UK: Greenleaf Publishing.

Laczniak, G.R. (2006). Some societal and ethical dimensions of the service-dominant logic perspective of Marketing. In R.F. Lusch and S.L. Vargo (Eds.), *The Service-Dominant Logic of Marketing: Dialog, Debate, and Directions* (pp. 279–85). New York: M.E. Sharpe.

Laczniak, G.R., and Murphy, P.E. (2006). Normative perspectives for ethical and socially responsible marketing. *Journal of Macromarketing*, 26(2), 154–77.

Laczniak, G.R., and Santos, N.J.C. (2016). The Integrative Justice Model: fair, ethical, and innovative marketing to the poor. In G. Enderle and P.E. Murphy (Eds.), *Ethical Innovation in Business and the Economy* (pp. 261–80). Cheltenham, UK: Edward Elgar Publishing.

Murphy, P.E. (1999). Character and virtue ethics in international marketing: an agenda for managers, researchers, and educators. *Journal of Business Ethics*, 18(1), 107–24.

Murphy, P.E., Laczniak, G.R., and Harris, F. (2017). *Ethics in Marketing: International Cases and Perspectives*. New York: Routledge.

Murphy, P.E., Laczniak, G R., and Wood, G. (2007). An ethical basis for relationship marketing: a virtue ethics perspective. *European Journal of Marketing*, 41(1–2), 37–57.

Oxfam (2020). Half a billion people could be pushed into poverty by COVID-19. Oxfam, April 8. Retrieved April 14, 2020 from https://www.oxfamamerica.org/press/half-billion-people-could-be-pushed-poverty-covid-19/

Porter, M.E., and Kramer, M.R. (2006). Strategy and society: the link between competitive advantage and corporate social responsibility. *Harvard Business Review*, 84(12), 78–92.

Prahalad, C.K., and Ramaswamy, V. (2002). The co-creation connection. *Strategy+Business*, 27 (Second Quarter), 1–12.

Prahalad, C.K., and Ramaswamy, V. (2004a). Co-creation experiences: the next practice in value creation. *Journal of Interactive Marketing*, 18(3), 5–14.

Prahalad, C.K., and Ramaswamy, V. (2004b). *The Future of Competition: Co-creating Unique Value with Customers*. Boston, MA: Harvard Business School Pub.

Samli, A.C. (2008). *Globalization from the Bottom Up: A Blueprint for Modern Capitalism*. New York: Springer.

Santos, N.J.C. (2013). Social entrepreneurship that truly benefits the poor. *Journal of Management for Global Sustainability*, 2, 31–62.

Santos, N.J.C., and Laczniak, G.R. (2009). Marketing to the poor: an Integrative Justice Model for engaging impoverished market segments. *Journal of Public Policy & Marketing*, 28(1), 3–15.

Santos, N.J.C., and Laczniak, G.R. (2012). Marketing to the base of the pyramid: a corporate responsibility approach with case inspired strategies. *Business and Politics*, 14(1), Article 4.

Santos, N.J.C., Laczniak, G.R., and Facca-Miess, T.M. (2015). The "Integrative Justice Model" as transformative justice for base-of-the-pyramid marketing. *Journal of Business Ethics*, 126: 697–707.

Sen, A. (1999). *Development as Freedom*. Cambridge, MA: Belknap Press of Harvard University Press.

Sen, A. (2009). *The Idea of Justice*. Cambridge, MA: Belknap Press of Harvard University Press.

Sprague, C. (2007). Amanz' Abantu: water (and sanitation) for the people. United Nations Development Programme. Retrieved April 14, 2020 from http://growinginclusivemarkets.org/media/cases/SouthAfrica_AmanzAbantu_Summary.pdf

Thomas, M. (2002). Thoughts on building a just market society. *Journal of Public Affairs*, 2(2), 9–15.

United Nations (2015). Sustainable Development Goals for 2030. Retrieved January 3, 2019 from https://www.nature.com/articles/495305a

United Nations Global Compact (UNGC) (2020). Uniting business to respond to COVID-19 outbreak. Retrieved March 12, 2020 from https://www.unglobalcompact.org/news/4523-02-17-2020

Vargo, S.L., and Lusch, R.F. (2004). Evolving to a new dominant logic for marketing. *Journal of Marketing*, 68 (January): 1–17.

Vargo, S.L., and Lusch, R.F. (2006). Service-dominant logic: what it is, what it is not, what it might be. In R.F. Lusch and S.L. Vargo (Eds.), *The Service-Dominant Logic of Marketing: Dialog, Debate, and Directions* (pp. 43–56). New York: M.E. Sharpe.

Vargo, S.L., and Lusch, R.F. (2008). Service-dominant logic: continuing the evolution. *Journal of the Academy of Marketing Science*, 36 (Spring), 1–10.

Vesoulis, A. (2020). Coronavirus may disproportionately hurt the poor – and that's bad for everyone. *Time*, March 11. Retrieved March 12, 2020 from https://time.com/5800930/how-coronavirus-will-hurt-the-poor/

Further reading

Borchardt, Miriam, et al. (2019). The evolution of base of the pyramid approaches and the role of multinational and domestic business ventures: value-commitment and profit-making perspectives. *Industrial Marketing Management*. Retrieved January 29, 2020 from https://www.sciencedirect.com/science/article/pii/S0019850119300574

Dembek, K., York, J., and Singh, P.J. (2018). Creating value for multiple stakeholders: sustainable business models at the Base of the Pyramid. *Journal of Cleaner Production*, 196, 1600–12.

Gebauer, H., Haldimann, M., and Saul, C.J. (2017). Business model innovations for overcoming barriers in the base-of-the-pyramid market. *Industry and Innovation*, 24(5), 543–68.

Heuer, M.A., Khalid, U., and Seuring, S. (2020). Bottoms up: delivering sustainable value in the base of the pyramid. *Business Strategy and the Environment*, 29(3), 1605–16.

Khalid, R.U., and Seuring, S. (2019). Analyzing base-of-the-pyramid research from a (sustainable) supply chain perspective. *Journal of Business Ethics*, 155, 663–86.

Palomares-Aguirre, I., Barnett, M., Layrisse, F., and Husted, B.W. (2018). Built to scale? How sustainable business models can better serve the base of the pyramid. *Journal of Cleaner Production*, 172, 4506–13.

Prahalad, C.K. (2019). The new fortune at the bottom of the pyramid. *Strategy+Business* (Spring). Retrieved January 29, 2020 from https://www.strategy-business.com/article/The-New-Fortune-at-the-Bottom-of-the-Pyramid?gko=c5f11

10 Innovative applications for transformative justice for quality of life

Tina M. Facca-Miess

Takeaways

- The IJM is used as tool to predict TQL.
- TQL as an outcome is grounded in the voices of beneficiaries, who are often vulnerable consumers.
- Transformative justice models are an operational tool to understand the drivers of TQL.
- TQL is a more reliable outcome measure than simple quantitative measures (e.g. number served, donations distributed, etc.).

Introduction

> **Business** is a vocation, and a **noble vocation**, provided that those engaged in it see themselves challenged by a **greater meaning** in life; this will enable them truly to **serve the common good** by striving to increase the goods of this world and to make them more **accessible to all**.
>
> (Pope Francis, *Evangelii Gaudium*, §203) [author's emphasis]

It seems that business is often to blame for many of the injustices we see in the world, yet we instinctively know that trade, or economic exchange, is essential for a community's development. Students study business practice, learn business skills, and build portfolios of experiential learning projects and internships while in business school, in order to be effective business leaders in the future. Yet how do we ensure that a business is dealing in fair exchange in the marketplace? Do we consider all the people impacted by a marketer's decisions? Are students prepared to evaluate fairness in the marketplace? Moreover, are we measuring the right things?

The Integrative Justice Model (IJM) (Santos & Laczniak, 2009a) is a normative ethical framework for marketing that can be used as a tool for measuring the extent to which justice is evident in a marketplace exchange, in a business, within a supply chain, or even in a live entertainment setting. The IJM was initially designed for multinational corporations engaged in impoverished markets, but is adaptable to nonprofit organizations, non-governmental organizations (NGOs),

DOI: 10.4324/9781003188773-10

and a variety of social innovations. The IJM provides guidance for fair and ethical marketplace exchanges, particularly when engagement with impoverished or marginalized populations is involved. We will discuss applications of the IJM to predict transformation in quality of life (TQL) for beneficiaries in varied settings. These will include beneficiaries of an NGO working at the margins of society, in this case refugee camps, as well as a Syrian refugee community in northern Iraq. We will discuss applications in nonprofit settings, including two Catholic parishes, and a men's shelter funded by local Orthodox churches. The IJM is applied as a tool for strategic planning for these organizations and communities as they identify the significant predictors of transformative outcomes, based on the voices of the impoverished or marginalized beneficiaries. Lastly, an experiential learning exercise is discussed which engages students as justice auditors as they apply the IJM to their own experiences of consumption of live entertainment. While discussion of the IJM in the classroom captures student interest, an experiential learning exercise, adapted to their personal interests, namely live entertainment, facilitates application and deeper analysis of justice in marketing practices and related managerial decision-making.

The context of the IJM, and why justice in marketplace exchange matters

The IJM postulates five interrelated components that are essential for treating consumers in a fair and just manner. These are: (1) authentic engagement without exploitative intent; (2) cocreation of value; (3) investment in future consumption; (4) genuine representation of stakeholders' interests; and (5) focus on long-term profit management. These elements have been arrived at following an examination of 13 frameworks in moral philosophy, marketing theory, and management, as well as religious doctrine (see Santos & Laczniak, 2009a, 2009b, 2012). The IJM gives special consideration to the poor and marginalized because, as consumers, they are often vulnerable due to resource constraints and availability of and access to products and services (Laczniak & Santos, 2011). Marginalized people include refugees and migrants, of whom there are more than 80 million as of 2020. For a marketer, or other type of business manager, it is critical to consider the consequences of one's decisions, and the impact that business decisions have on others, particularly vulnerable consumers.

Measuring the "impact" of social innovations at the margins of society is in many ways complicated and daunting. It is important to simplify impact measurement so global social entrepreneurs and the philanthropists who support them can more readily engage in scaling their efforts in ways that work best. Policymakers can hence benefit from a common language of impact assessment, more readily producing data-driven recommendations that are supported by evidence derived from commonly understood research methods and analytical techniques. Moreover, research and analysis that is cocreated with souls at the margins ought to be more highly valued than that which includes them merely as subjects. We intentionally use the word "souls" when referring to people at the margins in an effort to highlight and underscore the human dignity intrinsic to all, and respect for which is valued by all faith traditions. It is beyond the scope of this chapter to defend the notion that respect for human dignity is the catalyst for transformation, but nonetheless we commit to this critical perspective. The amplification of the voices of impoverished consumers (Facca-Miess & Santos, 2016) is a latent construct of the IJM, and can be predictive of TQL.

What outcomes? And why "transformation in quality of life"?

Another hurdle, if not roadblock, is reaching a shared understanding of desired outcomes. We submit that the most useful outcome variable is one that measures the extent to which the marginalized consumer (subject) perceives that an intervention (program, service, etc.) has not only improved but has also *transformed* their quality of life. Santos, Laczniak and Facca-Miess (2015) argue that, at the BoP, transformative justice can only be achieved when an agency actor facilitates the "power" portion of the justice equation proposed by McMahon (1999, 2004): namely, that Rights *plus* Power = Justice. To truly facilitate and sustain this power of agency, the research work needs to become an entrepreneurial endeavor of marginalized souls so that, ultimately, they can advocate for the social change they define as being warranted in order to improve TQL in their communities.

IJM applied to the evaluation of transformative justice in an NGO

Transformative justice is served when true improvement in quality of life is assured. Such transformation can best be articulated, or described, by the beneficiary, or the individual or community, who is actually experiencing the positive transformation. In this application, the firm is an NGO that serves higher education to people in resource-constrained environments, particularly refugee camps including Kakuma, Kenya, and Dzaleka, Malawi, and in post-conflict settings such as in Sri Lanka or Afghanistan. Jesuit Worldwide Learning (JWL) serves higher education at the margins, and maintains a mission of "learning together to transform the world." This is an innovative idea, and JWL has over 10 years of experience, with 5,000 students engaged in those 10 years. But how does one measure the extent to which transformation, or impact on quality of life, is happening? The IJM is used as a framework for measuring the extent to which transformative justice is evident within the JWL stakeholder community.

Methods

Nearly 200 surveys (n = 190) were collected from stakeholders via an online survey instrument distributed as a link by the NGO to its students and alumni. Respondents evaluated each tenet of the IJM by rating their agreement with a number of questions.[1] To measure authentic engagement, for example, items such as the ones listed in Table 10.1 are recommended, with which respondents

Table 10.1 IJM survey excerpt: "Authentic Engagement"

Authentic Engagement
AE – Improving the JWL community benefits all
AE – I feel accepted within the JWL community
AE – I feel respected within the JWL community
AE – JWL respects all people for who they are
AE – JWL helps me develop in ways that affect me long-term
AE – JWL helps develop critical thinking skills
AE – JWL helps me expand my capabilities
AE – JWL tries to make it easier for me to enjoy my educational experiences
AE – I get a lot of value out of my time with JWL
AE – I am involved with the JWL community because they consider the people, our environment, and use contributions effectively
AE – JWL works to bring together the learning community and the nearby community
AE – Overall, I feel engaged with the JWL community

Value Cocreation
VCC – I have opportunities to share in JWL resources (e.g. the learning center, programs, services)
VCC – What I value aligns with what JWL values
IFC – JWL helps me develop in ways that make my life better
IFC – JWL experiences help me understand my responsibility to contribute to the good of my community
IFC – I understand the information about programs and services available to me
AVOIC – JWL advocates for its stakeholders in socio-political arenas
VCC – Overall, I feel like I am a part of creating value in my experiences with JWL

Representation of Stakeholder Interests
STK – JWL views the challenges at the margins as opportunities for innovation
VCC – The JWL community makes me feel less vulnerable
AVOIC – JWL asks for input before deciding on major program changes
AVOIC – My opinion is valued at JWL
STK – Overall JWL understands what is important to me

Community Engagement
STK – I volunteer in my community
STK – I like to engage in dialogue with my community
STK – I have worked effectively alongside community residents on a project since my time with JWL
AVOIC – I would like to partner with local organizations to leverage my expertise and goodwill

Accessible Vision
VCC It is easy to participate within the JWL community
IFC – Overall, I expect to be part of the JWL community in the future

AE = Authentic Engagement; AVOIC = amplifying the voice of the impoverished consumer; IFC = investment in future consumption; JWL = Jesuit Worldwide Learning; STK = representation of stakeholder interests; VCC = value cocreation will rate their agreement on a scale from 1 (low) to 10 (high). An opening statement is provided before each tenet to clarify what is being measured, which helps to ensure validity (i.e. you are measuring what you set out to measure). The following is an example of an opening statement and instructions:

> For an organization to be fair or just, those who participate should feel like they trust the organization and that it does not exploit anyone or put anyone at risk in any way. These questions are about your **participation (or engagement)** with [organization x] and **our long-term relationship**. To what extent do you agree with **each** of the following statements? **Rate each statement on a scale from 1 = strongly disagree to 10 = strongly agree.**

A similar introduction is repeated for the remaining tenets of the IJM, including VCC, representation of stakeholder interests (STK), investment in future consumption (IFC), and long-term sustainability, also understood as "amplifying the voice of the impoverished consumer" (AVOIC). Essentially, we perceive the key to the long-term sustainability of an organization as being the extent to which the organization authentically engages with its stakeholders (particularly the poor and/or vulnerable that are affected by the organization) to cocreate value in their exchange, with a shared long-term vision that benefits all stakeholders. One might consider these benefits to be those that facilitate the common good; that VCC with consumers respects their human dignity; that representing the interests of all stakeholders means working in collaborative solidarity with them; and that local engagement can be viewed as subsidiarity, or helping those closest first, and allowing the self-governance of small communities with common interests, rather than imposing a higher level of authority.

In Table 10.1 are the variables, or items measured that yield the most reliable responses from JWL stakeholders. They can also be adapted to suit other organizations. In Table 10.1, the IJM tenet prefaces the statement to provide clarity.[2] Factor analysis was used to isolate the most fruitful questions, where items with correlated responses "load" onto the same factor. The factor is essentially an overarching concept, such as authentic engagement, VCC, or representation of stakeholder interests. In this case, two latent factors emerge, which we name "community engagement" and "accessible vision" to reflect the theme measured with the items loading onto the factor.

The items (also called measured variables) that comprise our factors in one study will sometimes load onto a different factor in another study. This is because contexts differ. In the case of JWL, we see items that previously loaded onto our IFC (investment in future consumption) factor now loading onto the VCC factor. Keep in mind that all stakeholders are represented in the analysis; some are JWL donors, or faculty or board members, while others are students or alumni of JWL, seen as the beneficiaries. It is interesting to note that community engagement plays a prominent role in JWL's justice equation, as this is an expectation of students and alumni. Higher education at the margins is not about landing a job as much as it is about transforming your community in ways that make it better, more peaceful, healthier, and more self-sustaining. Entrepreneurial endeavors are encouraged, and many students teach at primary and secondary school level in the refugee camps. Ease of participation, or accessibility, coupled with overall expectations of being part of the organization in the future, load onto a new (latent or underlying) factor which we name "accessible vision." These items can be adapted for surveys in other contexts, but to ensure accurate measurement of the IJM, they should be changed as little as possible (e.g. just the name of the organization, slight contextual adaptations). Be sure to add an overall, or dependent, variable to each section that evaluates a tenet of the IJM (e.g. "Overall, I feel part of creating value in my experiences with [organization x]"). The independent variables, or experience-related variables, come before the dependent ones so that respondents have time to think about their experiences with the tenet of justice as applied to the organization evaluated. Be sure to use a scale from 1 (low) to 10 (high), with no midpoint, to ensure greater variation in responses (i.e. five levels of negative perceptions, from 1–5; and five levels of positive perceptions, 6–10). The added variance is especially helpful in predicting outcomes.

Analytical tools used to evaluate justice

The primary analytical tools include, naturally, descriptive statistics, means, and frequencies, to describe the data set. Pie and bar charts will suffice to graphically depict demographics and categorical questions. Next, correlation analysis should be conducted, as well as t-tests, to identify significant differences among stakeholder groups, gender, age groups, etc. Finally, multiple regression analysis (inclusive of analysis of variance, ANOVA) will identify the significant predictors, or drivers, of the desired justice outcomes. These results yield strategic, data-driven recommendations, based on stakeholder feedback. No market analysis is more powerful than that which is grounded in the voice of the consumer. A just organization considers the poorest and most marginalized first.

PRIMARY ANALYSES TO INCLUDE

- **Descriptive statistics:** To clarify the constitution of the data (demographics, mean scores, frequency of responses, etc.). Report the mean scores (averages) for all variables measured on 1–10 scales.
  - *Graphics.* Present these as bar charts. For categorical variables, report the valid percentage, which means the percentage of those who responded to the question. If these add up to 1, present in a pie chart. If respondents have the option of selecting more than one category, report in bar charts, in descending order, presenting the most common responses first, down to the least common.

- **Correlation analysis:** To note significant relationships between variables, helping to develop segment profiles (e.g. young people who are interested in accompanying a JWL student at the margins also tend to prefer to receive their communications via social media). Present the correlation coefficient with its corresponding p-value (e.g. $r = .73, p < .001$). The thresholds are as follows: .3–.4, slight correlation; .5–.6, moderate correlation; .7–.9, strong correlation.
    - *Graphics.* Depictions can include shapes with the name of the variable inside them, linked to one another with lines that imply the strength of the relationship (e.g. a dashed line for a slight correlation, a solid line for a moderate one, and a bold solid line for a strong correlation). It is advisable to include the correlation coefficient in a chart close to where these lines appear, for greater graphic clarity and ease of understanding.
- **Difference analysis.** To identify significant differences between stakeholder segments and address specific concerns, needs, or interests, use an independent samples t-test, where the test statistic $t > |2|$ indicates a significant difference between the means of two groups.[3] Validate with the corresponding p-value (<.05, <.01, <.001). Insignificant t-tests identify commonalities, suggesting opportunities for converging marketing efforts for two separate groups where no significant differences are observed between them, thus saving financial resources. Similarly, a justification for differentiated marketing messages is revealed when statistically significant differences are evident between segments: additional spending can be vindicated for two separate campaigns, each with its own messaging. In this regard, consider genders, age groups, or donors versus beneficiaries. For example, "Beneficiaries begin to deviate from other stakeholders regarding the extent to which they have opportunities to create value in their JWL experiences, where beneficiaries (students and alumni) rate the attribute significantly higher. Also, beneficiaries, as compared to other stakeholders, are significantly more likely to agree that JWL uses the ideas of students and alumni to improve their communities" (Facca-Miess & Santos, 2018).
    - *Graphics.* Compare the two groups' mean scores with a two-series bar chart, with one general topic per chart (e.g. social media preferences, Facebook, Instagram, Twitter, Snapchat, compared by two age groups, <40 and 40+).
- **Multivariate regression analysis:** used to clarify the significant drivers of stakeholder attitudes and behaviors as well as to explain the variance in outcome measures. Using the stepwise method, this analysis is most helpful in designing strategies to engage stakeholders in ways that resonate with their stakeholder group. For example, "Having opportunities to share in the resources of JWL explains the most variation in overall perceptions of VCC, and is especially predictive for beneficiaries" (Facca-Miess & Santos, 2018).
    - *Graphics.* Creativity can help here, but one suggestion is to use arrow shapes to indicate the drivers, or significant predictors, of the outcome

variables. Place the name of the variable inside the arrow along with relevant stats, including the mean, R^2, t, and its corresponding p-value.

Discussion of results

Here we analyze Jesuit Worldwide Learning: Higher Education at the Margins (JWL) through the lens of the IJM, with a special focus on TQL. While tertiary education is clearly understood as a means of facilitating employment opportunities, the organization's (i.e. JWL) focus is on developing leaders who will stay in or return to their communities as transformative leaders and change agents. Longitudinal, qualitative research is critical in assessing long-term impact, yet quantitative research methods, implemented among beneficiaries, can help the organization validate its shorter-term impact. Moreover, predictive analytics can satisfy funders that their resources are being well spent and are yielding truly transformative results.

Using an online survey tool, distributed to various JWL stakeholder groups, the tenets of the IJM are measured using items based on the decision principles outlined by Santos and Laczniak (2012), and later statistically vetted by Facca-Miess and Santos (2016). Items were adapted slightly to fit the context of the "margins": namely, refugee camps and post-conflict settings where JWL operates. Several iterations of factor analyses with data from a relatively comparable setting with marginalized, vulnerable consumers (e.g. from a homeless shelter) yielded the final items used for this study. We focus on a segment of responses, those from students and alumni (beneficiaries), to better understand the drivers behind their perceptions of the extent to which their experiences with JWL transformed their quality of life.

Each of the tenets of the IJM is assessed in a multiple regression analysis to identify the significant predictors of beneficiaries' overall rating for the tenet. For example, "Overall, I feel engaged with JWL" is the dependent variable with the various decision principles for authentic engagement with nonexploitative intent (AE) as independent variables. After building regression models for each of the tenets, inclusive of amplifying the voice of the consumer (AVOIC; see Facca-Miess & Santos, 2016), a final multiple regression model is built to identify the significant predictors of TQL. TQL is the dependent/outcome variable, and the various significant predictors of the various tenets of the IJM are independent variables. The IJM is used to evaluate the predictors of transformative justice as delivered by JWL, serving higher education at the margins. Summative highlights for each of the tenets of the IJM follow.

Authentic engagement with non-exploitative intent

In order to ensure perceptions of authentic engagement (AE), JWL needs to maintain a focus on ensuring beneficiaries feel respected. Further, it is critical that JWL explicitly and consistently considers the needs of the people in each of the communities it serves, reflective of the JWL cornerstone of "highest quality, fiscal stewardship grounded in student (and community) feedback." Community-based research is foremost on the JWL research agenda, and should ultimately be conducted by well-trained, certified, local researchers from JWL community-based organizations (CBOs).

Value cocreation

To continually increase perceptions of VCC, JWL can highlight its trust in its students by continuing to share resources (e.g. allowing tablets to be taken home for study) and by focusing on shared values among the various cultures and religious traditions served by JWL. The impact of alumni engagement at all levels cannot be underestimated, particularly given the predictive capacity of values alignment.

Representation of stakeholder interests

The extent to which beneficiaries agree that "JWL views challenges at the margins as opportunities for innovation" is the most explanatory and most significant predictor of the extent to which beneficiaries feel their interests are represented. This aligns with the JWL cornerstone of global thinking with a transformative perspective, integral to Jesuit higher education. Volunteering in one's community adds to the explanation of variance in overall perceptions that "JWL understands what is important" to its beneficiaries.

Investment in future consumption

Fascinatingly, the most significant predictor is "JWL experiences help me understand my responsibility to contribute to the good of my community," which explains over half of the variance in perceptions that JWL facilitates development that makes beneficiaries' lives better. This recognition of one's responsibility to contribute to the good of the community, coupled with the extent to which one agrees that "my experiences with JWL are worth my time spent," explain nearly 60% of the variance in perceptions that JWL makes one's life better. These predictors suggest JWL is effectively investing in the future of its beneficiaries, providing a transformative and valued higher education experience.

Amplifying the voice of the (marginalized) consumer

The extent to which beneficiaries feel their *opinion is valued* is the most significant predictor of "overall feelings that one's voice is heard at JWL." Again, a continued focus on developing training and curriculum on research methods and statistical analysis can further integrate the highest gifts of justice into JWL's offering to the marginalized. Equipped with skills in research and analysis, beneficiaries can advocate for themselves, with guidance from JWL on its advocacy efforts on behalf of stakeholders.

Transforming quality of life

Values alignment is the most significant predictor of TQL, while helping beneficiaries understand their *responsibility to contribute to their community* explains over 60% of their perceptions of JWL's ability to impact their quality of life. Programs and services *relevant to beneficiaries' needs*, coupled with perceptions that JWL views *challenges at the margins as opportunities for innovation*, completes the model. These elements should be highlighted in fundraising efforts, marketing messages, and commitments to beneficiaries. For example, when asked *how* JWL transforms quality of life for beneficiaries, it has been proven here that the organization is correct in asserting that "JWL views the challenges at the margins as opportunities for innovation by providing a values-based education, with relevant academic programs and services that instill a sense of responsibility to others and community." The IJM, applied this way, yields ample statistical evidence measuring JWL's outcomes and their impact on its beneficiaries. Further, we have identified the drivers of these outcomes and explained the impact that a focus on these drivers will have on continued improvement toward delivering transformative justice through higher education at the margins.

Case studies: applications of the IJM

Syrian refugee community, northern Iraq

In an effort to assess community peace and justice perceptions – and ultimately identify the predictors of TQL – 91 surveys were completed by Syrian refugees in the Kurdistan and Domiz regions of northern Iraq. The same analytical method is applied. First, the significant predictors of the tenets of the IJM are identified using the stepwise method in SPSS™. Then, each of these significant predictors of the varied tenets are used as independent variables to predict perceptions of TQL.

Authentic engagement with nonexploitative intent (AE)

Authentic engagement (AE), measured by "Overall, I feel engaged with my community," rated fairly low at 5.93 on a ten-point scale. AE is predicted by the extent to which community stakeholders agree that the "community **supports itself**," that they "feel **respected** within the community" and garner "**value** out of (their) **time** with the community." It is always important to note the most significant predictor of the dependent variable (outcome), which is, in this case, authentic engagement. Together, these variables explain nearly 60% of the variance in overall feeling of community engagement (R^2 = .59). Feeling

Table 10.2 Predictors of "Overall, I feel engaged with my community" (Syrian refugee data). Model is significant (F = 16.07, p <.001)

Significant predictors of authentic engagement (M = 5.93)	*Mean*	*SD*	R^2	t *statistic*	*p-value*
My community supports itself.	4.02	2.57	.42	2.04	<.05
I feel ***respected*** *within my community.*	6.85	2.80	.53	**2.30**	<.05
I get a lot of value out of my time with my community.	4.97	3.0	.59	2.13	<.05

Table 10.3 Predictors of "Overall, my community understands what is important to me." Model is significant (F = 16.92, p <.001)

Significant predictors of representation of stakeholder interests (M = 4.40)	*Mean*	*SD*	R^2	t *statistic*	*p-value*
My community is ***open to change****.*	5.89	2.91	.43	**4.47**	<.001
I have worked effectively alongside community residents on a project.	6.09	2.86	.52	2.14	<.05

respected within the community is the most significant predictor (highest t-statistic value) of respondents' perceptions of authentic engagement with nonexploitative intent. In order to increase perceptions of AE, it is important to focus on ensuring that community members feel respected, that they see the community as self-reliant, and that they value their time with the community. Table 10.2 provides the relevant statistics to validate the AE model:

$$Y_{AE} = X_{Self-reliant} + X_{Respected} + X_{Value}$$

Representation of stakeholder interests (STK)

The extent to which Syrian refugee community members agree that "Overall, my community understands what is important to me" is rated low, at 4.40. *Openness to change* and *working effectively alongside community residents on a project* are the predictors of STK. Thus, to increase perceptions of overall STK, community members should be open to change and willing to work with others on community projects (Table 10.3).

Value cocreation (VCC)

Value creation in the IJM follows the emergent thinking in the field of marketing that VCC should take place not only at the point of exchange, but also at every point of interaction between the firm and the consumer. In the IJM, a special focus is placed on the low-income consumer, consistent with the settings

Table 10.4 Predictors of "Overall, I feel like I am a part of creating value in my experiences with my community." Model is significant (F = 7.06, p <.05)

Significant predictors of value cocreation (M = 7.43)	*Mean*	*SD*	R^2	t *statistic*	*p-value*
My community makes me feel less vulnerable.	5.52	2.49	.21	**2.66**	<.05

Table 10.5 Predictors of "My community helps me develop in ways that make my life better." Model is significant (F = 7.01, p <.05)

Significant predictors of investment in future consumption (M = 7.65)	*Mean*	*SD*	R^2	t *statistic*	*p-value*
I understand the information about programs and services available to me.	6.70	2.06	.24	**2.65**	<.05

evaluated here. Among the Syrian refugees in northern Iraq, the only predictor ofVCC (rated 7.43) is the extent to which their community makes them *feel less vulnerable*. In order to impactVCC, the community needs to focus on helping its members in ways that make them feel less vulnerable (Table 10.4).

Investment in future Consumption (IFC)

Investment in future consumption (IFC) suggests that a just marketplace exchange requires an organization to work to foster social sustainability while ensuring profitability in the long run. An organization should partner with local NGOs to leverage their expertise and goodwill and network in a mutually advantageous manner. IFC is demonstrated by business policies and ethical audits (like the IJM) offering evidence that the organization, or community, considers the interests of all its stakeholders. For the Syrian refugee community, overall expectations of being part of the community in the future (7.65) are predicted solely by the extent to which community members *understand the information about programs and services available to me.* (Table 10.5). Thus, it is critical that the community shares information with all its members effectively and in a spirit of transparency in order to sustain their commitment to the community.

Amplifying the voice of the impoverished consumer (AVOIC)

As noted previously, amplifying the voice of the impoverished consumer is a latent construct of the IJM, consistently evident in humanitarian, nonprofit-type settings (e.g. JWL, a men's shelter, Catholic parish outreach programs). An overall feeling that one's voice is heard in the community (AVOIC) is very

Table 10.6 Predictors of "Overall, I feel my voice is heard in my community." Model is significant (F= 110.16, p <.001)

Significant predictors of amplifying voices of impoverished consumers (M = 3.96)	*Mean*	*SD*	R^2	t *statistic*	*p-value*
My ***talents are valued*** *by my community.*	3.76	2.15	.84	**9.26**	<.001
I feel like I have an ownership stake in my community.	5.21	2.80	.92	4.48	<.001

low on the ten-point scale, at merely 3.96. The predictors are feeling like one's *talents are valued* (3.76) and feeling like one has an *ownership stake* in one's community (5.21) (Table 10.6). It is important to note that feeling one's talents are valued explains 84% of the variance in perceptions that one's voice is heard. Programs that develop and value community members' talents, coupled with ensuring that people feel they have an ownership stake in the community, can substantially impact perceptions that their voices are heard.

Predicting transformation in quality of life (TQL)

Once the significant predictors of each of the tenets of the IJM are identified, we move to building the TQL model. Each of the predictors are regressed on ratings for the overall extent to which *my community has transformed my quality of life.* In the Syrian refugee case, only one variable of all the predictors identified is significantly predictive of TQL. The extent to which community members feel like they *have an ownership stake in the community* explains 53% of the variance in TQL. The predictive capacity (t = 4.77) is highly significant at $p < .001$, as is the model (Table 10.7). Thus, it is critical that the community focuses on collaborative programs and services to ensure members feel like they have an ownership stake or responsibility to the common good of the community. This focus on a shared commitment to the community is the key to transforming quality of life for the Syrian refugee community in northern Iraq.

Further, note that the concept of subsidiarity is also a predictor of TQL in the Syrian community studied here. In Catholic social teaching, subsidiarity is an organizing principle which suggests that local matters ought to be handled at a local level to the extent possible, rather than by a centralized authority. In the context of this survey, subsidiarity is measured as agreement with "All community members focus on helping others (subsidiarity)." The low mean score (5.52) suggests opportunity for more collaborative community engagement, grounded in the predictors of justice as summarized in Table 10.8.

Given that community members need to feel an ownership stake in the community in order to experience transformation in their quality of life, we focus on the predictors of justice to drive such transformation. In other words,

Table 10.7 Predictors of "Overall extent to which my community has transformed my quality of life." Model is significant (F = 22.75, p <.001)

Significant predictors of transformation in quality of life (M = 5.20)	*Mean*	*SD*	R^2	t statistic	*p-value*
I feel like I have an ownership stake in my community.	5.21	2.40	.53	**4.77**	<.001

Table 10.8 Significant predictors of the tenets of integrative justice for Syrian refugee community (most significant predictors for tenet bolded)

Authentic engagement	*Representation of stakeholder interests*	*Value cocreation*	*Investment in future consumption*	*Amplifying voices of impoverished consumers*
My community supports itself.	*My community is **open to change**.*	*My community makes me feel **less vulnerable**.*	*I understand the **information** about programs and services available to me.*	*My **talents are valued** by my community.*
*I feel **respected** within my community.*	*I have worked effectively alongside community residents on a project.*			*I feel like I have an ownership stake in my community.*
I get a lot of value out of my time with my community.				

we articulate *how* the community can implement TQL. For example, a shared vision statement for the community, based on the predictors of integrative justice, could be as follows:

> Our community respects its members for their talents, and values their contributions. We work together on projects, with an openness to change and transparency, so all feel less vulnerable, and derive value and a feeling of ownership from their commitment to our community.

American men's homeless shelter

St. Herman House is a men's shelter that provides temporary shelter, meals, clothing, and transitional shelter and services to local men. The shelter is managed by FOCUS North America, a national movement of Orthodox Christians "united in faith and joined by a desire to provide action-oriented and sustainable solutions to poverty in communities across America," with churches in the greater Cleveland, Ohio, USA area.[4] Volunteers flow steadily from local high schools and churches, and the "House" exudes a captivating spirit of peace and justice. Here we summarize findings from our research for strategic planning. The survey tool is based on the IJM, and is grounded in the voices of the primary stakeholders of the House: the men served and those serving.

Stakeholder research conclusions

Ratings for St. Herman's engagement with stakeholders in decision-making are low. It is important to continue to engage stakeholders, particularly residents and meal guests in the strategic planning process. Overall, stakeholders expect to be part of the community in the future and feel their experiences are affordable, accessible, and available. Stakeholders strongly agree that they are happier when serving others, and they see outreach as a way of living their faith. Two faith-based activities are highly encouraged: privately praying for others, and prayer before meals. Visioning and planning for the future are key to transformation. It is important to focus on the future, on personal development, on creating a shared vision, and on celebrating shared outcomes. Stakeholders are in favor of treating one another equally, and with kindness (i.e. with respect for others' dignity). Stakeholders envision skills training and the marketing of St. Herman's services. There is clear potential for entrepreneurship training and promotion of the House.

Elements of a transformative justice model: key areas of strategic focus for TQL

The most influential transformative elements reflective of Catholic social teaching (CST) include working toward the common good, and making sure there are options for the poor and vulnerable. VCC is predicted by the extent to which stakeholders have the opportunity to create a more valuable experience for themselves at St. Herman House. The beneficiaries place prominence on the dignity of work and want to collaborate with the neighborhood community, particularly on safety in the neighborhood. They are interested in participating in spiritual development (e.g. retreats, speakers, direction). In order to feel their voices are heard, they must have enough opportunities to share their ideas with the leaders at St. Herman. In order to maintain the beneficiaries' engagement and build a long-term relationship, St. Herman must work to bring together the House community and the neighborhood community. To ensure stakeholders' interests are represented, beneficiaries should be encouraged to engage in dialogue with neighborhood residents. With regard to investing in the future together, beneficiaries need to feel that St. Herman helps them develop in ways that make their life better. In order to ensure they feel their voices are amplified, the shelter community must value each individual's opinion.

Catholic inner-city parish

In this case, the IJM is applied to a Catholic parish, St. Peter, in the inner city of Cleveland, Ohio, USA. The IJM is used as a framework for strategic planning aimed at sustaining and developing the parish community. Highlights from the study and strategic recommendations, based on the voices of stakeholders, are discussed.[5]

Predicting authentic engagement

To increase parishioners' and frequent visitors' perceptions of authentic engagement, all people need to feel *respected* and *accepted*. Given that male respondents are significantly more likely to feel that St. Peter helps develop their faith long-term, it is recommended to design outreach initiatives that engage men as leaders in neighborhood outreach activities, and mentors to men in need.

Predicting representation of stakeholder interests

To increase perceptions that stakeholder interests are represented, develop *relevant programs and services* based on stakeholders' needs. Provide ample opportunity for sharing ideas with parish leaders.

Predicting value cocreation

To increase parishioners' perceptions of VCC, it is critical that, when an individual contributes, they are made to feel that their *offering is valued*. This is essential for all types of contributions, including nonfinancial resources such as service to the church or neighborhood.

Predicting future consumption

To increase parishioners' and frequent visitors' expectations of being part of the parish's future, focus on ensuring that they feel they have an *ownership stake*. Create multiple *opportunities to share ideas* with parish leadership (e.g. community forums, surveys, follow-up discussions). Welcome and engage all stakeholders in the implementation of strategic initiatives. Potential parishioners (locals not currently engaged in the parish community) were also surveyed. To increase the likelihood of participation in the parish, be sure that the *availability of programs and services* is clearly articulated (e.g. social media to attract those under 40). The extent to which people feel the parish offers opportunities for *personal* (e.g. spiritual) *development* also drives interest. Programs offering opportunities for personal development should be created and clearly communicated to younger adults via social media.

Assessing perceptions regarding Catholic social thought (CST)

Perceptions regarding social justice as well as various tenets of CST were recorded among parishioner stakeholders and locals identified as potential parishioners, and evaluated by age. To increase perceptions of the overall importance of social justice, it is recommended to focus on programs or opportunities that increase understanding of the *right to political participation*. Further, increasing the extent to which *solidarity* resonates, will increase the community's perspectives of the overall importance of *social justice*. Note that young adults (under 30) are significantly less interested in *human rights*. Senior adults (56+) rate the resonance of varied tenets of CST significantly higher than their younger counterparts. This supports the idea of intergenerational projects to familiarize younger adults with challenges and social injustices regarding the *dignity of work*, *options for the poor and vulnerable*, *human rights*, *call to community*, *and respect for human dignity*. Experiential learning opportunities are most effective for younger adults.

To increase perceptions of the extent to which service deepens one's faith, it is essential to recognize that *outreach is a way that faith is lived*. Increasing service in the form of outreach will, in turn, deepen one's faith. Younger respondents, under 40, are more likely to *want to be more involved* than they currently are.

Predicting engagement in parish life

While attending mass is still the primary predictor of engagement, offering opportunities for *religious education* can have a significant impact on engagement in parish life. Further, offering opportunities to participate in *administrative* duties can enhance overall likelihood to engage. Although interest is currently mediocre, a focus on these two types of involvement can significantly increase engagement.

Predicting perceptions of living the mission

Respondents rated the extent to which they felt the parish is living the mission of the Catholic Church. To increase perceptions that the parish is doing this, focus on ensuring that all stakeholders *feel engaged* with the parish community. In turn, feelings of engagement are predicted by ensuring all people *feel accepted* and that they *feel respected* for who they are.

Summary of strategic recommendations

Revitalize St. Peter Parish as "a poor church for the poor." Currently, the parishioner base is well educated (60% having graduate degrees). CST resonates, yet involvement with poor and/or vulnerable stakeholders is limited. Utilize current resources (passionate parishioners) as collaborative leaders to attract young adults to "service in the city." Create opportunities for solidarity with the unchurched and the poor. Design intergenerational projects to familiarize younger adults with challenges and social injustices regarding *dignity of work*, *options for the poor and vulnerable*, *human rights*, *call to community*, and *respect for human dignity*.

Implementation insights include the following. Experiential learning opportunities are most effective for younger adults. Younger respondents are significantly more likely to feel part of creating value in their experiences at St. Peter Parish. Men are significantly more likely to agree that St. Peter Parish develops their faith with long-term effects; to feel their contributions are valued; and to trust St. Peter as a long-term partner. Social media is critical in reaching young adults and motivating engagement in service.

It is recommended to present CST as a framework for spiritual development through service, using concepts of *solidarity*, *human dignity*, and *call to community*. Focused workshops should also develop the less-understood concepts of *responsibility to peace in the world, rights of workers, care for creation and the environment, options for the poor and vulnerable*, and working toward the *common good*. Use tenets of the IJM as a guiding framework for engaging with the poor or marginalized, namely: (1) authentic engagement with nonexploitative intent, (2) VCC, (3) representation of stakeholder interests, (4) investment in future consumption, and (5) long-term financial sustainability. All effective strategies need to be grounded in the voices of, and with the involvement of, the parish community stakeholders.

Collaborative leadership is critical in developing the parish community. Create opportunities for collaboration on programs (e.g. with campus district partners, with the John Carroll University [JCU] Center for Service and Social Action, the Jesuit Volunteer Corps, or Inspired Foresight, LLC). Nurture a climate of acceptance and respect for all. Express gratitude for all contributions (including the nonfinancial, particularly when engaging with young adults). Create a culture of transformative justice. Recall that Rights + Power – Justice, and be the power-broker – the agency. Use the IJM as a measurement tool. Seek opportunities to engage in social enterprise with neighborhood partners, particularly the impoverished and marginalized. Utilize the expertise of suburban parish partners and engage them in service in the city. Use JCU marketing students and MA in nonprofit administration students as resource partners. Measure and monitor effects based on quality of life improvements versus quantity served, as reported and defined by parishioners, outreach volunteers, outreach beneficiaries, and neighborhood partners. Collaborate with these stakeholders to create metrics for measuring and monitoring quality of life improvements delivered by St. Peter Parish initiatives.

Reporting and presentation

Analyses should be presented in a concise and digestible PowerPoint or Google Slides format that is easily understood at all stakeholder levels and backgrounds. Analysis should include strategic recommendations for implementing a smooth transition that inspires a shared vision based on stakeholder feedback and interests.

Practical lessons learned

Prepare questions to allow your analyses to work (e.g. mutually exclusive questions; only ask one question at a time). Use a scale of 1–10, thereby allowing no midpoint for mediocrity. For example, if we rate from 1 to 5, then "1" and "5" are extremes indicating hyper-dissatisfaction or super-satisfaction and "3" means nothing (neutral), leaving us with just "2" (negative) and "4" (positive); in this case we might well have just asked for a response of either yes or no, and we have not learned much. With a ten-point scale there is no neutral, meaningless, midpoint, and there are five degrees of negative and five degrees of positive. A higher variance, or variety of responses, allows a higher-level statistical analysis, such as multiple regression analysis or analysis of variance (ANOVA).

Let the client, or firm leaders, or NGO directors' staff distribute the survey. Create a link and have them do the emailing, posting, etc. They thereby maintain the privacy of their contact list, absolving the researcher of such concerns. Conduct a purposive sampling, in that the survey is sent to those with a vested interest in the aims of the organization. Permit snowball sampling, whereby one respondent might send the link to another potential respondent whose voice they recommend be heard.

Prepare slides for presentation with enough data to support your findings when questioned. Prepare a few bullet points to offer a brief narrative about the graphics depicted on the slide. Be sure the presentation can stand on its own without your input. Assume the person(s) you present to will want to share your presentation with others. Will they understand it if you are not there to explain the analysis?

Conclusion

The IJM provides a framework, applicable in varied business disciplines, but particularly marketing, with which to consider the impact of managerial or marketing decisions on others. These "others" include *all* stakeholders, with a particular emphasis on the poor or marginalized who are considered vulnerable consumers. Moreover, the IJM can be used to predict the extent to which an organization is transforming quality of life for its stakeholders.

Collecting and amplifying the attitudes, behaviors, and concerns of vulnerable consumers is essential if an organization is to be socially responsible for its actions, often framed as "business decisions." Of course, reaching these consumers is a challenge, but the internet is a key resource in achieving this. In Africa, for example, more people have cell phones than electricity. Solar solutions abound. Marketer immersions into the supply chain field are critical in gathering the data necessary to make just business decisions. Take hard-copy surveys with you if need be, but most often you can take a laptop or smartphone and work with respondents to collect your data. People may be poor, but, more often than not, they are more innovative, more industrious, and more peaceful than those with more financial resources. Comparing their voices with those of your other stakeholders can be particularly enlightening for your corporate firm, nonprofit organization, or NGO.

Creating products and services that fulfill the most pressing needs of the global marketplace takes precedence over developing repetitive, mimicked, unsustainable products and services that yield overconsumption, debt, and unsustainable futures. Each of us has a role to play in working toward the common good by using our education to serve others. When we work with respect for the human dignity of each person affected by our decisions, we can expect more just outcomes that transform society in ways that enhance the common good, benefiting all. Thus, our vocations as business leaders are noble vocations.

Extra discussion questions

Small-group discussions about each of the following questions can be followed by short, informal presentations to others on the course to generate further discussion and engagement.

1 When you engage with a product or service, how do you personally determine if the engagement is authentic? Do you feel like you are part of the brand by wearing it, using it, or promoting it? How do marketers of the products or services you purchase encourage authentic engagement with you?
2 Have you ever been part of cocreating value in an exchange? Consider your insights from something in which you recognize your part (e.g. your team, your band, your project work group, etc.). What might that cocreation look like between a product or service you are marketing and its consumers?
3 Think about the groups in which you are a stakeholder? Are your interests represented? How? Do other stakeholders understand what is important to you? Develop examples as a small group and present to others in the class.
4 Consider the marketer's role in the cases discussed. Who are the varied stakeholder groups to be evaluated? What should the just marketer be watching carefully?

Experiential learning exercise: IJM and the experience of consuming live entertainment

This (three-page) essay will focus on your application of the IJM to an experience of consuming live entertainment. You will want to review materials on the IJM prior to your experience. Use the IJM framework to evaluate the extent to which the live entertainment experience delivers a fair exchange of value to you, the consumer. In your essay be sure to provide your rating for each tenet of the IJM on a scale of 1 to 10 and explain why you rated each variable the way that you did. Your essay should persuade the reader that you (the marketing expert) have evaluated the "fairness" or justice delivered with regard to the experience.

Notes

1 While it is beyond the scope of this chapter to discuss the analytical methods behind the choice of questions, see Santos and Laczniak (2012) and Facca-Miess and Santos (2016) for further clarification about the development of the IJM.
2 For a thorough discussion on IJM item (i.e. question) selection, see Facca-Miess and Santos (2016).
3 Levene's F-test for equality of variances between the groups offers increased accuracy and is produced within an independent samples t-test output accessible in IBM SPSS™.
4 https://sainthermans.org/
5 Statistical evidence is available on request; write tfacca@jcu.edu.

References

Facca-Miess, T.M. and Santos, N.J.C. (2016). Assessing perceptions of the Integrative Justice Model propositions: a critical step toward operationalizing a macro model. *Journal of Macromarketing,* 36(1) (March), 68–77.

Facca-Miess, T.M., and Santos, N.J.C. (2018). Measuring Impact at the Margins: Applying the Integrative Justice Model to Predict Transformative Impact. Working Paper.

Laczniak, G.R., and Santos, N.J.C. (2011). The Integrative Justice Model for marketing to the poor: an extension of S-D Logic to distributive justice and macromarketing. *Journal of Macromarketing,* 31(2), 135–47.

McMahon, T.F. (1999). Transforming justice: a conceptualization. *Business Ethics Quarterly*, 9(4), 593–602.

McMahon, T.F. (2004). *Ethical Leadership through Transforming Justice.* Lanham, MD: University Press of America.

Santos, N.J.C., and Laczniak, G.R. (2009a). "Just" markets from the perspective of Catholic Social Teaching. *Journal of Business Ethics*, 89 (supplement 1), 29–38.

Santos, N.J.C., and Laczniak, G.R. (2009b). Marketing to the poor: an Integrative Justice Model for engaging impoverished market segments. *Journal of Public Policy & Marketing*, 28(1), 3–15.

Santos, N.J.C. and Laczniak, G.R. (2012). Marketing to the Base of the Pyramid: a corporate responsibility approach with case inspired strategies. *Business and Politics,* 14(1), 1–42.

Santos, N.J.C., Laczniak, G.R., and Facca-Miess, T.M. (2015). The "Integrative Justice Model" as transformative justice for Base-of-the-Pyramid marketing. *Journal of Business Ethics,* 126, 697–707.

Appendix: explanation of terms used in statistical analysis

Term	*Definition*	*Regression steps in SPSS™*	*Form or test statistic*	*Application to measuring impact at the margins*
Multivariate regression analysis	Analytical test used to create predictive model	From the ribbon select *Analyze → Regression → Linear → Stepwise* *Use "stepwise" method to identify only statistically significant predictors*	$Y = X_1 + X_{2...} + X_n$	Use to understand *why* or *how* a desired outcome is happening; identify variables that increase likelihood of desired outcome
Scale	Respondent's rating scale for each measured variable; use 1 = low to 10 = high, no midpoint, usually no additional explanatory words required	In online survey form (Qualtrics™ recommended) use ten-point scale; radial bubbles or dropdown for mobile device displays	*Xbar*; mean score, average for each measured variable	Respondent rating scales 1 = low to 10 = high to ensure variation in responses; no midpoint
Outcome variable	Variable measured on a scale; outcome to be predicted; desired outcome to be achieved by increasing scores on significant predictors	Select from variable list and enter as sole *dependent* variable	*Y*, dependent, or outcome variable	E.g. variable that measures the extent to which the program or intervention transformed respondent's quality of life
Predictors	Independent "experience-related" variables that have potential to explain variance in and predict desired outcome	Select from variable list and enter as *independent* variables	$X_1 + X_{2...} + X_n$	Predictive model works best when experience-related variables (*xs*) are evaluated consecutively, followed by outcome variable or overall perception (*y*) of topic, program, intervention being evaluated

(continued)

Term	*Definition*	*Regression steps in SPSS™*	*Form or test statistic*	*Application to measuring impact at the margins*
Significant predictors	Each significant predictor explains a portion of the variation in ratings for the dependent (outcome) variable and is predictive of outcome	Identified first in output, these are the variables on which to focus in order to increase probability of desired outcome	$t \geq +/- 2.0$, each with a p-value of <.05, .01, or .001	E.g. significant predictors of TQL for JWL students include the extent to which JWL (1) helps me understand my responsibility to my community, (2) values alignment, (3) relevant programs and services, (4) views challenges as opportunities for innovation
Variance explained	Analyzing variation in ratings for outcome	Output under model summary; cumulative, each significant predictor adding to total variance explained	R^2 for each significant predictor; report total variance explained	Percentage of variance in dependent/outcome variable explained by each of the predictors
Total variance explained	Cumulative total of variance in dependent variable (Y) explained by set of significant predictors	Output under model summary; use final R^2 which is total variance explained	Final R^2; includes variance explained by combination of all significant predictors	Percentage of variance in dependent variable explained by all significant predictors together; e.g. (R^2 = .72), "Together these variables explain over 70% of variance in [outcome variable]"

Most significant predictor	Significant predictor with strongest potential to predict/drive outcome	Output under coefficients; use final model inclusive of all significant predictors	Highest $t \geq \pm 2.0$, validate with p-value <.05, .01, or .001	Not necessarily the first significant predictor in the model, but the one with the highest t statistic. Should be the primary area of focus because it has the most impact on ratings for the dependent variable. It is the most predictive of the outcome.
Model significance	Significance of the model including all variables identified as significant predictors	Output under ANOVA table; use final F stat which includes all significant predictors	F, with corresponding p-value	Confidence in the predictive model itself
Transformation	Substantial change in perceptions, worldview, quality of life, either for self or others but must be *self-reported*	Select as dependent variable to be predicted	Y_{Trans}	Self-reported on 1–10 scale by respondent; e.g. extent to which program helps me improve others' lives

Part 4

Implications for a broader societal perspective for challenge-driven transformation practice

11 Marketing ethics and corporate social responsibility for a broader societal perspective

Patrick E. Murphy and Gene R. Laczniak

Takeaways

- Essential to nurturing "fair" and sustainable exchange in the global marketplace is the ideal of *ethical marketing*. Ethical marketing is *normative*: that is, "prescriptive" in its recommendations.
- The distinction between *marketing ethics* (ME) and *corporate social responsibility* (CSR) in marketing is important because each concept typically has a distinct focus within the firm. ME addresses the behavior of managers in the organization while CSR is targeted primarily at the policy level of the corporation.
- Stakeholder theory (ST) has too often become associated with managing trade-offs among various parties connected with the organization: employees, suppliers, customers, etc. "Hard form" ST advocates putting the stakeholder focus at the societal level and considering its systemic effects.
- Unilever, while not perfect, is an example of a large MNC that has been innovatively proactive in its thinking about sustainable and responsible business practices.

Introduction

This chapter is about the basic considerations inherent in the creation and maintenance of fair and effective market exchange. It embraces as one of its foundations the major guidelines published by the United Nations Global Compact (i.e. their Principles for Responsible Management Education (PRME) and the UN Sustainable Development Goals (SDGs)), which are designed to motivate enlightened business practice. In particular, we focus on SDG #12, which requires responsible organizations to "Ensure sustainable consumption and production patterns." Since all the SDGs are treated at length in the overview of this book and in subsequent chapters, we raise them only briefly here to underscore that they serve as foundational principles that should guide responsible business worldwide. We concur that the major themes of this volume – sustainability, innovation, and transformation – are all contributory to successful

DOI: 10.4324/9781003188773-11

business enterprises in the 21st century. These ideas will be woven throughout this chapter and we envision our contribution helping to set the theoretical "stage" for the more pragmatic chapters in this volume.

This chapter covers four major areas. First, we briefly define and discuss the *normative* theories that underpin marketing ethics. Second, we elaborate on the important difference between *marketing ethics* and *corporate social responsibility*. Third, since *stakeholder theory* is one of the pivotal concepts for both these areas, we propose an aggressive, "hard form," version of this perspective. Finally, we utilize a case study of Unilever to illustrate the importance of both CEO leadership as well as the application of ethical and sustainable marketing to the three themes of this anthology. As subsequent references will make clear, this chapter draws on multiple articles that we have published on connected topics over the past 45 years. Several of them simply will be referenced as "L&M" followed by the year of publication. Readers are encouraged to consult these publications for further details and citations regarding the topics addressed. The emergent reality behind all our remarks is that innovative, sustainable business practices that transform society are unlikely to occur unless they are based on an ethical and responsible business system.

Theoretical foundations of marketing ethics

We begin with a commentary about marketing ethics because sustainable business practices become nearly impossible without fair and ethical exchange. Since marketing ethics (ME) has had multiple interpretations over the years, we proposed a workable definition in our writings almost three decades ago. We stated that "Marketing Ethics is defined as *the systematic study of how moral standards are applied to marketing decisions, behaviors, and institutions*" (L&M, 1993, p. x). We continue to endorse this *descriptive* definition of ME. But the subdiscipline of marketing ethics draws on both positive (descriptive) and normative (prescriptive) components. Thus, more recently, we promulgated a *normative*, proactive, and idealized definition of ethical marketing (EM):

> *Ethical marketing* (EM) refers to the practices that emphasize transparent, trustworthy, and responsible personal and/or organizational marketing policies and actions that exhibit integrity as well as fairness to consumers and other stakeholders.
>
> (Murphy, Laczniak, & Harris, 2017, p. 5)

The latter definition spells out the pathway for marketing to be truly ethical. And, to fully understand the nature of "ethical marketing," it is necessary to discuss the abstract components: transparency, trust, responsibility, and integrity. Obviously, ethical marketing consists of far more than good intentions. There are, unfortunately, numerous instances where firms practice *unethical* marketing, such as the price gouging that occurred in the sale of ventilators and personal protective equipment (e.g. masks) during the recent COVID-19 global pandemic.

Four major philosophical ethical theories undergird the field of normative marketing ethics. They are: *consequences-based theories*, which say that marketing decisions are ethical or unethical exclusively based on whether they produce good or bad outcomes (e.g. utilitarianism); *duty-based theories*, which state that intentions or motivations (not outcomes) are what determines whether a marketing action is ethical (e.g. Kant's categorical imperative); *contract-based theories*, which propose that companies should fashion a hypothetical contract with their stakeholders and the broader society (e.g. Rawlsian "justice as fairness"); and the *ethics of virtue*, which focuses on the decider and his/her moral character rather than on the particulars of a decision. (These theories and the literature in marketing ethics supporting them are further explained and can be consulted in L&M, 2019.)

Normative marketing ethics can inform marketing practice on several levels. Among those identified by L&M (2019) that are discussed in both this chapter and throughout this volume are sustainable consumption and marketing, the interface between corporate social responsibility (CSR) and marketing ethics, the indispensability of a stakeholder orientation, and "base of the pyramid" issues that address the special obligations to the disadvantaged. In sum, a theoretical and normative perspective can prove to be quite useful in examining a host of pragmatic issues facing business practitioners trying to create a sustainable and better society. Why? Ethical theory provides a roadmap for judging whether particular practices are ethical or unethical, sustainable or not, responsible or damaging to society, etc. Ethical theory helps establish whether particular organizational practices are good or bad for the commonweal, what the intention of economic actors might have been, and whether they were guided by a defensible framework in their selection of tactics and strategies.

The distinction between ME and CSR

There are some important differences between ME and CSR. We raise this point because the distinction has some pragmatic value for managers seeking business applications that are more sustainable. Most scholars and practitioners recognize that the two concepts – ME and CSR in marketing – are related and somewhat intertwined. However, they are not synonymous. Both ME and *ethical marketing* have been defined and discussed above. ME, always important, is more focused on the managerial level. It presumes that moral, "ethically aware" managers will make better decisions for the long-run health of the organization. CSR in marketing is concerned to a greater degree with a company's operational procedures and policies that affect the external environment. CSR encompasses marketing's obligation to all stakeholders to "fairly" integrate their claims with the firm's moral and legal duties to all its constituencies, including society. Similar to ME, CSR contains both positive and normative components. But we see CSR as inherently a normative concept since, as its name implies, certain societal obligations of marketing and business extend beyond basic fiduciary duties to shareholders. In fact, we and a coauthor (Murphy, Oberseder, & Laczniak, 2013) propose corporate *societal* responsibility as a superior term (to corporate *social* responsibility) because it captures this broader stance.

In L&M, 2014, we lay out in some detail the similarities and differences between ME and CSR and offer four major observations about these two concepts. While theoretical in nature, the observations have considerable utility in helping managers visualize an innovative path that might lead to responsible business practice. Below we summarize them and tie each to a few of the themes of this volume.

The first observation is a corollary of the *proportionality principle.* Davis (1960) proposed the *iron law of responsibility,* which says that social responsibility should be proportional to the economic power of the actor. Thus, the greater the power of an organization, the higher the level of responsibility it should exercise. As we will discuss later, Unilever, a major multinational corporation (MNC), should embrace and pursue sustainability with greater vigor (which the firm has done) than a smaller regional firm with fewer economic resources. Walmart (another huge MNC) has also touted sustainability in the last decade, especially with its construction of environmentally compatible facilities and offering many newer and more sustainable products in the stores. However, the firm's checkered past in dealing with suppliers and low pay for its many employees has somewhat undermined this effort (Gunther, 2006). Another large firm with a history of controversy, Coca-Cola, inspired by the UN Sustainable Development Goals (SDGs), has pledged to seek 100% water replenishment in its operations and to fully implement "zero waste packaging" by 2025 (Kent 2012).

The second observation regarding CSR is that the adoption of a *stakeholder orientation* is critical to fostering ethical decision-making in socially responsible organizations. We address stakeholders in more detail in the next section, but it should be noted here that firms have too often examined stakeholders through mainly a cost–benefit lens. As we argue later, this is a myopic, dysfunctional perspective that thwarts real innovation. One point that relates to stakeholders and sustainability, a viewpoint we hope is now changing, is that few firms have historically stipulated *future* generations as stakeholders to be considered in current marketing decisions with environmental impact (Murphy, 2005). As we discuss in the Unilever case study below, such a broadened stance toward the environment will require both innovative metrics and transformational thinking at many levels of the organization.

The third observation pertains to the *social contract* used to implement marketing strategies. What is required for ethical and socially responsible marketing under this "contract-based" approach is an examination of *distributive justice.* The analysis requires a determination of whether the benefits and burdens of market exchange systems are fairly allocated among stakeholders (L&M, 2008), with special consideration given to those groups that are most vulnerable. Regarding environmental damage, Pope Francis (2015) and others have forcefully argued that stakeholders in the developing world are impacted much more severely than many individuals and businesses in the more affluent areas. Similarly, the ramifications of COVID-19 have harmed the poor and vulnerable (i.e. those who are older, impoverished, minorities and/or having underlying conditions) more seriously than the rest of society. One of the chapters in this volume (Santos & Laczniak, 2021) proposes a framework that helps management focus on the special needs of vulnerable consumers.

The fourth observation states that marketing firms and their managers who desire to practice EM and CSR should follow the *stewardship principle*, thereby taking a longer-term and more sustainable perspective than other companies. The stewardship principle states that everyone, including corporations, has the responsibility to care for the earth. The principle has its moral grounding in both theological and philosophical literatures (Pontifical Council, 2005). A good illustration of the embrace of stewardship is Costco (the large US-based retailer). One of its founders, Jim Sinegal, stated that he is managing the business to be in operation for at least the next 50–60 years. The company has also been on the forefront in fighting climate change, in that 95% of its Kirkland (store) brand paper products have been certified by the Forest Stewardship Council or the Sustainable Forestry Initiative (Ward, 2019).

In other writings, two additional concepts (L&M, 2014) that relate to EM and CSR are the *common good* and *hyper-norms*. Both require a multi-stakeholder focus and a broad vision of marketing's role in society; thus, these two ideas have the potential to be transformational in how an organization perceives its mission. The "common good" is the focus of a recent anthology (Murphy & Sherry, 2014) which addresses sustainable and ethical marketing in several of its chapters. By extension, the common good follows the *societal marketing concept* (Kotler, 1972). The general idea is that, as most people live in community, the rules of social action (including economic actions) should be of benefit to the society. One chapter in the referenced text (Wilkie & Moore, 2014) examines the multitude of ways in which marketing contributes to positive societal impact. Another (Nahser, 2014) discusses the "Great Lakes Commons" and illustrates how the five "great fresh water lakes" have a significant influence on the biosphere of seven US states and two provinces in Canada "with interconnected systems of civil, social, economic and environmental resources" (p. 145).

"Hyper-norms" are guiding values that are both fundamental and universal. Conducting a content analysis of six well-known codes of global codes of conduct, Laczniak and Kennedy (2011) found that three hyper-norms emerged: (1) a comprehensive *stakeholder orientation* motivated by the centrality of human dignity; (2) a commitment to *sustainable business practices* that includes both protection of the physical environment as well as a dedicated effort to ongoing local operations; and (3) an *authentic compliance* that involves adherence to the letter *and* spirit of the law, including a demonstrated advocacy against bribery and corruption in business practice. The identification of such hyper-norms helps refute the mistaken notion that, because global business cultures and markets are very diverse, one cannot expect to find universal ethical norms for responsible economic behavior.

Stakeholder theory and marketing

Although stakeholders have been mentioned several times already in this chapter, we would like to spell out in more detail our conception of this widely used and important term. Indeed, as the logic chain of this narrative indicates, whether one is discussing business ethics, corporate social responsibility, sustainable business practice, or innovative economic approaches, the notion of *stakeholders* is a common denominator. Since its early examination by Freeman (1984), the ethics and CSR literature has argued for going beyond the traditional constituents of stockholders, customers, employees, and suppliers and viewing other groups as legitimate stakeholders, including distributors, the host community, and society. In fact, recently, the Business Roundtable, a long-standing association of corporate CEOs, added "serving all stakeholders" (e.g. customers, employees, suppliers, communities, and shareholders) as one of the basic purposes of business corporations (Business Roundtable, 2019). Marketing scholars also have been paying increasing attention to stakeholders, evidenced by a special issue of the *Journal of Public Policy & Marketing* (2010), which featured ten articles addressing the strategic value of a stakeholder orientation. Our (L&M, 2012) general conclusion was that the bulk of the articles conceived of stakeholders from a *micro-managerial* and mostly utilitarian perspective. From a societal point of view, that is not necessarily a good thing.

We advocate an innovative "hard form" of stakeholder management (SM) with three characteristics: (a) it is normative and aspirational in its ethical standards; (b) it is *macro* in orientation rather than firm-centric; and (c) it promotes greater engagement with external stakeholders beyond the traditional ones. The creation of transformational change in the business environment requires the constant review of stakeholder impact, broadly envisioned.

The first characteristic of SM implies ethical mandates requiring managers to come to grips with negative societal outcomes (Laczniak, 2017). For example, environmental degradation caused by mining companies would necessitate timely determination, clean-up, and restoration of any damaged native habitats. Second, "hard form" stakeholder theory's macro (system) orientation questions a micro (firm-centric) strategy. This means that firms ought *not* to embrace stakeholder theory merely because it brings economic advantage. If stakeholder theory is used merely because (for example) treating employees well reduces employee turnover, such a rationale is micro and instrumental. The recent pandemic in the US (and worldwide) has brought into focus not only working conditions, but also ignorance of the living conditions of meat-packing plant workers. A macro stakeholder analysis would have proactively identified some of the underlying inequities of this economic sector before the situation turned dire. The third characteristic of hard-form SM deals with the larger stakeholder network of a firm. Such thinking engages stakeholder groups with management in regular, impactful dialogue. Practices that reflect such networking would be, for example, employee representation at the directors' level in German companies, the liberal return policies for customers at US retailers such as Costco and Nordstrom, and the partnerships with environmental groups at McDonald's to improve packaging.

Unilever: a commentary addressing company leadership and commitment

Although no company is without its faults, Unilever comes closer than any other multinational firm to personifying the principles outlined in this chapter. It was founded over 90 years ago by Lord Lever, who envisioned a broad social mandate for his fledgling company. It now operates in over 100 countries with millions of customers and 400 brands. Despite its growth, the firm has remained true to its original principles. A good example is the Marine Stewardship Council, which was formed in the 1990s as a partnership between Unilever and the World Wide Fund for Nature (WWF); it certifies the sustainability of commercial fish catches.

In 2009, Paul Polman became the CEO. He was the first "outsider" to head the company but came with an extensive background, having held major managerial positions at Procter & Gamble and Nestlé. As one of his first acts, he instituted the Sustainable Living Plan, which decoupled economic growth from environmental impact. In fact, the firm's ambitious goal was to double sales and also cut its environmental impact by half. In addition, he had the company discontinue reporting of quarterly earnings, instead steering it to make investments over a longer horizon that would benefit both the firm and society (Murphy & Murphy, 2018). In 2014, the *Economist* reported on a survey of "experts" in which Unilever was far ahead of other companies in terms of sustainability policies, with over 30% of the experts stating the company was an environmental "leader," while the second-most-mentioned firm managed less than 10% (*Economist*, 2014).

While many additional actions taken by the company over the last decade have cemented its reputation, it is to Unilever's embedding of CSR, ME/EM, and stakeholder thinking into its policies and programs that our analysis now turns. In terms of the ethical theories, it appears that Unilever is driven more by duty or virtue than utilitarianism. We believe that for some firms like Unilever the term "sustainability" has supplanted CSR as the overarching concept that characterizes its approach to societal obligations. In fact, Polman was called "Captain Planet" by the *Harvard Business Review* (Ignatius, 2012). Its partnership with an NGO to form the Marine Stewardship Council is an illustration of a "common good" perspective extending beyond corporate objectives.

In terms of ethical marketing practices, Unilever has demonstrated its commitment to the virtues of transparency and responsibility to stakeholders. On the company's website at the time of writing, the firm openly acknowledges that it has not accomplished every goal of its Sustainable Living Plan, even while noting successes. Its tea brands, Lipton and PG Tips, display the Rainforest Alliance logo on all their packaging to show that the tea is "sustainably sourced." Recently, Ben & Jerry's (a Unilever subsidiary) announced that it was replacing plastic spoons with wooden ones and offering paper straws instead of plastic ones (Ward, 2019). The firm also practices the "hard form" of stakeholder management. Polman (2016) stated: "I think you can develop a model that balances the interests of stakeholders over the long term." In terms of the three major themes of this book, Polman can be characterized as a sustainable, transformative, and innovative leader with his overriding emphasis on making the company more responsive to societal challenges than his predecessors.

One concept that has not yet been introduced but relates to Unilever is the "triple bottom line" (TBL; Elkington, 1998). This overarching approach captures many of the ethical and responsible marketing practices discussed above and identifies "people, planet, and profits" (or social, environmental, and economic criteria) as its components. The "planet" aspect as it relates to Unilever has been discussed above. The profit dimension arose during the Polman years with some critics arguing that the tension between profits and TBL considerations was often hard to reconcile (Dupont-Nivens et al., 2017). However, social and business goals need not be mutually exclusive, as one writer (Lozanova, 2015) concludes in her examination of Unilever:

> Many of us get skeptical when we hear of a big company doing good and wonder if it is more of a green-washing campaign than a genuine paradigm shift. It does seem Unilever is sincere in seeing the business opportunity in CSR and is successfully benefiting the bottom line by mitigating risk and creating trust. Of course, no CSR initiative is impeccable, and a "business as usual" mentality may sneak in at times as the new paradigm takes hold.

Unilever's innovative human resources (i.e. people) strategies are also a hallmark of the company and have been discussed elsewhere. For example, in 2013, Unilever held a global "Winning with Integrity" week which encouraged its suppliers to operate at a higher ethical standard; it also helped Unilever to learn more about the concerns of partners around the world (Bazil, 2014).

Polman's tenure concluded in 2019, and one can never be certain whether a firm will continue with the policies of its departed CEO. Nonetheless, his successor, Alan Jope, a long-time Unilever employee who is well versed in the company's history, has retained the Sustainable Living Plan and other Polman-era goals. A recent op-ed by Jope (2020), responding to the COVID-19 pandemic, was entitled "Capitalism must adapt and evolve if we are to end this crisis." It seems to suggest that the current CEO has the same, broad social vision for Unilever as his predecessor. Jope writes, "We need a new normal. One that doesn't fall back on old familiar ways of unsustainable production and consumption, environmental degradation and widening inequality."

As for Paul Polman, he has founded an NGO called *Imagine One*, which seeks collaboration as a means of attaining sustainability goals; he also serves as the chair of the board of the UN Global Compact. These two Unilever executives help illustrate that genuine CEO leadership makes it easier for a company to carry out its larger ethical and CSR mission. They give credibility to the old managerial adage that "an organization is but a lengthened shadow of the person at the top."

Conclusion

This chapter has endeavored to lay out what it means for a company to be normatively ethical and societally responsible. Such an approach needs to be grounded in a theory of the firm that goes beyond financial considerations. Concepts such as practicing a "hard form" stakeholder perspective, enhancing the common good, and subscribing to the stewardship principle are part of such a long-term view of the enterprise. We use Unilever as one example of a company that possesses many of these characteristics. Our hope is that more firms, both large and small, will begin to consider the ethical characteristics necessary to create a more sustainable economy and society.

References

Bazil, M. (2014). Human resource management and employee motivation at Unilever. Benzinga, August 6. Retrieved from https://www.benzinga.com/14/08/4761762/human-resource-management-and-employee-motivation-at-unilever

Business Roundtable (2019). Business Roundtable redefines the purpose of a corporation to promote "An economy that serves all Americans." Business Roundtable, August 19. Retrieved from https://www.businessroundtable.org/business-roundtable-redefines-the-purpose-of-a-corporation-to-promote-an-economy-that-serves-all-americans

Davis, K. (1960). Can business afford to ignore social responsibilities? *California Management Review*, 2(3), 70–77.

Dupont-Nivet, D., Ruhaak, A., Schuurs, M., Tielbeke, J., and Woutersen, E. (2017). Inside Unilever's sustainability myth. *New Internationalist*, April 13. Retrieved from https://newint.org/features/web-exclusive/2017/04/13/inside-unilever-sustainability-myth

Economist. (2014). In search of good business. *The Economist*, August 9, 55–56.

Elkington, J. (1998). *Cannibals with Forks: The Triple Bottom Line of 21st Century Business*. Oxford, UK: Capstone.

Freeman, R.E. (1984). *Strategic Management: A Stakeholder Approach*. Boston, MA: Pitman.

Gunther, M. (2006). The green machine. *Fortune*, 154(3), 42–57.

Ignatius, A. (2012). Captain Planet: interview with Paul Polman. *Harvard Business Review*, June, 112–18.

Jope, A. (2020). Capitalism must adapt and evolve if we are to end this crisis. *The Telegraph*, May 28. Retrieved from https://www.telegraph.co.uk/business/2020/05/28/capitalism-must-adapt-evolve-end-crisis/

Journal of Public Policy & Marketing, (2010). 29(1), 1–102.

Kent, M. (2012). Coca-Cola CEO address at Bentley College (April). Retrieved from https://www.bentley.edu/news/coca-cola-ceo-muhtar-kent-discusses-sustainable-business-practices-bentley-university-raytheon

Kotler, P. (1972). What consumerism means for marketers. *Harvard Business Review*, 50, 48–57.

Laczniak, G.R. (2017). The hidden costs of hidden costs. *Journal of Macromarketing*, 37(3), 324–27.

Laczniak, G.R., and Kennedy, A.M. (2011). Hyper norms: searching for a global code of conduct. *Journal of Macromarketing*, 31(3), 245–56.

Laczniak, G.R., and Murphy, P.E. (1993). *Ethical Marketing Decisions: The Higher Road*. Boston, MA: Allyn & Bacon.

Laczniak, G.R., and Murphy, P.E. (2008). Distributive justice: pressing questions, emerging directions, and the promise of Rawlian analysis. *Journal of Macromarketing*, 28(1), 5–11.

Laczniak, G.R., and Murphy, P.E. (2012). Stakeholder theory and marketing: moving from a firm-centric to a societal perspective. *Journal of Public Policy & Marketing*, 31(2), 284–92.

Laczniak, G.R., and Murphy, P.E. (2014). The relationship between marketing ethics and corporate social responsibility: serving stakeholders and the common good. In R.P. Hill and R. Langan (Eds.), *Handbook of Research on Marketing and Corporate Social Responsibility* (pp. 68–87). Cheltenham, UK: Edward Elgar.

Laczniak, G.R., and Murphy, P.E. (2019). The role of normative marketing ethics. *Journal of Business Research*, 95, 401–407.

Lozanova, S. (2015). How Unilever converges doing good and strong performance. *Triple Pundit*, June 9. Retrieved from https://www.triplepundit.com/story/2015/how-unilever-converges-doing-good-and-strong-performance/57816

Murphy, P.E. (2005). Sustainable marketing. *Business & Professional Ethics Journal*, 24(1–2), 171–98.

Murphy, P.E., Laczniak, G.R., and Harris, F. (2017). *Ethics in Marketing: International Cases and Perspectives*. London: Routledge.

Murphy, P.E., and Murphy, C.E. (2018). Sustainable living: Unilever. in E. O'Higgins and L. Zsolnai (Eds.), *Progressive Business Models: Creating Sustainable and Pro-social Enterprise* (pp. 263–86). Cham, Switzerland: Palgrave Macmillan.

Murphy, P.E., Oberseder, M., and Laczniak, G.R. (2013). Corporate societal responsibility: normatively broadening the concept. *AMS Review*, 3(2), 86–102.

Murphy, P.E., and Sherry, Jr., J.F. (2014). *Marketing and the Common Good: Essays from Notre Dame on Societal Impact*. London: Routledge.

Nahser, F.B. (2014). Consumption in the un-commons: the economic case for reclaiming the *commons* as unique *markets*. In P.E. Murphy and J.F. Sherry, Jr. (Eds), *Marketing and the Common Good: Essays from Notre Dame on Societal Impact* (pp. 137–52). London: Routledge.

Polman, P. (2016). Personal interview with P. Murphy, August 15.

Pontifical Council for Justice and Peace. (2005). *Compendium of the Social Doctrine of the Church*. Rome: Pontifical Council.

Pope Francis (2015). *On Care for our Common Home*. Encyclical Letter "Laudato Si" of the Holy Father Francis. Retrieved from http://www.vatican.va/content/francesco/en/encyclicals/documents/papa-francesco_20150524_enciclica-laudato-si.html.

Santos, N., and Laczniak, G.R. (2022). The integrative justice model as a challenge-driven normative framework for sustainable and just business practice" in S.P. Sebhatu, B. Enquist, and B. Edvardsson (Eds.), *Business transformation for a sustainable future*. London: Routledge.

Ward, M. (2019). How brands are working to fight climate change: here's how. *USA Today*, September 20. Retrieved from https://www.today.com/news/brands-fighting-climate-change-costco-gap-ikea-trader-joe-s-t163026

Wilkie, W.L., and Moore, E.S. (2014), A larger view of marketing: marketing's contributions to society. in P.E. Murphy and J.F. Sherry, Jr. (Eds), *Marketing and the Common Good: Essays from Notre Dame on Societal Impact* (pp. 13–40). London: Routledge.

12 PRME: impact for transformative change

Samuel Petros Sebhatu

Takeaways

- Transformation is crucial if leading organizations are to navigate – innovatively and sustainably – the new landscape of the SDG challenges.
- Multi-stakeholder dialogue contributes to creating a sustainable business, its governance guided by social and environmental perspectives.
- A dynamic service ecosystem (at micro, meso, and macro levels) can create new meaning and result in genuine transformative change toward sustainability through value creation in a global organization/initiative.
- Value is networked and cocreated through a transformation in specific contextual settings to address what comprises moral and/or ethical value and what should be reinforced legally.
- PRME, as part of the UN Global Compact, has grown to become the largest organized relationship between the United Nations and business schools.

Introduction

The COVID-19 crisis has highlighted the urgent need to rethink the human ecosystem, the relationship between humanity and nature, and, more specifically, the service ecosystem. PRME (the United Nations Principles for Responsible Management Education), a proactive initiative for business schools and other tertiary educational institutions, launched its first virtual global forum in response to the COVID-19 pandemic and the restrictions it is imposing. This innovation accompanies a new leadership and governance structure within PRME, after over a decade of work on organizing and leading business schools, in the new era of the Agenda 2030 Sustainable Developmental Goals (SDGs) (UN, 2015)[1] and transformative business-societal practices. "2020 is also a pivotal year for the PRME initiative with a new PRME Secretariat team, the appointment of a new Head of PRME, the creation of a new PRME Board, and the largest convening of the wider community at the 2020 Virtual PRME Global Forum" (PRME, 2020, p. 6).

DOI: 10.4324/9781003188773-12

In the last decade, PRME, as part of the UN Global Compact, has grown to become the largest organized relationship between the United Nations and business schools. The mission of PRME is partly a response to those business leaders committed to the Global Compact's ten principles who were asking the following question of educational institutions: *What are you doing to help future business leaders understand the challenges of responsible management?* Tertiary educational institutes and business schools must accept the challenge of transforming their responsible management education in an innovative and sustainable way. And a long-term consideration of responsible management needs to include educational institutions as important players in the transformation (Rasche, 2010). In this chapter, rather than describing a challenge-driven transformative change within PRME, we will investigate PRME's new vision, strategy, and governance structure as part of its ongoing process of transformation.

PRME's mission is to transform management education by developing the responsible decision-makers of tomorrow in order to advance the agenda of sustainable development. This is driven by its vision "to create a global movement and drive thought leadership on responsible management education." This chapter is an empirical study of how PRME has been engaging with that mission and how its achievement of this transformation has been driven by self-assessment and communication of innovative solutions to stakeholders.

This study examines the organization's proactive and innovative thinking, under the aegis of the UN Global Compact, and its impact on its member schools and other stakeholders. PRME works in a complex environment based on a principle of a "network of networks," which represents a multi-stakeholder dialogue at every level, vertically and horizontally. Creating value for all stakeholders requires sympathetic engagement (Freeman, Phillips, & Sisodia, 2020), based on the value network, a concept that is vital for cocreating value and making good decisions. This chapter also assesses the societal and environmental impact of PRME's multi-stakeholder dialogue across the whole service ecosystem (at micro, meso, and macro levels) (Lusch & Vargo, 2014). We present the case of Karlstad Business School (KBS)'s transformation as part of PRME's self-assessment approach. The chapter concludes by examining PRME's new vision and mission as drivers for future aspirations in which new governance structures enable the implementation of the SDGs in business schools, both in curriculum and in research, and in tertiary educational institutes (Wersun et al., 2020). The chapter uses the lens of a global transformation agenda – namely, the UN 2030 Agenda SDGs for addressing global challenge through multi-stakeholder dialogue and service research – to examine the service ecosystem at all levels.

Theoretical foundations

Transformational change and multi-stakeholder dialogue

PRME uses multi-stakeholder dialogue at every level in its work of guiding tertiary educational institutions in cocreating societal value by implementing the

SDGs. Stakeholder theory is about "knowing how" to engage stakeholders and create value for them, as opposed to the more technical "knowing that" something is the case for all organizations and institutions, always, for all problems, and for all configurations of stakeholders (Freeman, Phillips, & Sisodia, 2020, p. 217). According to Waddock (2008) and Waddock and Bodwell (2004), adopting a genuine stakeholder perspective involves commitment; but this commitment is vital for transformative change. A transformation to the new kinds of business practice we are discussing requires values-based thinking (Edvardsson & Enquist, 2009), a stronger stakeholder orientation (Freeman, 1984), and achievement of genuine societal and sustainability impact. The SDGs, which necessitate stakeholder engagement, offer the societal and environmental perspectives needed (Van Tulder, 2018; Van Zanten & Van Tulder, 2018; Bowen et al., 2017). In fact, the challenges of a complex and dynamic world require the kind of transformation that is ideally based on sustainability thinking underpinned by the SDGs (Waddock et al., 2015; Van Tulder & Keen, 2018; Van Tulder, 2018; Bowen et al., 2017).

Transformation can be defined as the implementation of a change management process. In the field of service research, transformative service research (TSR) – which lies at the intersection of service research and transformative consumer research and focuses on well-being outcomes related to service and services (Anderson et al., 2012; Ostrom, Mathras, & Anderson, 2014) – is opening the door for well-being not just at an individual level but also from a societal perspective by delivering service in a sustainable manner (Ostrom et al., 2010), and furthermore in a manner that can be aligned with prosperity. Anderson et al. (2012) have also identified sustainability as one of many possibilities on the future TSR agenda and offered three early references (Grove et al., 1996; Edvardsson & Enquist, 2009; Sebhatu, 2010). Although it is worthwhile here to highlight the link between TSR and sustainability/CSR, this chapter largely focuses on assessing the role of transformation to address business and societal challenges and can therefore be considered an extension of research into innovation addressing sustainability/CSR challenges. This chapter also takes into account the service research priorities identified by Ostrom and her coauthors (Ostrom et al., 2015), through which service is stimulated by understanding it in the context of global business practices.

This chapter adopts a broad perspective on management, one that considers governance and stewardship using a stakeholder orientation. The real global transformation agenda in practice is based on Agenda 2030, a plan of action for people, planet, prosperity, and partnership (Van Tulder, 2018). Because sustainability is complex and dynamic (Waddock et al., 2015; Van Tulder & Keen 2018), such transformation must happen within a new paradigm of positive change in a complex environment (Van Tulder, 2018; Van Tulder & Keen, 2018).

The PRME initiative is a framework for change for tertiary educational institutions in the area of business and societal ethics and responsibility. Its guide for progress reporting lays out the voluntary nature of its self-assessment process, which forms the central commitment made by institutions who participate in the PRME initiative, and through which there is regular sharing of information with stakeholders on progress in implementing PRME's six principles. It can be viewed as a kind of CSR addressing business-societal practices. Sustainability and CSR both offer a means for creating value, through the application of stakeholder approaches in different contexts (Wheeler & Thompson, 2006; Grosser, 2016). Sustainability implies the strategic commitment of an organization to social and ecological value, created through its own activities (Wheeler, Colbert, & Freeman, 2003). In parallel, CSR is a global phenomenon which creates a "market for virtue" (Vogel, 2005), although it can also manifest as greenwashing. It can also be an important element of a new type of business model, providing a strategy for service development and innovation (Edvardsson & Enquist, 2009; Sebhatu, 2010) and a resource for creating stakeholder value (Enquist, Johnson, & Skålén, 2006). Bhattacharyya (2010) called for strategic CSR in every organization, using a model that integrates different perspectives on strategic CSR to provide a unified, holistic, and conceptual view. It is important to understand the tension between an idealization of CSR dialogue versus its realistic execution (Høvring, Andersen, & Nielsen, 2018). The business case for CSR relates more closely to doing well (Enquist, Edvardsson, & Sebhatu, 2008; Sebhatu, 2010) as a means of securing sustainable service business (Edvardsson & Enquist, 2009) and multi-stakeholder dialogue (Høvring, Andersen, & Nielsen, 2018). This form of CSR is a proactive strategy to find smart solutions and build new types of global business models in which environmentally and socially responsible practice is part of the solution (Edvardsson & Enquist, 2009), rather than being handled as an externality (Von Weizsäcker & Wijkman, 2018; Van Zanten & Van Tulder, 2018), and is operationalized according to different stakeholders (Høvring, Andersen, & Nielsen, 2018).

To conclude, Van Tulder (2018) discussed the complexity of "wicked problems" in connection with how companies can contribute to the SDGs. He identified four levels of corporate engagement with the SDGs, each with its own logic, based on what CSR stands for in each case. "Level 1" and "level 2" are where green-, blue- or SDG-washing take place; at "level 3," CSR is strategic or active; and, in "level 4," CSR is systemic. We consider these levels useful in this chapter in building our framework of the service ecosystem in the value network.

Ecosystem and value cocreation for a "network of networks"

As described, PRME works in a complex environment based on the principle of a "network of networks." The issue of management in institutions understanding value cocreation in value networks is an ongoing discussion in service research. A "network of networks" is a value network that creates value by facilitating a network relationship between the organization and its stakeholders at every level. One way that a value network creates value is by facilitating a network relationship between an organization and its customers, using mediating technology (Stabell & Fjeldstad, 1998, pp. 414–15). Value is networked and cocreated through a steering and navigation processes in specific contextual settings to identify what comprises moral and/or ethical value and what should be reinforced legally (Sebhatu & Enquist, forthcoming). Several authors have used Normann's (2001) "value-creating system" to describe the process of creating value in networks by taking full responsibility (Enquist, Camén, & Johnson, 2011; Gummesson, 2008; Lusch, Vargo, & Tanniru, 2010; Lusch & Webster, 2011). According to Lusch, Vargo, and Tanniru (2010, p. 21), a "value creation network" or ecosystem is built on loosely connected social and economic actors who interact through institutions and technology, held together by "the trinity of competences, relationships, and information," and can be "understood as a complex network mechanism linking customer value and the value of the firm for all of its stakeholders" (Lusch & Webster, 2011, p. 131). The value network or ecosystem perspective is important as a platform for stakeholder interaction (Lusch, Vargo, & Tanniru, 2010; Freeman, Phillips, & Sisodia, 2020) that is multilevel in nature: micro, meso, and macro (Lusch & Vargo, 2014).

We are, therefore, framing PRME as a value network or ecosystem related to steering in a broader sense than just management (Enquist, Camén, & Johnson, 2011). Rather, it is a holistic perspective on business (Freeman, Phillips, & Sisodia, 2020). It is the difference between a value chain (linear and singularly focused on financial value) and a value network (which includes the importance of shared purpose and values) (Freeman, Phillips, & Sisodia, p. 217). Therefore, we must expand the service research theory that relies on marketing discourse (Skålén, 2010) in order to adopt a more inclusive stakeholder orientation for interaction that focuses not only on customers, but also on all stakeholders (Laczniak & Murphy, 2012; Lusch & Webster, 2011).

It is also important to understand an organization's structure if we are to understand the complexity of an ecosystem. Understanding complexity, as with sustainability, requires an openness to the reality of change, in both supply and demand, and the continual appearance of new ideas and innovation. It, therefore, replaces the aim of "maximal efficiency" to that of "sufficient efficiency," combined with a capacity to adapt, change, and learn (Allen, 2011). As emphasized many times already, transformative change requires a new paradigm for a positive change in a complex environment (Van Tulder, 2018; Van Tulder & Keen, 2018) and, for this, "sufficient efficiency" in running organizations and initiatives is the goal.

Service ecosystems need shared institutions (rules) to function effectively and coordinate activities among actors (Lusch & Vargo, 2014) in a complex environment. Vargo and Lusch define a service system as "a relatively self-contained system of resource-integrating actors connected by shared institutional arrangement and mutual value creation through service exchange" (Vargo & Lusch, 2016, pp. 10–11). In the same article, the researchers further develop the idea of institutions as an extension and update of S-D logic, using a new axiom and some fundamental premises.

> Axiom 5/FP11: Value co-creation is coordinated through actor-generated institutions and institutional arrangements.
>
> (Vargo & Lusch, 2016)

Lusch and Vargo (2014)'s model includes an actor-to-actor perspective of processes in different levels of exchange. As argued in Chapter 2, the theoretical and conceptual framework points to an actor-to-actor-to-nature interaction. The ecosystem perspective entails seeing all levels – *micro*, *meso*, and *macro* – by zooming out to see the bigger picture (see Lusch & Vargo, 2014, p. 169). A service ecosystem perspective is also a *processual*, *systemic*, and *institutional* one (Koskela-Huotari and Vargo, 2018).

- **Macro level**. Focusing on the planet/global society to identify planetary boundary/global challenges. The level is more *systemic* in character.
- **Meso level.** The level that focuses on societal and business institutional networks searching for societal practice. This level is more *institutional* in character.
- **Micro level.** The level that focuses on a stakeholder-centric point of view searching for a new business-societal practice. This level is more *processual* in character. Key actors are of great importance, allowing for legitimation in a systemic governance structure to create a challenge-driven transformation agenda for *implementation*.

Depending on perspective, zooming out or zooming in, the model shown in Figure 12.1 can be viewed as either systemic, institutional, or processual.

The dynamic ecosystem model in Figure 12.1 presents the different levels of the service ecosystem and multi-stakeholder dialogue based on an actor-actor-to-nature relationship. The PRME case presented in this chapter will help us further understand the model, which will be developed in subsequent sections. PRME's impact for *challenge-driven transformative change through multi-stakeholder dialogue in a dynamic ecosystem* will be discussed in the concluding part.

Transformation through responsible management education

PRME: the initiative

Hansen (1980) identified the importance of business schools in training future managers. He highlighted the need to understand the continuously changing environment and develop an ability to confront new facts and problems. Sustainability and social responsibility are now part of this dynamic environment and the new reality for business leaders. Tertiary educational institutions must address these dynamics and challenges not only by providing factual knowledge about responsible business practices, but also (and maybe more importantly) by inspiring students to reflect on their values. Business and management education institutions have faced criticism for falling short on a number of

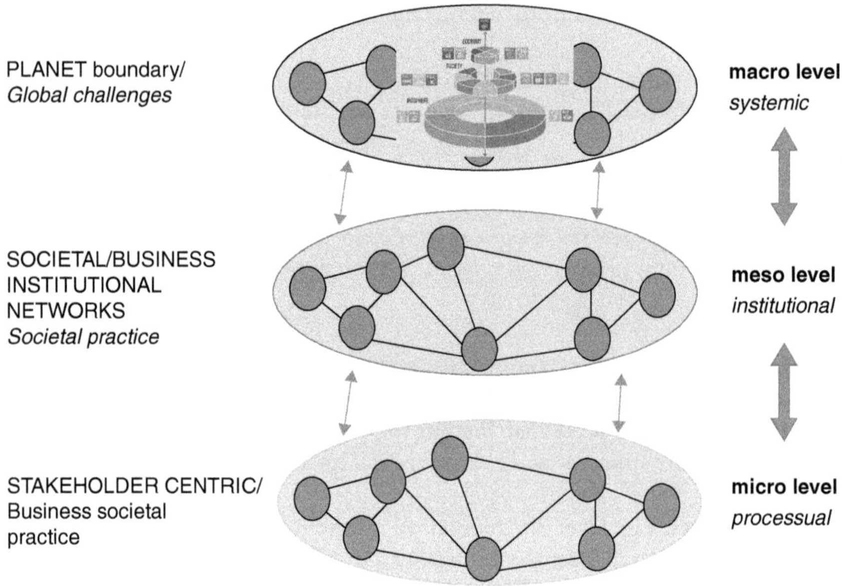

Figure 12.1 A business ecosystem in a business-societal perspective (see Chapter 2 for further discussion).

issues, including their capacity to produce leaders and managers who are not just successful but also ethical (Ghoshal, 2005), and a failure to promote sustainability in a way that converts into practice (Crawford & Wall, 2018). Thus, demand has been growing for an organized response from such institutions.

The need for a coordinated response to the complex and changing demands of sustainability creates an opportunity for new collaborations and initiatives between business and other institutions – enter PRME. This UN Global Compact sponsored initiative seeks to establish a process for continuous improvement among institutions of management education and develop a new generation of business leaders capable of managing the complex challenges faced by business and society in the 21st century. PRME from its inception has worked on transforming business schools and higher education institutions by understanding the challenges of sustainability and business-societal practices.

PRME was developed between October 2006 and July 2007 by an international task force of 60 deans and university presidents, along with scholars committed to the idea of responsible management education (Rasche, 2010). It was formally launched with its first 100 business and management signatories at the 2007 Global Compact Leaders' Summit, declaring its primary objective as being "encouraging higher education institutions to develop students who, as potential business leaders, would be responsible for enacting sustainable business practices in their future organizations"[2] (PRME, 2017). During its first two years, the initiative enjoyed tremendous growth in terms of participating institutions (from around 40 in July 2007 to 225 in April 2009). The interest in PRME and its underlying premise was also reflected by the high participation rate in the first Global Forum for Responsible Management Education held at UN headquarters in December 2008. In its early years, PRME aimed at promoting responsibility and sustainability through business and management curricula. To enhance multi-stakeholder dialogue and the perceived legitimacy of the development process, the drafting of the principles was supported by representatives from the Global Compact and other institutions, all of whom remain partners of the initiative, being members of the steering committee that guides PRME.

The PRME concept

The PRME concept is a framework for the progressive, challenge-driven systemic transformation of higher education institutions in the area of business and societal ethics and responsibility. It aims to transform management education, research, and thought leadership globally. The preamble to the PRME principles states: "As institutions of higher learning involved in the education of current and future managers, we are voluntarily committed to engaging in a continues process of improvement of the following Principles, reporting on progress to all stakeholder and exchange effective practices with other academic institutions."[3]

PRME is based on six voluntary principles and their implementation[4] (PRME, 2017) (see below). In adhering to these six principles, schools and universities can provide future leaders with the necessary insights and skills to reflect on, critically analyze, and provide leadership about corporate responsibility (PRME, n.d.). In its guide for progress reporting, PRME describes the voluntary nature of the challenge and the central commitment of institutions participating in PRME to regularly share information with their stakeholders on progress made in implementing the principles via Sharing Information on Progress (SIP) reports. As a key integrity measure, the main objective of this voluntary reporting is to serve as a public vehicle for information on responsible management education. The six principles in the SIP report are as follows:

- **Purpose**. We will develop the capabilities of students to be future generators of sustainable value for business and society at large and to work for an inclusive and sustainable global economy.
- **Values**. We will incorporate into our academic activities, curricula, and organizational practices the values of global social responsibility as portrayed in international initiatives such as the United Nations Global Compact.
- **Method**. We will create educational frameworks, materials, processes, and environments that enable effective learning experiences for responsible leadership.
- **Research**. We will engage in conceptual and empirical research that advances our understanding about the role, dynamics, and impact of

corporations in the creation of sustainable social, environmental, and economic value.

- **Partnership**. We will interact with managers of business corporations to extend our knowledge of their challenges in meeting social and environmental responsibilities and to explore jointly effective approaches to meeting these challenges.
- **Dialogue**. We will facilitate and support dialogue and debate among educators, students, business, government, consumers, media, civil society organizations, and other interested groups and stakeholders on critical issues related to global social responsibility and sustainability.

Higher-education signatories to the PRME initiative have to declare their willingness to implement the six principles within their institution. They begin with those that are more relevant to their capacities and mission. Through the SIP reports they can share good practice. The SIP policy was developed based on a consensus reached at the 1st PRME Global Forum for Responsible Management Education in 2008 and was updated in consultation with the PRME Working Group on SIP and PRME Advisory Committee in 2015. The revised policy was endorsed by the 2015 Global Forum for Responsible Management Education – 6th Annual Assembly in the Outcomes Declaration.[5]

The PRME structure and network

The PRME initiative includes the PRME framework, the development of learning communities, and promotion of awareness about the SDGs (PRME, 2020). For the last 12 years, PRME has been overseen by a steering committee comprising key stakeholders in higher education, with an advisory committee comprising members of different PRME networks. These networks include PRME Champions (38 schools), PRME Regional Chapters (15 schools), and PRME Working Groups (six schools), including the new Working Group on Humanistic Management. The PRME engagement model is built on UN organizational models and organized under a governance structure as an enabler to drive the platforms in facilitating and driving the business schools (see Figure 12.2).

The PRME engagement model is built on transforming management education, research, and thought leadership globally based on the challenges of the SDGs. This transformative change should be the result of the engagement of different actors at each level to help the educational institutions implement the six principles. Educational institutions are tasked with becoming innovative in their work and in their self-assessments, and communicating with their stakeholders. As outlined above, this transformative change is part of a new paradigm of a positive change in a complex environment with the goal of having "sufficient efficiency" in order to run the initiative.

As already mentioned, the entire organizational structure of PRME is based on the United Nations and the SDGs. An understanding of the engagement model is helpful in understanding the structure of the initiative and the complexity of

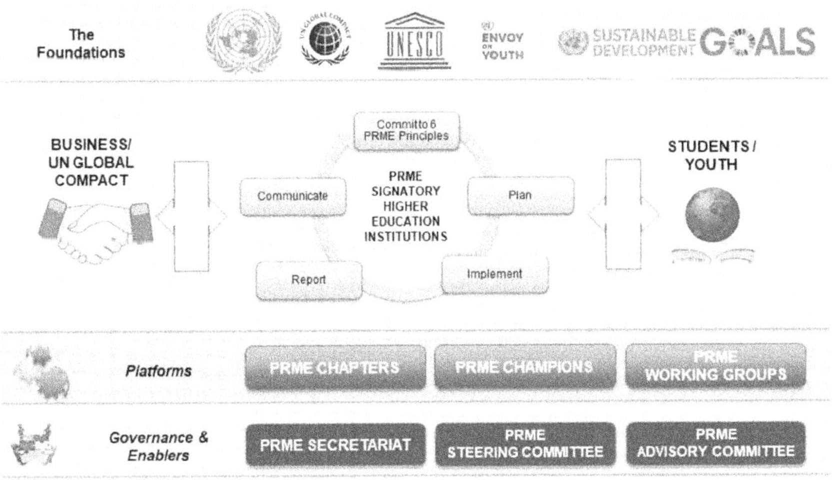

Figure 12.2 The PRME engagement model (PRME, 2020, p.23).

the whole ecosystem. Service ecosystem thinking, based on service logic, which entails developing a systems view of exchange, is a lens through which to view the institutional structure of PRME in a simplified way (see Figure 12.3).

The PRME initiative can be understood as a dynamic service ecosystem framework that meets global challenges. This underlines the need for a dynamic service ecosystem to handle the complexity of the organization, where the educational institutions and their stakeholders are interconnected and live in a balance between individual and collective interests within planetary boundaries. Innovation and sustainability for societal practice in responsible management acquires new meaning in such a dynamic and integrative service ecosystem. The above framework provides foundations on which to build such a model.

Adopting self-assessment for transformative change: the case of Karlstad Business School

Karlstad Business School (KBS) was established in 2009 as part of Karlstad University. It is one of the youngest business schools in Sweden. KBS has a staff of approximately 130, with around 2,500 students every year, either first cycle (nine programs), second cycle (nine programs), or third cycle (doctoral studies). Many of the KBS lecturers are also conducting research, in one of the multidisciplinary research centers or one of its five discipline areas: Business Administration; Economics and Statistics; Information Systems; Law; and Working Life Science. Also connected to KBS is a research center, the Service Research Centre, and two fora: the Forum for Accounting and Control and the Insolvency Law Academy. What brings the people at KBS together is a deep interest in economics and business.

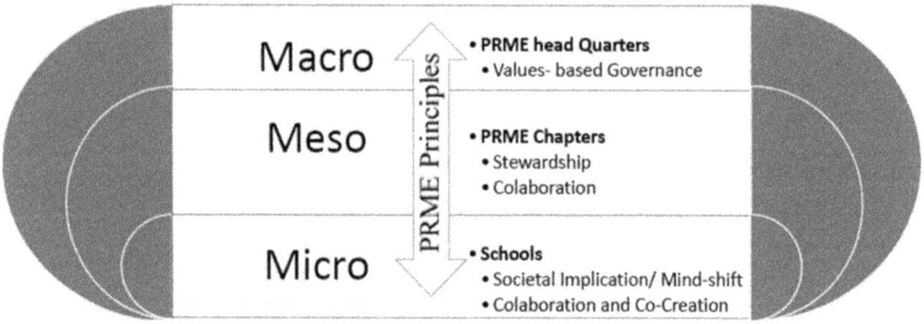

Figure 12.3 The PRME service ecosystem.

On 19 October 2016, KBS, with regard to its aims of integrating sustainability and societal practices into its curriculum and other activities of the school, took a major step forward. This author, along with this book's coeditor Bo Enquist, organized a day around investigating the SDGs under the theme "Meeting the challenges of tomorrow today." The morning session started with a transformation lab (T-Lab) discussion about implementation of the SDGs, members of which included: two world-renowned professors of marketing ethics and CSR; a manager and designer from IKEA; the Chairman of the Board and Head of Sustainability of Löfbergs (a Nordic coffee-roasting company); and representatives of an innovation park. The afternoon comprised the inauguration of KBS's first "Sustainability Day," which transmitted the signal that KBS was ready to apply PRME's ideas and principles.

This journey had begun before October 2016, however. It started out as part of a research journey and the need to integrate sustainability research and education within our business school leads. Bo and I had taken an interest in PRME having learned about the initiative in the Marketing Ethics and CSR Symposium instigated by Professor Patrick Murphy of Notre Dame University. We had the insight that PRME had a role to play in our existing international network on marketing ethics and CSR as a means for transformation as well as assessing our engagement and communication to our stakeholders. Once we looked into it, we appreciated that the self-assessment and SIP report represent tremendous challenges for the school and require an innovative approach to addressing the SDGs. It took about two years before KBS was ready to be a PRME member. An report on KBS's work on ethics and sustainability was presented in June 2015 to the KBS Advisory Board, who gave their approval for taking the next step toward PRME membership. The preparatory work for the PRME application supported KBS's ongoing accreditation implementation process. Further reports on KBS's status were undertaken during 2016, which included curriculum footprints, alumni footprints, and research footprints. KBS joined PRME in February 2017, four months after its first "Sustainability Day," and published its first SIP report in 2019.

The KBS case provides a good example of challenge-driven transformation. The school was investigating transformative change by implementing the SDGs and looking to develop its curriculum based on sustainability and business-societal practices. Its ambition is also to integrate its distinctive ongoing studies, research, and stakeholder dialogues with its responsible management education curriculum. After joining PRME in February 2017, the school committed to sharing information with its stakeholders on its progress via an SIP. Both before and after that time, the school worked to implement the six principles of Purpose, Values, Method, Research, Partnership, and Dialogue. KBS realized early in the process that many good examples from education and research were already aligned with the principles. The self-assessment process revealed that the school had no systematic method for advancing corporate social responsibilities via the incorporation of universal values into curricula and research. This first progress report was therefore useful in visualizing the status of KBS's day-to-day-operations with regard to its embedding of the PRME principles and institutionalizing the learning process in pursuit of continuous improvements.

Implementation of the PRME principles in the school over the past two years has allowed better coordination in developing a new generation of business and societal members capable of managing the complex challenges faced by business and society in the 21st century. The implementation of these principles is embedded in the SDG goals, and the SDGs demonstrate the scale and ambition of this new universal agenda, with all countries and all stakeholders acting in collaborative partnerships to implement it. The UN Global Compact makes it clear that this plan means a new era for responsible business:

> The adoption of the United Nations Sustainable Development Goals (SDGs) and the Paris Climate Agreement has provided a powerful common agenda for achieving peace and prosperity on a healthy planet by 2030 – with an essential role spelled out for business. The SDGs provide a blueprint for how to address the complex challenges the world faces.
>
> (Global Compact, 2017)

The close connection between research and education allows KBS to meet the vision while delivering high-quality and responsible education to its students. KBS's vision is articulated as: "Karlstad Business School is influential and highly visible in society – the first choice for students, employees, and partners," while its mission reads: "Educating responsible professionals and conduct research with high societal impact." The main mantra of KBS is built on a culture of responsibility: "how we work and what we value is fundamental to achieving our vision. In other words, it is not only what we do, but how we do it that matters." The main challenge of the SDGs is that they require systemic thinking and a holistic approach. PRME acknowledges that integrating and/or mainstreaming the SDGs into a business school context is a dynamic process with no "one size fits all" solution (Wersun et al., 2020, p. 6).

During 2017–18 PRME implementation for KBS has been about focusing on the adoption of the six principles. In the next stage, 2019–20, KBS will focus on four of the SDGs: number 4, Quality Education; number 5, Gender Equality; number 12, Responsible Consumption and Production; and number 13, Climate Action. These were voted for on Sustainability Day, 3 December 2018, the participants choosing what they believed to be the most relevant SDGs to be implemented in the following two years, and which are seen as drivers for the other SDGs (KBS, 2019). KBS has already committed to these four goals, and the implementation process commenced on 1 January 2019.

PRME is a tool that allows KBS to meet its vision and mission statement in daily practice, and an excellent way to coordinate its ambition toward sustainable development. However, it is not a quick fix.

Conclusion and implications

Transformation: the outlook

The main purpose of this chapter has been to discuss how an initiative, via a multi-stakeholder approach based on sustainability, innovation, and transformation can be used as a foundation on which to develop a dynamic service ecosystem for challenge-driven transformative change. At a macro level, Stiglitz (2006) describes a need for transformation to address globalization's economic, social, and environmental challenges; this is the main purpose of the PRME initiative. Sustainability is not only an environmental challenge, but also an economic and social one, too. This chapter has contributed to the discussion on PRME as a continuing process to remain a strong voice in confronting the sustainability challenges of the globalized world generally and cocreating a new meaning. It has focused on global challenges by zooming in on PRME's transformation processes, searching for innovative and sustainable practices within PRME Chapters and business schools, and learning how to use these practices to come closer to implementation.

Transformation is defined as the implementation of a change management process. While 2020 will see the continuation of existing platforms and projects, PRME will also provide an opportunity to reaffirm KBS's commitment to the 2030 Agenda for Sustainable Development. In the new PRME blueprint for SDG integration, Wersun and coauthors (2020) provide concepts and frameworks to support business schools in integrating the SDGs into their curricula, research, and partnerships with practical examples of approaches already adopted by business schools. PRME is introducing new work streams and strengthening its engagement with key stakeholders (PRME, 2020):

- There will be a new PRME board for the PRME initiative going forward, with a specific focus on the strategic direction of PRME in terms of governance, identity, and balanced growth.

- The engagement and structure of PRME Chapters will be reviewed in order to strengthen the development of existing ones but also to support the establishment of new Chapters in underrepresented regions.
- A new two-year cycle of the PRME Champions begins in 2020 to develop resources and materials that will showcase high-level engagement with the SDGs in teaching, research, and partnership.
- The programmatic work of PRME will align even further with the work of the UN Global Compact in key areas in which PRME and UN Global Compact networks and platforms complement each other to deliver greater overall impact with regard to the SDGs.

The new look PRME of 2020 marks the beginning of the "Decade of Action," which calls for accelerated sustainable solutions to the world's greatest challenges, such as climate change, poverty, gender inequality, and the COVID-19 pandemic. It is a call to all sectors of society, including the private sector, academia, youth, and civil society, among other key stakeholders (PRME, 2020, p. 6). PRME's three new focus areas represent the new service ecosystem at all the three levels: macro, setting the identity; meso, identifying the organizational structure; and micro, the impact, in implementing the SDGs (Wersun et al., 2020) by creating balanced growth (see Figure 12.4).

We have seen in this chapter that value is networked and cocreated through a transformation in specific contextual settings to address what comprises moral and/or ethical value, particularly at the social level, and what should be reinforced legally. This impacts the ability of related stakeholders to work together toward a common vision driven by the SDG challenges, which determine the effectiveness of the chosen involvement. It is the stakeholder engagement element that contributes to creating a sustainable business, its governance guided by social and environmental perspectives, within a context of multi-stakeholder dialogue. We have found that transformation is what is necessary in order for leading organizations to navigate the new landscape of SDG challenges and steer through different networks to cocreate value for tertiary educational institutions and other stakeholders.

In this empirical study, the theoretical and conceptual framework and model confronted the case of the PRME initiative – to reveal new meaning. Figure 12.3 demonstrates the dynamic ecosystem of a PRME network. We extended the model to consider the transformative change process as being vision- and goal-driven to meet the global challenges of complexity and "wicked" problems. That new model is illustrated in Figure 12.4, which shows transformative change in which the SDGs are used as a proactive tool for identifying global challenges and also for developing a transformation agenda for change in multiple institutions and organizations in the direction of greater sustainability and social justice. The network of complexity, where service innovation, social innovation, and corporate social responsibility meet global challenges in the light of Agenda 2030 to handle transformation, innovation, and sustainability, needs to shift from a firm-centric to a societal perspective.

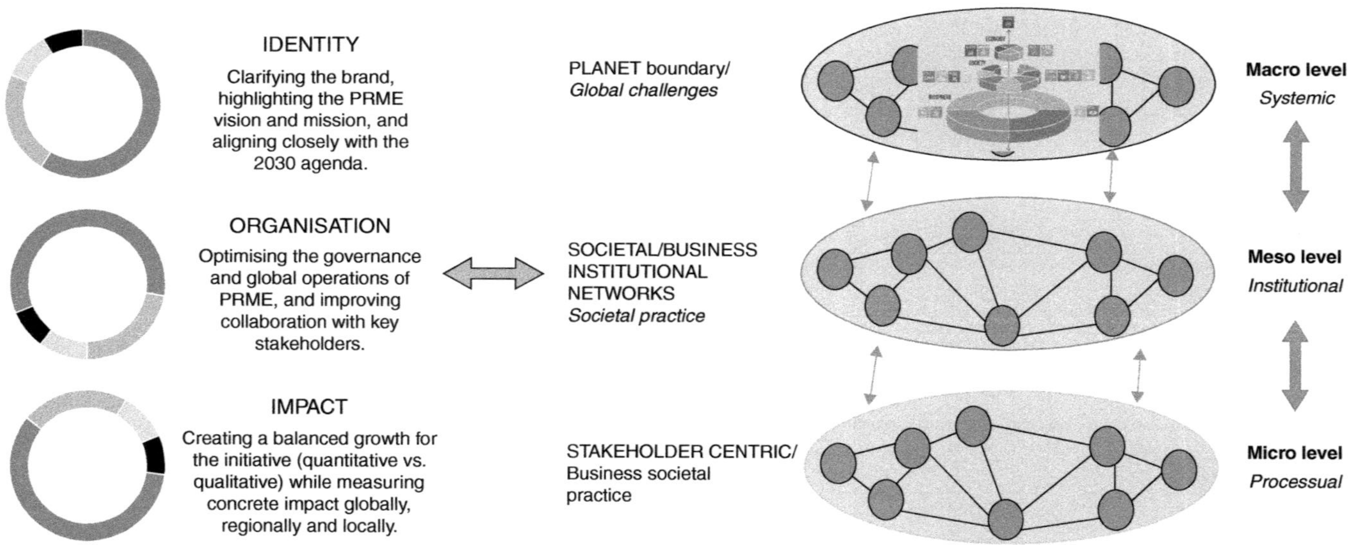

Figure 12.4 A dynamic ecosystem with a business-societal perspective for challenge-driven transformative change in PRME.

Figure 12.4 elaborates the transformation agenda of PRME based on I identity, organization and impact toward achieving the vision and mission-driven by the SDGs for societal perspectives. The transformation is steering sustainability/ governance through the strategy and values of PRME to create value to the stakeholders. Navigating societal business practices in the value network based on multi-stakeholder dialogue is also indicated in this transformation process.

The following challenges and implications can be identified:

- Transformation is crucial if leading organizations are to navigate the new landscape of SDG challenges.
- Stakeholder engagement plays a key role in creating a sustainable business, its governance guided by social and environmental perspectives, in accordance with multi-stakeholder dialogue.
- A dynamic ecosystem with a business-societal perspective is essential for challenge-driven transformative change.
- Value is networked and cocreated via a transformation in specific contextual settings to address what comprises moral and/or ethical value and what should be reinforced legally.

Notes

1 Hence forth, in this chapter, Agenda 2030 SDGs are described using UN 2015 reference unless it is referenced.
2 See also https://www.unprme.org/about. Historical background here is partly taken from the PRME website.
3 Ibid.
4 https://www.unprme.org/what-we-do
5 https://www.unprme.org/sip-policy-1

References

Allen, P.M. (2011). Complexity and management. in C. Hooker (Ed.), *Philosophy of Complex Systems* (pp. 783–808). Handbook of the Philosophy of Science, Vol. 10. Amsterdam:NorthHolland.https://doi.org/10.1016/B978-0-444-52076-0.50025-0

Anderson, L., Ostrom, A.L., Corus, C., Fisk, R.P., Gallan, A.S., Giraldo, M., Mende, M., Mulder, M., Rayburn, S.W., Rosenbaum, M.S., Shirahada, K., and Williams, J.D. (2012). Transformative service research: an agenda for the future. *Journal of Business Research*, 66(8), 1203–10.

Bhattacharyya, S.S. (2010). Exploring the concept of strategic corporate social responsibility for an integrated perspective. *European Business Review*, 22(1), 82–101.

Bowen, K.J., Cradock-Henry, N.A., Koch, F., Patterson, J., Häyhä, T., Vogt, J., and Barbi, F. (2017). Implementing the "Sustainable Development Goals": towards addressing three key governance challenges – collective action, trade-offs, and accountability. *Current Opinion in Environmental Sustainability*, 26–27, 90–96.

Crawford-Lee, M., and Wall, T. (2018). Sustainability 2030: a policy perspective from the University Vocational Awards Council. *Higher Education, Skills and Work-Based Learning*, 8(3), 233–42. https://doi.org/10.1108/HESWBL-03-2018-0043

Edvardsson, B., and Enquist, B. (2009). *Values-Based Service for Sustainable Business: Lessons from IKEA*. London: Routledge.

Enquist, B., Camén, C., and Johnson, M. (2011). Contractual governance for public service value networks. *Journal of Service Management*, 22(2), 217–40.

Enquist, B., Edvardsson, B., and Sebhatu, S.P. (2008). Corporate social responsibility for charity or for service business? *Asian Journal of Service Quality Management*, 9(1), 55–67.

Enquist, B., Johnson, M., and Skålén, P. (2006). Adoption of corporate social responsibility: incorporating a stakeholder perspective. *Qualitative Research in Accounting & Management*, 3(3), 188–207.

Freeman, R.E. (1984). *Strategic Management: A Stakeholder Approach*. Boston, MA: Pitman.

Freeman, R.E., Phillips, R., and Sisodia, R. (2020). *Tensions in stakeholder theory. Business & Society*, 59(2), 213–31.

Ghoshal, S. (2005) Bad management theories are destroying good management practices. *Academy of Management Learning & Education*, 4(1), 75–91.

Global Compact. (2017). *Making Global Goals Local Business: A New Era for Responsible Business*. New York: UN Global Compact. Retrieved from https://d306pr3pise04h.cloudfront.net/docs/about_the_gc%2FMakingGlobalGoalsLocalsBusiness2017.pdf

Grosser, K. (2016). Corporate social responsibility and multi-stakeholder governance: pluralism, feminist perspectives and women's NGOs. *Journal of Business Ethics*, 137, 65–81.

Grove, S.J., Fisk, R.P., Pickett, G.M., and Kangun, N. (1996). Going green in the service sector: social responsibility issues, implications and implementation. *European Journal of Marketing*, 30(5), 56–66.

Gummesson, E. (2008). *Total Relationship Marketing: Marketing Management, Relationship Strategy, CRM, and a New Dominant Logic for the Value-Creating Network Economy*. Oxford, UK: Butterworth-Heinemann.

Hansen, H.L. (1980). Business schools and management education in the world: present and future. *Vikalpa: The Journal for Decision Makers*, 5(3) (July).

Høvring, C.M., Andersen, S.E., and Nielsen, A.E. (2018). Discursive tensions in CSR multi-stakeholder dialogue: a Foucauldian perspective. *Journal of Business Ethics*, 152, 627–45.

Karlstad Business School (KBS). (2019). *Sharing Information on First Progress Report: 2017–2018*. Karlstad, Sweden: Karlstad Business School PRME Office.

Koskela-Huotari, K., and Vargo, S.L. (2018). Why Service-Dominant Logic? In S.L. Vargo and R.F. Lusch (Eds.), *The SAGE Handbook of Service-Dominant Logic* (pp. 40–57). London: SAGE Publications Inc.

Laczniak, G.R., and Murphy, P.E. (2012). Stakeholder theory and marketing: moving from a firm-centric to societal perspective. *Journal of Public Policy & Marketing*, 31(2), 284–92.

Lusch, R.F., and Vargo, S.L. (2014). *Service-Dominant Logic: Premises, Perspectives, Possibilities*. Cambridge, UK: Cambridge University Press.

Lusch, R.F., and Webster Jr., F.E. (2011). A stakeholder-unifying, co-creation philosophy of marketing. *Journal of Macromarketing*, 31(2), 129–34.

Lusch, R.F., Vargo, S.L., and Tanniru, M. (2010). Service, value networks and learning. *Journal of the Academy of Marketing Science*, 38(1), 19–31.

Normann, R. (2001). *Reframing Business: When the Map Changes the Landscape*. Chichester, UK: John Wiley & Sons.

Ostrom, A.L., Mathras, D., and Anderson, L. (2014). Transformative service research: an emerging subfield focused on service and well-being. In R. Rust and M.-H. Huang, *Handbook of Service Marketing Research* (pp. 557–79). Aldershot, UK: Edward Elgar.

Ostrom, A.L., Bitner, M.J., Brown, S.W., Burkhard, K.A., Goul, M., Smith-Daniels, V., Demirkan, H., and Rabinovich, E. (2010). Moving forward and making a difference: research priorities for the science of service. *Journal of Service Research*, 13(1), 4–36.

Ostrom, A.L., Parasuraman, A., Bowen, D.E., Patrício, L., and Voss, C.A. (2015). Service research priorities in a rapidly changing context. *Journal of Service Research*, 18(2), 127–59.

Principles for Responsible Management Education (PRME). (2017). *Impact: A Decade of Principles for Responsible Management Education*. New York: United Nations Principles for Responsible Management Education.

Principles for Responsible Management Education (PRME). (2020). *2018–2019 Annual Report & 2020 Outlook*. New York: United Nations Principles for Responsible Management Education.

Principles for Responsible Management Education (PRME). (n.d.). *A Basic Guide to the Sharing Information on Progress (SIP): For Current and Prospective Signatories of the Principles for Responsible Management Education* (version 1.0). New York: United Nations Principles for Responsible Management Education.

Rasche, A. (2010), The Principles for Responsible Management Education: A call for action for German Universities. In M. Haase, S. Mirkovic and O.J.S chumann (Eds.), *Stand und Perspektiven der unternehmens- und wirtschaftsethischen Ausbildung in Deutschland*. Mering: Hampp. Retrieved September 16, 2020 from https://www.researchgate.net/publication/228285524_The_Principles_for_Responsible_Management_Education_PRME_-_A_%27Call_for_Action%27_for_German_Universities.

Sebhatu, S.P. (2010). *Corporate Social Responsibility for Sustainable Service Dominant Logic*. Doctoral thesis. Karlstad University Studies, No. 10. Karlstad, Sweden.

Sebhatu, S.P., and Enquist, B. (forthcoming). *Steering and Navigating UN Sustainability Developmental Goals (Agenda 2030) for Multi-Stakeholder Dialogue: Sustainability and Sustainable Business Societal Practice for a Real Transformation*.

Skålén, P. (2010). *Managing Service Firms: The Power of Managerial Marketing*. London: Routledge.

Stabell, C.B., and Fjeldstad, D.O. (1998). Configuring value for competitive advantage: on chains, shops, and networks. *Strategic Management Journal*, 19(5), 413–37.

Stiglitz, J.E. (2006) *Making Globalization Work*. New York: W.W. Norton.

UN (2015). Transforming Our World: The 2030 Agenda for Sustainable Development. United Nations. New York: A/RES/70/1

Van Tulder, R. (2018). *Business and the Sustainable Development Goals: A Framework for Effective Corporate Involvement*. Rotterdam School of Management, Erasmus University, Rotterdam, Netherlands.

Van Tulder, R., and Keen, N. (2018). Capturing collaborative challenges: designing complexity-sensitive theories of change for cross-sector partnership. *Journal of Business Ethics*, 150(2), 315–32.

Van Zanten, J.A., and Van Tulder, R. (2018). Multinational enterprises and the Sustainable Development Goals: an institutional approach to corporate engagement. *Journal of International Business Policy*, 1(3–4), 208–33.

Vargo, S.L., and Lusch, R.F. (2016). Institutions and axioms: an extension and update of service-dominant logic. *Journal of the Academy of Marketing Science*, 44(1), 5–23.

Vogel, D. (2005). *The Market for Virtue: The Potential and Limits of Corporate Social Responsibility*. Washington, DC: The Brookings Institution.

Von Weizsäcker, E.U., and Wijkman, A. (2018). *Come On! Capitalism, Short-termism, Population and the Destruction of the Planet.A Report to the Club of Rome 50th Anniversary in 2018.* New York: Springer Science + Business Media.

Waddock, S. (2008). Building a new institutional infrastructure for corporate responsibility. *Academy of Management Perspectives*, 22(3), 87–108.

Waddock, S., and Bodwell, C., (2004). Managing responsibility: what can be learnt from the quality movement? *California Management Review*, 47(1), 25–37.

Waddock, S., Meszoely, G.M., Waddell, S., and Dentoni, D. (2015). The complexity of wicked problems in large scale change. *Journal of Organizational Change Management*, 28(6), 993–1012.

Wersun, A., Klatt, J., Azmat, F., Suri, H., Hauser, C., Chur, G., Bogie, J., Meaney, M., and Ivanov, N. (2020). *Blueprint for SDG Integration into Curriculum, Research and Partnerships*. New York: United Nations Principles for Responsible Management Education.

Wheeler, D., and Thomson, J. (2006). Business and sustainability: implications for corporate governance theory and practice. In M.J. Epstein and K.O. Hanson (Eds.), *The Accountable Corporation*. Vol. 1: *Corporate Governance* (pp. 243–70). Westport, CT: Praeger (Greenwood).

Wheeler, D., Colbert, B., and Freeman, R.E. (2003). Focusing on value: reconciling corporate social responsibility, sustainability and a stakeholder approach in a network world. *Journal of General Management*, 28(3), 1–28.

APPENDIX: DATA IN NUMBERS (2019)

PRME

- Over 800 signatories
- 95 Countries
- 38 Champions institutions
- 12 Regional Chapters
- 8 Working Groups

PRME progress

- 18.6% average global growth
- 142 new signatories joined PRME between 2018 and 2019
- 470 SIP Reports submitted in 2019
- 35% advanced signatories in 2019

KBS

- ~2,500 students
- ~130 employees
- 9 programs at undergraduate level
- 9 programs at graduate level
- Doctoral program
- 5 discipline areas

13 Implications from business transformation for a sustainable future

Bo Enquist, Samuel Petros Sebhatu, and Bo Edvardsson

Takeaways

- Sustainability needs to be embedded in a wider framework, theoretically as well contextually, within the business-societal practice.
- Challenge-driven business and societal transformation need to transcend green-, blue- and SDG-washing to the point where sustainability thinking acquires a more circular and societal meaning in an interrelationship with both innovation and transformation.
- The UN SDGs, as a hyper-norm, can be used as a compass to mobilize change for sustainable business practice; and, vice versa, sustainable business practice can contribute to the achievement of the SDGs.
- A business practice with a more societal perspective will have a stakeholder orientation that addresses the question "value for whom?" in its value cocreation transformation process.

Introduction

The purpose of this final chapter is to summarize the lessons learned. The various chapters have focused on global challenges by zooming in on transformation processes and searching for innovative and sustainable business practices. This concluding and reflexive chapter, therefore, examines the implications of each of the preceding chapters by raising the questions "Why?", "What?", "Who?", and "How?".

Why this book?

This book focuses on transformation processes by discussing and presenting innovative and sustainable business practices, and showing how to implement those practices. In a globalized world, businesses need to transform from a strictly firm-centric and economic perspective to a societal one (Laczniak & Murphy, 2012) in order to lead the way to a sustainable future. A wide range of researchers have engaged herein with business and societal practice, with all the chapters being grounded in business and societal research, and, more

DOI: 10.4324/9781003188773-13

specifically, on the interdependencies between sustainability, innovation, and transformation.

What and who?

We learned from Chapter 2 that to tackle global challenges we need to be aware of the complexity of "wicked" problems when contemplating large-scale change. These challenges have to be tackled holistically because their various components are interconnected, interdependent, and interrelated. Wicked problems are also dynamic and unpredictable, which has been exemplified dramatically in 2020 by the COVID-19 pandemic.

The father of Triple Bottom Line (TBL) thinking, John Elkington, argues that it is time to rethink the TBL and see it as a genetic code for tomorrow's capitalism, spurring the regeneration of our economies, societies, and biosphere (Elkington, 2019). To achieve this, we believe that sustainability needs to be embedded in a wider framework, theoretically as well as contextually, by business-transformation practice. We agree with the message coming from the Club of Rome's 50th Anniversary in 2018 that it is clear that current trends are not sustainable (von Weizsäcker & Wijkman, 2018). This book aims to contribute to the wider discussion about sustainability.

The interrelationship between sustainability, innovation, and transformation is the foundation of this book. Its authors have contributed to the discussion of how sustainable societal practices can contribute to business transformation, and vice versa, in the interrelationships among different theories and different contexts.

Part 1, *Transforming firm-centric business and societal practices*, adopted a stakeholder perspective in different business contexts in seeking to move from a firm-centric to a more societal perspective.

Chapter 2 focused on *fossil-free transformation*, as illustrated by the case of Fossil Free Sweden. Theoretically, a multilevel business ecosystem with an actor-to-nature relationship was developed. Sustainability, innovation, and transformation are used as the pillars of such an ecosystem which takes a business-societal perspective for challenge-driven transformative change. The SDGs are used as a proactive tool in order to identify global challenges and develop a transformation agenda for change in multiple institutions and organizations in the direction of greater sustainability and social justice.

Chapter 3 focused on the *circular economy and values-based sustainability business practice* in the context of the global retailer IKEA. IKEA makes plans over the long term to achieve a positive sustainability footprint and introduce innovative change with a circular-economy effect. It is a continuous transformative process, which addresses complexity and "wicked" problems, led by a strong culture, stakeholder engagement, and its own IKEA values, with the mission of creating "a better life for the many people." IKEA shows that the SDGs can be used in practice as a compass to mobilize transformative change for sustainable business practice; and, vice versa, sustainable business practice can contribute to the aims of the SDGs.

Chapter 4 focused on the global enterprise Eataly and highlighted the contribution of sustainable business practice in a service ecosystem to the scaling-up process. The central idea is one of "no waste" as a transformative driving force for changing attitudes, creating opportunities, and disseminating a new culture. Important for Eataly's business practice is a continuous commitment to the development of innovative solutions. This includes collaboration with its partners as well as acquiring knowledge on transformation services to improve the well-being of individuals, organizations, and society. Eataly is a good example of a company that aims to contribute to sustainable transformative change through business strategies grounded in and supported by the values held by customers, employees, and collaborating actors. This requires an innovative mindset and a pragmatic strategy, not just exploiting the concept of sustainability for economic gain, nor using sustainable transformation merely as a communication or promotional tool.

Part 2, *The role of the individual in business and social transformation*, looked at how changes in individuals' mindsets can advance the processes of transformation.

Chapter 5 focused on how service design can be used in a proactive way for transformative collaboration in innovative and complex service systems to address emerging complex service problems – the role of design in creating service systems for sustainability. It looked at collaborative learning in three innovative service systems: *healthcare systems* – the Portuguese Electronic Health Record; *IKEA*'s collaborative service platform; and *ServCollab*, a nonprofit platform for transformative collaboration through service research projects that serve humanity. The chapter thereby offered a concept of transformative collaboration for sustainable service systems in the contexts of government, industry, and transnational collaboration.

Chapter 6 focused on steering toward happiness in sustainable travel. The empirical evidence came from travelers in the city of Helsinki (Finland is officially the happiest country in the world). An environmentally sustainability lifestyle is seen as a contribution to the mitigation of climate change. But it is necessary to use happiness as a metric in order to facilitate a transition to sustainable transport. High quality combined with a well-integrated ecosystem provides value in daily life and this has a positive influence on happiness. High-quality travel is related to happiness in terms of experience and satisfaction.

Chapter 7 focused on transforming people's lives and worlds for the better – "the real purpose of marketing." The key message is here is *breaking the story*. The chapter investigates what happens when a new "story," or narrative, is on the point of being accepted; what behavioral change occurs at an individual or group level when we have a new story to guide us. "Breaking the story" can be put into practice using a transformative collaboration design.

Part 3, *Base-of-the-Pyramid thinking for transforming business societal practice,* looked at the role of the BoP in transforming business practices and integrating justice, from both a theoretical and an empirical perspective.

Chapter 8 focused on service research at the BoP. The service ecosystem framework can help solve sustainability and scalability challenges at the BoP because of its wider scope, which allows for an inclusive perspective in which all socioeconomic actors can draw on resources and capabilities to contribute to sustainable services. Actor diversity is a vital factor in BoP service ecosystems because it allows the integration of different capabilities and resources, which are naturally scarce in this environment. This chapter's contribution is to bring a service ecosystem framework to the BoP context, and it highlights the key factors of actors' social embeddedness, private resources, and informal institutions in enabling value cocreation in service ecosystems.

Chapter 9 focused on an Integrative Justice Model (IJM) for sustainable and just business practice. The model can serve as an ethical guide when business practices engage with impoverished or BoP market segments. The IJM approach provides a defensible set of general ethical values, grounded in theory, which can help steer a fair, just, and sustainable course when marketing to vulnerable populations. Just, fair, and sustainable markets for disadvantaged consumers are more likely to come about when organizations aim and plan for such outcomes from the outset. The IJM approach is in line with SDG thinking about how businesses can operate in challenging situations (such as a pandemic) and still execute their operations in a socially responsible and sustainable manner.

Chapter 10 focused on the application of the IJM to predict transformation in quality of life (TQL) for beneficiaries in varied settings. The IJM is applied as a tool for strategic planning for organizations and communities as they identify the significant predictors of transformative outcomes, based on the voices of impoverished or marginalized beneficiaries. These include the beneficiaries of an NGO working at the margins of society, in this case refugee camps, as well as Syrian refugee communities in northern Iraq and Lebanon. An experiential learning exercise is discussed which engages students as justice auditors as they apply the IJM to their own experiences of consuming live entertainment. Transformative justice models are an operational tool to understand the drivers of TQL.

Part 4 looked at *Implications for a broader societal perspective for challenge-driven transformation practice.*

Chapter 11 focused on *marketing ethics and corporate social responsibility for a broader societal perspective.* The distinction between marketing ethics (ME) and corporate social responsibility (CSR) in marketing is important because each concept typically has a distinct focus within the firm. ME addresses the behavior of managers in the organization while CSR is targeted primarily at the policy level of the corporation. Stakeholder theory (ST) has too often become associated with the management of trade-offs among various parties connected to the organization – employees, suppliers, customers, etc. "Hard form" ST advocates, however, maintain the stakeholder focus at a societal level and its systemic effects. In this chapter, Unilever is used as a real-world example of a large MNC which, while not perfect, has been innovatively proactive in its thinking about sustainable and responsible business practices.

Chapter 12 focused on the PRME initiative, which aims to transform tertiary business education in the era of the SDGs and business-societal practices. PRME emerged partly because business leaders committed to the ten principles of the Global Compact were working to help the business leaders of the future understand the challenges of responsible management. The challenge is to inculcate in business schools a long-term consideration of innovative responsible management education. PRME works in a complex environment based on the principle of a "network of networks," which represents multi-stakeholder dialogue at every level of the service ecosystem (micro, meso, and macro). PRME's innovative route toward transformation is by means of voluntary self-assessment by schools of their progress against PRME's six principles. This chapter can be seen as a CSR business case of business-societal practices.

How?

To address the "how?" aspect of business transformation for a sustainable future meeting global challenges, we need to highlight the following key concepts which have emerged in the preceding chapters: values (V); value cocreation (VCC) responsibility (R1); resilience (R2); regeneration (R3); transformative collaboration (TC); and ecosystem humanity–nature (ES). These concepts are both conceptually and theoretically covered in the following works:

Values-based thinking (Edvardsson & Enquist, 2009; Enquist, Sebhatu, & Johnson, 2015);

Value (co)-creation (Lusch & Vargo, 2014);
The three Rs: responsibility, resilience, and regeneration (Elkington, 2020);
Transformative collaboration (Fisk et al., 2019);
Ecosystem, as developed in service research in an actor-to-actor context (Lusch & Vargo, 2014); ecosystem humanity–nature (Rockström & Klum, 2015) is further developed in Chapter 2 of this book.

These concepts will be used as modules within an overarching model of business transformation to meeting global challenges. We explain below how the preceding chapters have contributed to the formation of these concepts.

Values

"Values" as a concept is made explicit within many of the chapters; in some it remains hidden, but it is still there. It is one of the six PRME principles; a business school in the PRME program commits to "incorporate into its academic activities, curricula, and organizational practices the values of global social responsibility as portrayed in international initiatives such as the United Nations Global Compact." Implementation of the SDGs is now also part of the Global Compact initiative. In a business context, we have learned that IKEA, Unilever, and Eataly are acting as values-based companies in pursuit of a broader societal perspective, and that the SDGs are important to them. IKEA's values have undergone a transformation in the last decade to become more innovative, more circular/regenerative, and more caring/responsible. Separating marketing ethics (ME) from corporate social responsibility (CSR) in marketing, and hard stakeholder theory, represent values-based theories in pursuit of a broader societal perspective. The two chapters in Part 4 illustrate this. Transformation to fossil-free industry, complex service systems, and city transformation are all values-based in the direction of greater sustainability and social justice. "Breaking the story" is a values-based vision of transforming people's lives for the better and emerges from the starting point of a challenging – often "wicked" – problem.

Value (co)creation

Value creation is a key concept in service research (Lusch & Vargo, 2014). The mission statement of the Service Research Center at Karlstad University is: "We research value creation through service with a particular emphasis on the needs of individuals, organizations, and the wider society." This book's aim is to identify business practice with a more societal perspective where value creation has a wider meaning than merely profit maximization (i.e. a shareholder value perspective). In Chapter 1 we referred to Mazzucato (2018), who addresses distribution of value, making the distinction between who is taking and who is making. Her message is one of a more inclusive and collective creation of value: "If the goal is to produce growth that is more innovation-led (smart growth), more inclusive and more sustainable, we need a better understanding of value to steer us" (Mazzucato, 2018). "Values drive value" is the conclusion of Edvardsson and Enquist (2009) discussing a values-based company (i.e. IKEA). Rockström and Klum (2015) see smart growth as "an abundance within planetary boundaries," where value creation is about prosperity and growth within the limits of societal and ecological responsibility. Raworth (2018) envisages a distribution of value among humanity constrained between two boundaries: ecological and social. "Between the social and planetary boundaries lies an environmentally safe and socially just space in which humanity can thrive" (Raworth, 2018). Adopting a more societal perspective, the chapters in this book address a stakeholder orientation with a value cocreation approach where value has different meanings depending on the different needs of individuals, organizations, and the wider society. In Chapter 2, a transformation of value cocreation processes is manifested through a shifting from a fossil-free vision to the gradual creation of a fossil-free industry in practice. In Chapter 3, the value cocreation process at IKEA is about "meeting customer needs for affordable sustainable living and, at the same time, creating a positive impact for people, society, and the planet." In Chapter 4, the value cocreation process at Eataly is expressed as "to offer value propositions of transformation services to improve the well-being of individuals, organizations, and societies." Chapter 5 focused on how to construct value cocreation processes for emerging complex service problems through transformative collaboration and service design in service networks or complex service systems. Chapter 6 addressed value cocreation in the context of sustainable travel, with sustainability and happy citizens going hand in hand. Value cocreation can also be seen in the TQL improvements being sought for vulnerable consumers in different settings, or at the BoP.

Responsibility

Responsibility is a key values-based concept within a broader societal perspective and appears either explicitly or implicitly in most of the chapters. Responsibility is about corporations', and other organizations', duty of care for nature and for social justice. Van Tulder (2018) devised a categorization to measure the extent to which enterprises accept responsibility: level 1 is corporate self-responsibility; level 2 is corporate social responsiveness; level 3 is proactive corporate social responsibility; and level 4 is corporate societal (or sustainable) responsibility. For an organization to be proactively operating with a societal perspective, it needs to be at level 3 or 4. The cases presented in this book are examples of high-level responsibility.

Resilience

Resilience is systemic in nature and related to an ecosystem (Rockström & Klum, 2015). The Stockholm Resilience Center defines it as follows:

> Resilience is the capacity of a system, be it an individual, a forest, a city, or an economy, to deal with change and continue to develop. It is about the capacity to use shocks and disturbances like a financial crisis or climate change to spur renewal and innovative thinking. Resilience thinking embraces learning, diversity, and above all the belief that humans and nature are strongly coupled to the point that they should be conceived as one social-ecological system.[1]

In their book about social innovation (Westley, McGowan, & Tjörnbo, 2017; see also Chapter 2), the authors talk about building *resilience through transition*; this is related to the interrelationship between sustainability, innovation, and transformation. Many of the chapters look at this through an ecosystem lens. This interrelationship appears in different contexts across the chapters, and so the resilience aspect is often expressed in different ways. The Helsinki case, where quality improvement combined with a well-integrated ecosystem to provide value in daily life, is a good example of how to build resilience through a transition in a city context. IKEA, Unilever, and Eataly are building resilience through transformative change to their business ecosystems, again based on the three-way interrelationship – an interrelationship that makes the system more robust. Resilience is also reflected in designing transformative collaboration in complex service systems, as shown in Chapter 5.

Regeneration

Eataly's mantra of "no waste" provides a robust illustration of regenerative thinking. Regenerative thinking is important in Kate Raworth's Doughnut model (Raworth, 2018; see also Chapter 2), the one with the two boundaries: planetary and social. One of her seven principles concerns regeneration (Raworth, 2018). We introduced the "full world" idea in Chapter 3, which offers a more regenerative and societal meaning.

In Chapter 3, we discussed circular systems which, through reuse, sharing, repair, refurbishment, remanufacturing, and recycling, create a closed loop, minimizing the use of resource inputs and the creation of waste, pollution, and carbon emissions. This is a key insight in IKEA's business practice, forming a pillar of its People & Planet 2030 strategy which aims to make IKEA "circular" in all aspects. In shifting linear systems to circular ones, circular economy thinking is related to regenerative thinking. The roadmaps for the different industry sectors in the Fossil Free Sweden initiative are specifically designed to pursue this path, the goal being the more sustainable use of resources.

Transformative collaboration

Transformative collaboration (TC) occurs when all participants can contribute to their full human potential (see Chapter 5). The concept of TC can be used as a foundation to transform vulnerable service systems into sustainable and resilient ones. Chapter 5 presents an overview of how service design can be used in a proactive way to embed TC learning within different innovative service systems contexts. *Breaking the story* is an example of a challenge that can be tackled using the TC concept. A "business as usual" stakeholder orientation with different actors playing their different roles will not lead to transformation. If TC is to transform (service) systems into sustainable and resilient ones, it must do so using a "hard form" of stakeholder orientation, which places the stakeholder focus on the societal level and its systemic effects. Such a societal-level stakeholder orientation is clearly seen in Part 3 with the BoP cases and the use of IJM in improving TQL for beneficiaries in varied settings (e.g. refugees).

Ecosystem (humanity–nature)

The book provides examples of ecosystems that were designed for different purposes. In Chapter 2, a model of a business ecosystem is developed as a platform for stakeholder interaction between people and nature. The ecosystem can be viewed from a processual, systemic, or institutional point of view and at different levels (micro, meso, or macro). In Chapter 12, the PRME initiative is described as a multilevel ecosystem. Chapter 4 highlights the contribution to the scaling-up processes of sustainable business practice in Eataly's service ecosystem. In Chapter 6, the city is seen as a complex ecosystem in which public transport is embedded and which includes political, technical, and social dimensions. Chapter 8, which covers the BoP context, has a service ecosystem perspective, highlighting the key role of actors' social embeddedness, private resources, and informal institutions in enabling value cocreation in the service ecosystem. Chapter 10 used the IJM as a tool to predict the TQL and understand the ecosystem of vulnerable consumers. Chapter 5 developed the idea of sustainable service systems in which the TC concept can be used as a foundation. Such a system can be seen as a service ecosystem.

A concluding model

The above concepts and their interdependencies, as illustrated in all the chapters in this book, form the constituent parts of a concluding model. The concluding model is built to illustrate the resonance of value and values in organizations. This illustration on the resonance of value and values is used to clarify the way value is innovated and cocreated for a sustainable transformative change. This forms a *Business Transformation for sustainable future model* (see Figure 13.1). The formula is:

$$(V + VCC + R1 + R2 + R3 + TC) \leftrightarrow ES$$

V = values
VCC = value cocreation
R1 = responsibility

R2 = resilience
R3 = regeneration
TC = transformative collaboration
ES = ecosystem

The message in this book is clear. Sustainability needs to be embedded in a wider framework, theoretically as well contextually, by business-societal practice in the broadest sense, which will cocreate a new meaning for the interrelationship between sustainability, innovation, and transformation to meet the complex challenges facing business and society in the 21st century.

The model in Figure 13.1 is a *values-based sustainable and innovative transformative loop* –where sustainable business-societal practice in real-world contexts engages with transformative change processes – within a *multilevel ecosystem from a business-societal perspective.*

Values (V) is in the center of the loop which gives us the formula:

V =VCC + R1 + R2 + R3+ TC

The multilevel ecosystem within a business-societal perspective takes its inspiration from the dynamic ecosystem in Chapter 2. To enhance the societal perspective in this ecosystem, the SDGs at the macro level gives directions to all levels. In our new model, we want to provide a universal values-based guide for operating with a societal perspective. This is something that can be found in the concluding part of Laczniak and Murphy (2012) with their discussion of *hyper-norms*, a term that was taken from the article "Hyper norms: searching for a global code of conduct" (Laczniak & Kennedy, 2011). We favor this label, seeing as it is more universal in nature, rather than referring to any specific norm or code of conduct.

The model can be further explained by applying it to the chapters and cases studies in this book. This will help to illuminate the implementation process

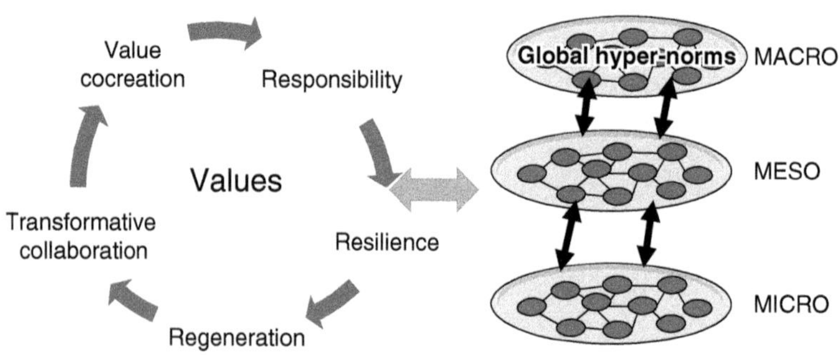

Figure 13.1 Values-based sustainable and innovative transformation loop *within a* multi-level business ecosystem transformation for a sustainable future.

of challenge-driven transformation and create a holistic understanding of the whole ecosystem, including how values drive value for engaged actors. Here, we will use IKEA as an example.

Business transformation practices for sustainability at IKEA

IKEA's vision is "to create a better everyday life for the many people." This value cocreation vision goes beyond home furnishings and includes an ecosystem in which its products and services are designed and produced. IKEA's value cocreation process is about meeting customer needs for affordable sustainable living while, at the same time, creating a positive impact for people, society, and the planet. Thus, we can understand IKEA as doing business in a global **ecosystem** with multiple collaborating actors. **Global hypernorms** such as human rights (as per the UN – Universal Declaration of Human Rights) and environmental codes of conduct had already been adopted by IKEA in the 1990s to tackle challenges around child labor and environmental issues. From 2000, IKEA has been guided by the Global Compact's ten principles and the company is now, proactively, applying the 17 UN SDGs goals to guide its societally driven transformation. This ongoing transformation is **values-based, sustainable, and innovative-loop**. The IKEA **values** represent the compass that guides its workers, and those values propagate themselves when they are put into practice within the ecosystem.

The IKEA values are part of the company's DNA and way of doing business. The values around *caring for people and planet* have become more prominent in recent decades, and reflect the hyper-norms of the SDGs. Over the last decade, IKEA has become more interactive and collaborative in cocreating value in **responsible** ways with customers and other stakeholders for mutual gain. This is expressed, for example, through "Democratic Design," a guiding philosophy for all its value cocreation processes, including design of products, service, logistics solutions, and service platforms. It includes form, function, sustainability, quality, and affordability. Furthermore, Democratic Design informs the way IKEA is building **resilience** through its physical materials infrastructure, through its wide range of facilities, through its legal configuration, and through its construction of scalable collaborative product and service platforms. Finally, IKEA has introduced a circular business model as a **regenerative** sustainable strategy, now being implemented in the global ecosystem. This gives energy and direction to IKEA's journey of transformation to become people and planet-positive. This is a **transformative collaboration** process and it means rethinking every aspect of how to do business.

Concluding remark: lessons learned

In the words of the PRME mission, this is "a new era for responsible business." This book has provided knowledge and experience in business and societal research from a range of scholars and academic disciplines who have explained why and how to proceed. It takes the firm-centric view and extends it into a broader, systemic, and dynamic understanding of business and societal transformation. Rather than a *how-to* handbook, this book is based on business research meeting business and societal practice to tackle global challenges characterized by complexity and wicked problems, such as the ongoing pandemic and climate change. A recurring theme is how business practice and societal practice are part of the same mission: a transformation from "business as usual" to more inclusive and sustainable businesses and society. This is not a "quick fix," as we have shown. It requires the use of resources through the interactions between sustainability, innovation, and transformation, in a smarter but also more inclusive way. What is needed is more transformative collaboration under a joint vision or joint roadmap. It can be the beginning of a new mission to address our global challenges.

Implications and future research

Below are some general implications about the new landscape in which we find ourselves. They raise important points and point to further study in different contexts and within different theoretical conceptualizations:

- To address global challenges, we need to be aware of the complexity of wicked problems in the context of large-scale change.
- Sustainability needs to be embedded in a wider framework, theoretically as well contextually, within business-societal practice.
- Challenge-driven business and societal transformation need to transcend green-, blue- and SDG-washing to the point where sustainability thinking acquires a more circular and societal meaning in an interrelationship with both innovation and transformation.
- The UN SDGs, as a hyper-norm, can be used as a compass to mobilize change for sustainable business practice; and, vice versa, sustainable business practice can contribute to the achievement of the SDGs.
- A business practice with a more societal perspective will have a stakeholder orientation that addresses the question "value for whom?" in its value cocreation process.
- Transformative collaboration – transforming (service) systems into sustainable and resilient ones – needs "hard form" stakeholder orientation, which places the stakeholder focus at the societal level and its systemic effects.
- Service design can assist in transformative collaboration in innovative and complex service systems, addressing emerging complex service problems; design has a role in creating service systems for sustainability.
- High quality in combination with a well-integrated ecosystem provides value in daily life.
- Looking at the role of the Base of the Pyramid in transforming business practices and integrating social justice, we must understand the key roles of actors' social embeddedness, private resources, and informal institutions in enabling value cocreation in an ecosystem.

- A dynamic ecosystem for stakeholder interaction that is of an actor–actor–nature configuration needs societal implementation based on responsibility–resilience–regeneration thinking.

Note

1 https://www.stockholmresilience.org/

References

Edvardsson, B., and Enquist, B. (2009). *Values-Based Service for Sustainable Business: Lessons from IKEA*. London: Routledge.

Elkington, J. (2019). 25 years ago I coined the phrase "Triple Bottom Line": here's why it's time to rethink it. *Harvard Business Review*, June 25, 2019.

Elkington, J. (2020). *Green Swans: The Coming Boom in Regenerative Capitalism*. New York: Fast Company Press.

Enquist, B., Sebhatu, S. P., and Johnson, M. (2015). Transcendence for business logics in value networks for sustainable service business. *Journal of Service Theory and Practice*, 25(2), 181–97.

Fisk, R., Fuessel, A., Laszlo, C., Struebi, P., Valera, A., and Weiss, C. (2019). Systemic social innovation: co-creating a future where humans and al life thrive. *Humanistic Management Journal*, 4, 191–214.

Laczniak, G.R., and Kennedy A.-M. (2011). Hyper norms: searching for a global code of conduct. *Journal of Macromarketing*, 26 (December), 154–77.

Laczniak, G.R., and Murphy, P.E. (2012). Stakeholder theory and marketing: moving from a firm-centric to societal perspective. *Journal of Public Policy & Marketing*, 31(2), 284–92.

Lusch, R., and Vargo, S. (2014). *Service Dominant Logic: Premises, Perspectives, Possibilities*. Cambridge: Cambridge University Press.

Mazzucato, M. (2018). *The Value of Everything: Making and Taking in the Global Economy*. London: Penguin.

Raworth, K. (2018). *Doughnut Economics: Seven Ways to Think Like a 21st-Century Economist*. Paperback Ed. London: Penguin Random House.

Rockström, J., and Klum, M. (2015). *Big World Small Planet: Abundance within Planetary Boundaries*. Stockholm: Max Ström Publishing.

van Tulder, R. (2018). *Business and Sustainable Developments Goals: A Framework for Effective Corporate Involvement*. Rotterdam School of Management, Erasmus University, Rotterdam.

von Weizsäcker, E.U., and Wijkman, A. (2018) *Come On! Capitalism, Short-termism, Population and the Destruction of the Planet. A Report to the Club of Rome's 50th Anniversary in 2018*. New York: Springer Science + Business Media.

Westley, F., McGowan, K., and Tjörnbo, O. (Eds.). (2017). *The Evolution of Social Innovation: Building Resilience through Transitions*. Cheltenham, UK: Edward Elgar Publishing.

Index

Note: Page numbers in *italics* indicate figures, **bold** numbers indicate tables, on the corresponding pages.

Milton Keynes UK
Ingram Content Group UK Ltd.
UKHW022150071123
432171UK00004B/23

9 781032 037431